MUSTANG BON FOUNDATION

These advanced practices should only be practiced after getting the appropriate transmission, and done only by practitioners with appropriate qualifications, permissions, and pith instructions. Without such qualifications, permissions, and instructions these practices can be dangerous, so do not put yourself at risk.

The Six Lamps According to the Zhang Zhung Oral Transmission Lineage of Bon Dzogchen

ISBN: 978-1-956950-04-5
Library of Congress Control Number: 9781732157965

Copyright © 2022 Mustang Bon Foundation
All rights reserved. No part of this book may be reproduced without prior written permission from the publisher.

Published by Mustang Bon Publishing

Second Edition

Front cover: Tapihritsa (photograph of thangka taken by Gary Freeman)

MustangBonFoundation.org

Printed and Bound in the United States of America

Layout and design by Brad Reynolds integralartandstudies.com

The Six Lamps

Tapihritsa
8th century C.E.

The Six Lamps
According to the Zhang Zhung Oral Transmission Lineage of Bon Dzogchen

Root Text by Tapihritsa
and
Gyerpung Nangzher Lodpo

Explanatory Commentaries:
The Ornamentation of Sunlight Commentary
by Uri
The Intention and Ultimate Meaning Commentary
by Drugom Gyalwa Yungdrung

Practical Guidance Commentaries:
The Six Essential Points of *Bodhicitta*
Transmitted from the Lineage of Yangal Gongtra ba
The Six Energy Drops
Transcribed by Tsangpa Jadral

translated under the guidance of
His Holiness the thirty-third
Menri Trizin

by Geshe Sonam Gurung and Daniel P. Brown, Ph.D.

for Mustang Bon Foundation

*May the translation of these precious lineage teachings
cause their benefits to flourish everywhere
and serve the welfare of all beings.*

Geshe Sonam Gurung grew up in an indigenous Bon Tibetan region of Nepal, in the Pangling Village area of Central Mustang. When he was nine years old he was sent by the local Bon lama to become a monk at Menri Monastery, the seat of the indigenous Bon religion, now located in the Dolanji area of India. He spent fourteen years obtaining his Geshe degree (the equivalent of a doctoral degree in Bon spiritual studies) under the guidance of His Holiness Menri Trizin, the spiritual leader and lineage holder of the Bon and the 33rd Head Abbott of Menri Monastery. After obtaining his Geshe degree he served as treasurer, guest master, and personal assistant to His Holiness Menri Trizin at Menri Monastery. Recently, Geshe Sonam returned to the Jomsom area of Central Mustang to reestablish and spread the indigenous Bon teachings in his country of origin. Two documentaries have been made about Geshe Sonam's life and work: *Bon: From Mustang to Menri*, and a follow-up film about his return home, *Returning the Blessings*.

Daniel P. Brown, Ph.D. is an Associate Clinical Professor in Psychology, Dept. of Psychiatry, at Harvard Medical School at Beth Israel Deaconess Medical Center. He teaches a variety of clinical assessment and treatment courses and also a course on performance excellence for physicians, CEOs, and judges. In graduate school at the University of Chicago he studied Sanskrit, and at the University of Wisconsin he studied Tibetan, Buddhist Sanskrit, and Pali. In the 1980s he wrote *Transformations of Consciousness* with Ken Wilber and Jack Engler. He is also the author of *Pointing Out the Great Way: The Stages of Meditation in the Mahamudra Tradition*. More recently, under the guidance of H.H. Menri Trizin, he and Geshe Sonam translated Bru rGyal ba g.Yung drung's *The Pith Instructions for the Stages of the Practice Sessions of Bon rDzogs Chen [Great Completion] Meditation*, and a collection of eleven advanced yogic texts, Shar rdza bKra' shis rGyal mtshan's *sKu gsum rang shar [Self-Arising Three-fold Embodiment of Enlightenment]*.

Table of Contents

Acknowledgments xxiii

INTRODUCTION 1
Appropriate and Inappropriate Recipients of These Teachings 2
The Six Lamps Teachings 2
The Lamp of the Universal Base 3
The Lamp of the Fleshy Heart-Mind 11
The Lamp of the Soft White Channels... 13
The Fluid Eye Lamp of the Extensive Lasso.................................. 14
The Condensed Style; All Four Lamps at Once............................. 15
The Development of the Visions; The Lamp of the *Buddha*-fields... 16
The Lamp of the After-Death States... 23

THE SIX LAMPS ACCORDING TO THE ZHANG ZHUNG 27
A.1.0 **The Meaning of the Previous Described Preliminaries**... 29
B.1.0 **The Overall Meaning**.. 30
A.1.1 **The Homage** 30
A.1.1.1 **Expounding on Compassion** 30
A.1.1.1.1 **The Object of Homage** 30
A.1.1.1.2 **Explaining the Necessity of Homage** 31
A.1.1.1.2.1 **Explaining the Necessity of Homage** 31
A.1.1.1.2.2 **The Actual Meaning of the Homage**.............................. 31
B.1.1 **Homage** 32
A.1.2 **The Actual Teachings on the Preliminaries**.................. 33
A.1.2.1 **The Way to Establish the Pith Instructions in Your Mind-Stream** 33
A.1.2.2 **Explaining the Greatness of the Pith Instructions**... 34
B.1.2 **The Way the Instructions are Described** 35
B.1.2.1 **The First Meeting**.. 35

B.1.2.2 **The Second Meeting** 35
A.1.2.2.1 **Explaining the Instructions for Reaching the Final State of Everything About Bon** 37
A.1.2.2.2 **Explaining How These Instructions Enable Making a Determination about Awakened Awareness Without Which you will Not come to the Gateway of Nothing More Profound than the Vehicle of Bon** 37
B.1.3 **Explaining the Way it Really is and Extolling its Greatness** 38
B.1.3.1 **The Extraordinary Instructions, the Teachings for Reaching the Ultimate End of Everything** 38
B.1.3.2 **Numerous Ordinary Instructions, the Teachings on the Concealed Meaning** 39
A.1.2.2.3 **Explaining How to Directly Draw Forth [the Realization]** 40
B.1.3.3 **Extolling the Greatness, the Precious Qualities of These Teachings** 41
B.1.3.3.1 **Explaining the Unique Positive Qualities of These Instructions** 41
A.1.2.3 **Explaining the Enumeration of the Pith Instructions** 42
B.1.3.3.2 **Explaining the Numerous Designations** 42
A.1.2.3.1 **The Teachings are Secret for Those Without a Vessel** 43
A.1.2.3.2 **The Instructions [for Those Who Have Built the] Vessel** 43
B.1.3.3.3 **Explaining Who Should be Accepted or Rejected Regarding these Teachings** 44
B.1.3.3.3.1 **The Necessity of Who Should be Accepted or Rejected** 44
A.1.3 **A Brief Conclusion** 45
B.1.3.3.3.2 **A Brief Summary** 45
B.2 **An Explanation of the Meaning of the Six** 45
A.2.0 **Making a Determination of the Meaning of the Essence of the Main Practices** 45

B.2.1 **The Lamp of the Basis that Stays** 46
A.2.1 **Homage** 46
A.2.2 **Elucidating the Meaning** 46
A.2.2.1 **The Synopsis** 47
B.2.1.1 **A Brief Explanation** 47
A.2.2.2 **The Extensive Explanation** 47
B.2.1.2 **An Extensive Explanation** 47
A.2.2.2.1 **The Teachings on the Natural State, the Basis, the Essence-Itself**.. 48
A.2.2.2.1.1 **The Brief Explanation** 48
B.2.1.2.1 **The Explanation of the Natural State of Universal Ground**... 48
A.2.2.2.1.2 **The Extensive Explanation** 49
B.2.1.2.1.1 **Universal Ground**... 49
A.2.2.2.1.2.1 **Explaining the Natural State of Groundless-ground**... 49
A.2.2.2.1.2.1.1 **Explaining the Essence of Groundless-ground**... 49
A.2.2.2.1.2.1.2 **Explaining the Natural State of Groundless-ground**.. 50
B.2.1.2.1.1.1 **A Brief Explanation** 50
A.2.2.2.1.2.1.2.1 **Explaining the Natural State as Original Purity** 50
A.2.2.2.1.2.1.2.2 **Explaining the Natural State as Spontaneously Present**.................................. 51
A.2.2.2.1.2.1.2.3 **Explaining the Natural State as Not Prophesied**... 51
A.2.2.2.1.2.1.2.4 **Explaining the Natural State as a Single Thread of Energy** 52
A.2.2.2.1.2.1.2.4.1 **Brief Explanation**.. 52
A.2.2.2.1.2.1.2.4.2 **Extensive Explanation** 53
A.2.2.2.1.2.1.2.4.2.1 **Explaining the Three—Space, Sphere, and Expanse—as the Same Single Thread of Energy** 53

A.2.2.2.1.2.1.2.4.2.2 **Explaining the Three—Example, Meaning, and Sign—as the Same Single Thread of Energy** 55
A.2.2.2.1.2.2 **Explaining the Natural State of Awakened Awareness** 56
B.2.1.2.1.1.2 **An Extensive Explanation** 56
B.2.1.2.1.1.3 **A Brief Summary** 58
A.2.2.2.1.2.2.1 **Explaining the Basis of Arising of Primordial Wisdom's Awakened Awareness** 59
A.2.2.2.1.2.2.2 **Explaining the Essence of Primordial Wisdom's Awakened Awareness** 59
A.2.2.2.1.2.2.3 **Explaining Liveliness** 60
A.2.2.2.1.2.2.4 **Explaining the Enumeration of the Names** ... 61
A.2.2.2.1.2.2.5 **Explaining the Way it Arises in Anyone's Mind-stream** 62
A.2.2.2.1.2.2.6 **The Way it Exists as the Foundation of all *Saṁsāra* and *Nirvāṇa*** 63
B.2.1.2.1.2 **Primordial Wisdom's Awakened Awareness** 64
B.2.1.2.1.2.1 **The Subject, the Natural State of Primordial Wisdom's Awakened Awareness** 64
B.2.1.2.1.2.2 **The Object, How Ultimate Sound, Light, and Light-rays Arise** 65
B.2.1.2.1.2.3 **Explaining the Inseparable Non-dual Pair of Subject/Object** 65
B.2.1.2.1.2.4 **Explaining the Enumerations and Distinctions Regarding Awakened Awareness** 66
B.2.1.2.1.2.5 **How *Saṁsāra* and *Nirvāṇa* Arise from Making a Connection with the Non-dual Inseparable Pair** 66
A.2.2.2.1.2.3 **Explaining the Natural State of Ordinary [Conceptual] Thought** 67
A.2.2.2.1.2.3.1 **Explaining the Basis of Arising of Ordinary Thought** 68
A.2.2.2.1.2.3.2 **Explaining the Basis of Arising of Ordinary Thought** 68

A.2.2.2.1.2.3.3 **Explaining the Enumeration of Ordinary Thought** 68
B.2.1.2.1.3 **The Explanation About Ordinary Conceptual Thought** 69
B.2.1.2.1.3.1 **How Four Kinds of Conceptual Thought Arise in the Basis** 69
B.2.1.2.1.3.2 **An Enumeration of the Kinds of Thought That Arise** 69
A.2.2.2.1.3 **A Brief Conclusion** 70
A.2.2.2.1.3.1 **Summary Regarding the Natural State** 70
A.2.2.2.1.3.2 **Explaining the Way this Stays Every Moment in an Individual's Mind-stream** 71
B.2.1.3 **A Condensed Summary** 72
B.2.1.3.1 **An Enumeration of the Three—Subject, Mother and Son, and Liveliness** 72
B.2.1.3.2 **How [Awakened Awareness] Stays in the Mind-stream of Any Individual Being** 73
A.2.2.2.2 **The Teachings on How *Saṁsāra* and *Nirvāṇa* Become Divided in a Duality** 74
A.2.2.2.2.1 **A Brief Summary of How *Saṁsāra* and *Nirvāṇa* Become Divided** 74
A.2.2.2.2.2 **An Extensive Explanation** 75
A.2.2.2.2.2.1 **The Way of the Primordial *Buddha*, Kun tu bZang po** 76
B.2.1.2.2 **The Way *Saṁsāra* and *Nirvāṇa* Become Divided into Two [as a Duality]** 76
B.2.1.2.2.1 **The Teachings** 76
A.2.2.2.2.2.1.1 **Explaining the Way Primordial Wisdom's Awakened Awareness Arises** 77
A.2.2.2.2.2.1.2 **Explaining the Way to Attain the Self-influence of Awakened Awareness** 78
A.2.2.2.2.2.1.3 **Explaining the Way the Emanations of *Nirvāṇa* Arise** 79
B.2.1.2.2.2 **The Extensive Explanation.** 80
B.2.1.2.2.2.1 **How *Nirvāṇa* Gets Separated** 80

B.2.1.2.2.2.1.1 **How the Realization Comes From the Natural State Just As It Is** 80
B.2.1.2.2.2.1.2 **How *Nirvāṇa* is Attained Through Realization** 81
A.2.2.2.2.2.2 **The Way Delusion Arises from the Karma of Sentient Beings of the Three Realms** 82
A.2.2.2.2.2.2.1 **Explaining the Way Delusion Arises from Not Recognizing Awakened Awareness** 83
B.2.1.2.2.2.2 **How *Saṁsāra* Gets Separated** 84
B.2.1.2.2.2.2.1 **With Respect to Ultimate Truth, in What Way Delusion Arises** 84
B.2.1.2.2.2.2.1.1 **How Non-recognition of Awakened Awareness and Simultaneousness [of Appearance] Occurs** 84
A.2.2.2.2.2.2.2 **Explaining the Way *Saṁsāra* Arises** 85
A.2.2.2.2.2.2.2.1 **A General Explanation of the Way *Saṁsāra* Arises** 86
A.2.2.2.2.2.2.2.1.1 **The Way Sense-objects and Ordinary Knowing Arise** 86
B.2.1.2.2.2.2.1.2 **How Non-recognition of Groundless-ground Occurs** 87
B.2.1.2.2.2.2.1.3 **How the Self-grasping and Afflictive Emotions of the Ordinary Sense-mind Occurs** 89
A.2.2.2.2.2.2.2.1.2 **The Way the Habitual Karmic Propensities Accumulate** 89
B.2.1.2.2.2.2.1.4 **How Habitual Karmic Propensities [Accumulate in the Basis]** 91
A.2.2.2.2.2.2.2.1.3 **The Way the Three Realms and the Body Arise** 92
B.2.1.2.2.2.2.2 **Through Delusion How One Wanders in *Saṁsāra*** 93
B.2.1.2.2.2.2.2.1 **The Divisions of *Saṁsāra*** 94
B.2.1.2.2.2.2.2.1.1 **Realms** 94
B.2.1.2.2.2.2.2.1.2 **Support** 95

B.2.1.2.2.2.2.2.1.3 **Types of Beings** 95
B.2.1.2.2.2.2.2.1.4 **Paths** 95
B.2.1.2.2.2.2.2.1.5 **Opening the Gateways of Birth** 95
B.2.1.2.2.2.2.2.1.6 **The Unique Kinds of Suffering** 95
A.2.2.2.2.2.2.2.2 **A Specific Explanation of the Way** *Saṁsāra* **Arises** 95
A.2.2.2.2.2.2.2.2.1 **Brief Explanation** 95
A.2.2.2.2.2.2.2.2.2 **The Extended Explanation** 96
A.2.2.2.2.2.2.2.2.2.1 **An Explanation of the Way the External Container, the Known Ordinary World, Arises from Mind** 96
B.2.1.2.2.2.2.2.2 **The Essence** 97
B.2.1.2.2.2.2.2.2.1 **The Way the External Container Arises** 97
A.2.2.2.2.2.2.2.2.2.2 **An Explanation of the Way the Internal Contained Contents, the Mind of Sentient Beings, Arises from Mind** 98
B.2.1.2.2.2.2.2.2.2 **The Way the Seeming Internal Content Arises in the Mind** 100
B.2.1.2.2.2.2.2.3 **The Way** *Saṁsāra* **Actually Is** 101
B.2.1.2.2.2.2.2.3.1 **Whatever the Causes** *Saṁsāra* **Depends On** 101
B.2.1.2.2.2.2.2.3.2 **Whatever the Essence of** *Saṁsāra* **Is** 101
B.2.1.2.2.2.2.2.3.3 **Whatever Outcome Develops** 101
A.2.2.2.2.2.2.2.2.3 **An Explanation of the Way** *Saṁsāra* **Arises from Not Knowing Awakened Awareness** 103
A.2.2.2.2.3 **A Brief Summary** 104
B.2.1.2.2.3 **A Brief Summary Regarding** *Saṁsāra* **and** *Nirvāṇa* 105
B.2.1.3 **Conclusion** 105
A.2.2.2.3 **The Lamp of the Fleshy Heart** 106
A.2.2.2.3.1 **Homage** 106
A.2.2.2.3.2 **The Extensive Explanation** 106
A.2.2.2.3.2.1 **A Brief Explanation** 106
B.2.2 **The Lamp of the Fleshy Heart-Mind** 107

Table of Contents

B.2.2.1 **A Brief Introduction** 107
A.2.2.2.3.2.2 **An Extensive Explanation** 108
A.2.2.2.3.2.2.1 **Within the Domain of Groundless-ground There is No Limit** 108
B.2.2.2 **An Extensive Explanation** 109
B.2.2.2.1 **Explaining How This Stays Just As it Is** 109
B.2.2.2.1.1 **Explaining What Stays, the Essence of Groundless-ground** 109
B.2.2.2.1.2 **Explaining What Stays, the Real Nature of the Heart-mind** 110
A.2.2.2.3.2.2.2 **Explaining How It Stays** 111
A.2.2.2.3.2.2.3 **Explaining How It Pervades the Body** 111
B.2.2.2.1.3 **The Special Distinction of Primordial Wisdom Staying Just As It Is** 112
B.2.2.2.1.3.1 **Explaining How Mother and Son Groundless-ground are Inseparable.** 112
A.2.2.2.3.2.2.4 **Explaining How Ordinary Thought Arises in Groundless-ground** 113
B.2.2.2.1.3.2 **How Ordinary Mindful Thought Arises** 114
A.2.2.2.3.2.2.5 **Explaining the Way to be Free From the Connection of Body and Mind** 115
B.2.2.2.2 **Explaining How the Body and Mind Become Connected and Become Separated** 116
A.2.2.2.3.3 **A Brief Summary** 117
B.2.2.3 **A Brief Conclusion** 117
A.2.2.2.4 **The Lamp of the Soft White Channels** 117
A.2.2.2.4.1 **Homage** 117
A.2.2.2.4.2 **The Extensive Explanation** 118
B.2.3 **The Lamp of the Soft White Channels** 118
B.2.3.1 **A Brief Introduction** 118
B.2.3.2 **The Extended Explanation** 119
B.2.3.2.1 **Whatever Arises As the Essence** 119
A.2.2.2.4.2.1 **A Brief Overview** 119
A.2.2.2.4.2.2 **An Extensive Explanation** 120
B.2.3.2.2 **Whatever Arises As Path** 121

B.2.3.2.2.1 How the Body and Mind Arise as a Support 121
B.2.3.2.2.2 Based on This Support, the Way the Winds in the Channels Develop 122
A.2.2.2.4.2.2.1 Explaining the Way the Body and Mind are Generated in the Mother's Womb Via the Five Elements 122
A.2.2.2.4.2.2.2 Explaining the Way the Three Channels and Six *Chakras* Develop 124
A.2.2.2.4.2.2.3 Explaining the Way Ultimate Truth Develops in the Vessel Via the Arising of Branch Channels, and Further Branch Channels to the Sense-organs.. 126
B.2.3.2.2.2.1 The Way the Main Channel and the Branch Channels Develop.. 126
A.2.2.2.4.2.2.3.1 Explaining How Ultimate Truth Arises in the Heart-mind 129
B.2.3.2.2.2.2 How the *Chakras* and Branch Channels Develop... 130
A.2.2.2.4.2.2.3.2 Explaining How it Arises in the Ancillary Channels 131
B.2.3.2.2.2.3 How the Minor Branches Develop From the Elements.. 132
A.2.2.2.4.2.2.3.3 Explaining How It Arises in the Five Sense-organs... 133
B.2.3.2.2.2.4 How the Support of the Senses Develops From the Pure Essence of the Wind in the Channels 134
A.2.2.2.4.2.2.3.4 Explaining How Liberation Arises Inside the Vessel 136
B.2.3.2.2.2.5 The Meaning of the Impure Wind in the Channels and How It Develops Into the Sacred Substances of the [Suitable] Vessel 137
A.2.2.2.4.2.2.4 Explaining How the Branch Channels and Further Branch Channels Become Differentiated 138

A.2.2.2.4.2.2.5 **Explaining How Primordial Wisdom Arises in the Path of the [Upper] Central Channel** 138
A.2.2.2.4.2.2.5.1 **Recognizing the Lamp of the Channels** 138
B.2.3.2.2.3 **Based on the Support the Division of the Channels** 138
A.2.2.2.4.2.2.5.2 **Explaining the Way Primordial Wisdom Arises** 139
B.2.3.2.3 **The Way it Arises Just As It Is** 140
A.2.2.2.4.3 **A Brief Summary** 141
B.2.3.3 **The Conclusion** 141
A.2.2.2.5 **The Fluid Lamp of the Extensive Lasso** 141
A.2.2.2.5.1 **Homage** 141
B.2.4 **The Fluid Lamp of the Extensive Lasso** 141
B.2.4.1 **The Explanation** 142
B.2.4.2 **The Extensive Explanation** 142
B.2.4.2.1 **Whatever Arises as the Essence of Groundless-Ground** 142
A.2.2.2.5.2 **The Extensive Explanation** 143
A.2.2.2.5.2.1 **The Brief Explanation** 144
B.2.4.2.2 **The Gateway of the Lamp by Which it Arises** 144
A.2.2.2.5.2.1.1 **The Extensive Explanation** 145
A.2.2.2.5.2.1.1.1 **Explaining How it Stays as Complete in Itself** 145
A.2.2.2.5.2.1.1.2 **Explaining How it is Seen Nakedly** 146
B.2.4.2.3 **The Ultimate Truth of the Natural State of its Arising Just As It Is** 147
A.2.2.2.5.3 **A Brief Summary** 148
B.2.4.3 **The Conclusion** 148
A.2.2.2.6 **The Lamp of the *Buddha*-fields** 148
A.2.2.2.6.1 **Homage** 148
A.2.2.2.6.2 **The Extensive Explanation** 149
B.2.5 **The Lamp of the *Buddha*-fields** 149
A.2.2.2.6.2.1 **A Briefer Explanation** 149
B.2.5.1 **The Brief Explanation** 149
A.2.2.2.6.2.2 **A More Extended Explanation** 150

B.2.5.2 **The Extended Explanation**..150
A.2.2.2.6.2.2.1 **Pointing out the Three Enlightened**
        ***Buddha*-bodies**..151
B.2.5.2.1 **Pointing out the Three Enlightened**
        ***Buddha*-bodies**..151
B.2.5.2.1.1 **Pointing out the Enlightened *Dharmakāya*** 151
B.2.5.2.1.2 **Recognizing the *Buddha*-fields of the**
        Enlightened Completion Body..............................153
B.2.5.2.1.3 **Pointing out the *Nirmāṇakāyas* [Enlightened**
        Emanation Bodies] 156
A.2.2.2.6.2.2.2 **The Close-to-the-Heart Instructions**..............158
B.2.5.2.2 **The Close-to-the-Heart Instructions**......................158
B.2.5.2.2.1 **Pointing out the Enlightened *Dharmakāya*** 158
A.2.2.2.6.2.2.2.1 **With Respect to Pointing out the Essence-**
        itself of Awakened Awareness, the Close-
        to-the-Heart Instructions on the Body of
        Bon [*Dharmakāya*] 159
A.2.2.2.6.2.2.2.1.1 **Pointing out Instructions** 159
B.2.5.2.2.1.1 **Pointing Out** 160
B.2.5.2.2.1.1.1 **Recognizing the Basis, [Groundless-ground],**
        Through the Lamp of the Basis that stays....160
B.2.5.2.2.1.1.1.1 **Pointing out the Mother Consciousness** 160
B.2.5.2.2.1.1.1.2 **Pointing out the Son Consciousness**...........161
A.2.2.2.6.2.2.2.1.1.1 **Through the Lamp of Groundless-ground**
        that Stays, Recognizing the Basis..........162
B.2.5.2.2.1.1.1.3 **Pointing out Liveliness**................................163
B.2.5.2.2.1.1.2 **The Lamp of Illustrative Examples**...............164
A.2.2.2.6.2.2.2.1.1.2 **Through the Lamp of Illustrative**
        Examples, Illustrating Ultimate Truth by
        Example...165
A.2.2.2.6.2.2.2.1.1.3 **Through the Lamp of the Signs of**
        Primordial Wisdom, in Addition
        Recognizing the Signs............................166
A.2.2.2.6.2.2.2.1.2 **Close-to-the-Heart Instructions**...............167
B.2.5.2.2.1.1.3 **The Lamp of the Extent of the Signs**............167

Table of Contents   xvii

B.2.5.2.2.1.1.3.1 **Pointing out the Truth of Groundless-ground**.. 167
B.2.5.2.2.1.1.3.2 **Pointing out the Truth of Awakened Awareness**.. 168
A.2.2.2.6.2.2.2.1.2.1 **Explaining the Actuality of the Close-to-the-Heart instructions**............................ 169
A.2.2.2.6.2.2.2.1.2.1.1 **Close-to-the-Heart Meditation**........... 169
B.2.5.2.2.1.2 **The Close-to-the-Heart Instructions**................. 169
B.2.5.2.2.1.2.1 **Explaining What Kind of Close-to-the-Heart Instructions**.. 169
A.2.2.2.6.2.2.2.1.2.1.2 **Close-to-the-Heart View**...................... 170
B.2.5.2.2.1.2.2 **Close-to-the-Heart Instructions About Whatever**.. 171
A.2.2.2.6.2.2.2.1.2.2 **Showing the Fruition of the Close-to-the-Heart Instructions**........................... 171
B.2.5.2.2.1.2.3 **The Positive Benefit From the Close-to-the-Heart Instructions**........................... 172
A.2.2.2.6.2.2.2.2 **With Respect to Pointing out that Gives Special Insight into Awakened Awareness, the Close-to-the-Heart Instructions of the Enlightened Form-bodies**............................ 172
A.2.2.2.6.2.2.2.2.1 **Pointing out the Three Great Appearances**... 172
B.2.5.2.2.2 **Close-to-the-Heart Instructions on the Enlightened Form-bodies**.. 173
B.2.5.2.2.2.1 **Pointing out the Special Insight into Awakened Awareness**.. 173
A.2.2.2.6.2.2.2.2.1.1 **Explaining the Essential Points Regarding the Body**................................... 173
B.2.5.2.2.2.1.1 **The Skillful Means by which Special Insight Arises**.. 174
A.2.2.2.6.2.2.2.2.1.2 **Explaining the Actuality of What is Being Pointed Out**................................... 175
B.2.5.2.2.2.1.2 **Whatever Arises is Pointed Out as Self-appearing**.. 176

B.2.5.2.2.2.2 The Close-to-the-Heart Instructions on the
    Enlightened Form-bodies 177
B.2.5.2.2.2.2.1 The General Explanation 177
A.2.2.2.6.2.2.2.2.2 Close-to-the-Heart Instruction Regarding
    the Enlightened Form-body 177
A.2.2.2.6.2.2.2.2.2.1 Explaining the Close-to-the-Heart
    Instructions in General 178
A.2.2.2.6.2.2.2.2.2.1.1 The Way to Become Familiar with the
    Three Appearances as Mind 178
B.2.5.2.2.2.2.1.1 How to Take up the Meditative Experiences
    Like That 178
A.2.2.2.6.2.2.2.2.2.1.2 Explaining how the Maṇḍala of the
    Three Enlightened Buddha-bodies
    Shines Forth in the Mind 179
B.2.5.2.2.2.2.1.2 The Way the Experience of Clear-light
    Arises 180
B.2.5.2.2.2.2.2 The Specific Explanation 181
A.2.2.2.6.2.2.2.2.2.2 Specific Explanation of the Close-to-the-
    Heart Instructions 181
A.2.2.2.6.2.2.2.2.2.2.1 Explaining the Practice of Liveliness
    with Respect to the Three
    Appearances 181
B.2.5.2.2.2.2.2.1 How to Take up Whatever Kind of
    Meditative Experiences 182
B.2.5.2.2.2.2.2.2 From these Experiences how the Clear-light
    of Appearance Arises 183
B.2.5.2.2.2.2.2.2.1 How the Clear-light Arises 183
A.2.2.2.6.2.2.2.2.2.2.2 Explaining the Specialness of
    Familiarity 184
B.2.5.2.2.2.2.2.2.2 How to Develop Familiarity Through
    Meditative Experience 186
B.2.5.2.2.2.2.2.2.2.1 The Meditative Experience of
    Proliferating Visions 187
B.2.5.2.2.2.2.2.2.2.2 The Meditative Experience of
    Multiplying Visions 188

B.2.5.2.2.2.2.2.2.2.3 **The Meditative Experience of Quite Extensive Visions** 188
B.2.5.2.2.2.2.2.2.2.4 **The Meditative Experience of the Completion of the Visions** 189
B.2.5.2.2.2.2.2.2.2.5 **The Meditative Experiences of the Ultimate State of the Visions** 190
B.2.5.2.2.2.2.3 **The Manner of the Close-to-the-Heart Instructions** 191
A.2.2.2.6.2.2.2.2.2.3 **Explaining the Fruition of the Close-to-the-Heart Instructions** 192
A.2.2.2.6.2.2.2.2.3 **Explaining the Secret Pith Instructions** .. 193
B.2.5.2.2.2.2.4 **The Positive Qualities that Directly Become Manifest** 193
B.2.5.2.2.2.2.3 **The Instructions with the Authoritative Seal** 194
A.2.2.2.6.3 **A Brief Summary** 195
B.2.5.3 **The Conclusion** 195
A.2.2.2.7 **The Lamp of the After-Death States** 195
A.2.2.2.7.1 **Homage** 196
A.2.2.2.7.2 **An Extensive Explanation** 196
A.2.2.2.7.2.1 **A Brief Overview** 196
A.2.2.2.7.2.2 **An Extended Explanation** 197
B.2.6.1 **The Teaching** 197
B.2.6.2 **The Extended Explanation** 198
A.2.2.2.7.2.2.1 **How the Mind Separates from the Aggregates and the Ordinary Body** 198
B.2.6.2.1 **How the Mind Separates from the Aggregates and the Ordinary Body** 198
A.2.2.2.7.2.2.1.1 **How the Elements Dissolve** 199
B.2.6.2.1.1 **The Teachings on How the Elements Dissolve** 200
A.2.2.2.7.2.2.1.2 **How the Elements are Absorbed** 202
B.2.6.2.1.2 **The Way the Elements are Absorbed** 202
A.2.2.2.7.2.2.1.3 **Firmly Establishing these Teachings via the Special Essential Points** 204

A.2.2.2.7.2.2.2 **How Liberation Comes from the Realization [According to Capacity]**..................205
B.2.6.2.2 **How Realization Leads to Liberation**......................205
A.2.2.2.7.2.2.2.1 **Those of Great Capacity**..............206
B.2.6.2.2.1 **Those of Highest Capacity**........................207
A.2.2.2.7.2.2.2.2 **Those of Middling Capacity**........................208
A.2.2.2.7.2.2.2.2.1 **The Way of Arising**........................208
B.2.6.2.2.2 **Those of Middling Capacity**........................209
B.2.6.2.2.2.1 **At first, Liberation of the After-death State of the *Dharmadhātu***........................209
A.2.2.2.7.2.2.2.2.2 **The Way of Liberation**........................211
B.2.6.2.2.2.2 **Second, How Liberation Comes**........................212
A.2.2.2.7.2.2.2.2.3 **The Way Liberation Comes for Those of Lesser Capacity**........................216
B.2.6.2.2.3 **Those of Lesser Capacity**........................216
A.2.2.2.7.2.2.3 **How Delusion Ensues When There is No Realization**........................218
B.2.6.2.3 **An Explanation as to How Delusion Comes from Being Without Realization**........................221
A.2.2.2.7.2.3 **A Brief Summary**........................224
B.2.6.3 **Conclusion**........................224
A.3.0 **Concluding Practices**........................224
B.3.0 **Overall Conclusion**........................225
A.3.1 **Explaining the Greatness of These Instructions**........................225
B.3.1 **The Positive Qualities that Ensue from These Great Instructions**........................227
A.3.2 **Explaining How to Find and Keep up These Instructions**........................228
B.3.2 **How Whatever of This is Explained**........................228
B.3.3 **How the Enlightened Emanation Body came to Teach**........................229
A.3.3 **Explaining the Lineage of These Instructions**........................229
B.3.4 **The Way Followers Attain the Positive Qualities**........................230
B.3.5 **A Summary of the Basic Import of the Teachings**........................230

THE SIX ESSENTIAL POINTS OF *BODHICITTA* FOR PRACTICE 233

[Basis, Path, and Fruition Pith Instructions] 235
[The Manner of Arising of the Visions] 237
Separating the Brightness of Awakened Awareness From the Residual Dregs 240
Pointing Out 241
Delusion 242
Identifying the Conditions of Delusion 242
Making a Determination About Delusion 243
Meditation on the Heart-Lamp 244
Practicing Seeing Awakened Awareness Nakedly 245
Pointing Out Seeing the Essence Nakedly 246
Pointing Out Seeing the Clear-Light Nakedly 246
Making a Close-to-the-Heart Determination 246
Pointing Out the Three-fold Embodiment of Enlightenment 247
Making a Close-to-the-Heart Determination about the Three-fold Embodiment of Enlightenment 247
Determining the *Dharmakāya* 247
Determining the Enlightened Form-bodies 247
[The Lamp of the Dying Process and After-Death Bardos According to Capacity] 249
Conclusion 250

POINTING OUT THE SIX ENERGY DROPS 251

The Energy Drop of the Universal Ground 254

The Energy Drop of the Fleshy Heart 255

The Energy Drop of the Soft White Channel 257

The Energy Drop of the Fluid [Eye-Lamp] of the Extensive Lasso 258

The Energy Drop of Pointing Out the *Buddha*-fields 258

The Energy Drop of the After-Death Bardo 261

Bibliography 265

Acknowledgments

Our deepest gratitude to His Holiness the 33rd Menri Trizin. Without his support this work would never have been translated. Also, our deepest thanks to Kathleen McCarthy who did the initial copy editing on this manuscript, and to Susan Pottish who did the final stage of copy editing on this manuscript. Thanks to graphic artist Brad Reynolds for his masterful layout and sensitive handling of these complex scriptures. Our deepest gratitude goes to Dustin DiPerna of Bright Alliance Publishers for the personal touch he gave to the publication of this precious set of teachings. Thanks also to Roger and Brenda Gibson, whose generous donation paid for the translation, and to the Pointing Out the Great Way Foundation for sponsoring these translation projects.

Introduction

The *Instructions on the Six Lamps* (*sGron ma drug gi sdams pa*) is a major work from the Bon *Great Completion Oral Transmission Teachings from Zhang Zhung* (*rDzogs pa chen po zhang zhung snyan rgyud*). The teachings are attributed to Tapihritsa, who is believed to have practiced in the 8th century. Tapihritsa was the twenty-fifth lineage holder in an unbroken mind-to-mind transmission lineage of masters, all of whom are said to have attained great consciousness-transference, or the awareness-holder version of rainbow body, while dying. The twenty-fourth master was Zla ba rGyal mtsan, who is said to have passed the full collection of teachings to Tapihritsa. Tapihritsa is said to have had the intention to pass these lineage teachings to a worthy Bon *tantric* master, sNang bzher Lod po, but had reservations because Tapihritsa thought that sNang bzher Lod po had developed strong spiritual pride about the accomplishments of his *tantric* practice. Therefore, as an awareness-holder who had the capacity to emanate in whatever form he intended, he emanated in the form of a sixteen-year-old boy who appeared to sNang bzher Lod po and volunteered to serve sNang bzher Lod po at his hermitage site. Tapihritsa manifested certain paranormal attainments to sNang bzher Lod po in a way that subdued his spiritual pride. After that, sNang bzher Lod po understood that this boy was no ordinary being, and humbled himself, and received teachings from Tapihritsa. Five years later, after sNang bzher Lod po had been in a meditation retreat on a solitary island on a lake near Mt. Kailash, Tapihritsa emanated again, this time descending from the sky naked and sitting in a meditation posture. Then, he directly gave sNang bzher Lod po the pith instructions on the Six Lamps teachings.

Appropriate and Inappropriate Recipients of These Teachings

As secret and precious transmission instructions, they are given freely to appropriately qualified students and are not given to unqualified and inappropriate students. The root text begins with a list of qualifications of inappropriate recipients, saying, "...these instructions are not appropriate for those individuals: (1) who lack faith, (2) who have wrong views, (3) who lack confidence, and (4) who are easily distracted, spiritually immature, or who practice the lower vehicles. The root text next introduces the qualifications of those who are appropriate students, namely "...for those individuals who fear the cycling of rebirth and death, who seek enlightenment from the bottom of their hearts; for those who have tireless faith; for those who carry their lama on their crown [in Guru Yoga]; and for all those who abandon worldly activities and are seeking this profound truth." (334) The root text also refers to these Six Lamps teachings as the "six essential points of *bodhicitta*." (333) *Bodhicitta* represents enlightened intention. Enlightened intention means that the intention of Kun tu bZang po, the primordial *Buddha*, is for these precious pith instructions to be made available to qualified students as an intense means for attaining full *Buddhahood*. That is why the root text begins with an homage to Kun tu bZang po, whose enlightened intention is for awakened awareness to show itself to all sentient beings. The text says, "Homage to Kun tu bZang po, the primordial *Buddha* of self-awakened awareness." (332)

The Six Lamps Teachings

The Six Lamps is a very important teaching of by-passing Great Completion. There are two main types of Bon Great Completion meditations—thoroughly cutting through and by-passing. As the name implies, thoroughly cutting through teachings are designed to cut through the residuals of the "ordinary mind" (*sems*) so as to establish the unbounded wholeness of "awakened mind-itself" (*sems nyid*). However, despite the value of thoroughly cutting through practice in establishing the realization of awakened awareness, this meditation doesn't result in complete purification of the residual substantiality of perception and the physical body. For example, mountains still seem solid like mountains, and the physical body still seems solid and doesn't fully dissolve into light because some small particulate matter still exists after thoroughly cutting through practice. In contrast, by-passing practice completely dissolves the residual substantiality of perception and the physical body.

There are essentially four successive lamps teachings: teachings about the universal base; teachings on opening up the heart lamp for continuous realization of awakened awareness; teachings on opening the soft white channel pathway from the heart to the eye lamps; and teachings on setting up the view and gaze to experience the four levels of by-passing visions. Each set of teachings is introduced initially to be practiced in succession, until some degree of mastery is developed for each of the four lamps. Then, the practitioner meditates using all four lamps at once. The fifth lamp is essentially an extension of the fourth lamp. The fourth lamp sets up the initial meditation on the by-passing visions. The fifth lamp essentially describes the resultant meditative experiences, namely the four levels of by-passing visions. This is followed by a more refined level of practice called "making a close-to-the-heart determination." Tapihritsa uses six metaphors to introduce this closer, refined level of practice.

The sixth lamp describes a similar experience of visions during the dying process and after-death *bardos* because if the practitioner masters the four levels of visions during this lifetime, he or she is likely to find comparable visions appearing during the dying process very familiar, and can use recognition of the clear-light of death, and/or the visions in the *bardo* of the *dharmadhātu*, as the platform for attaining complete *Buddhahood* during the dying process or the after-death states.

The Lamp of the Universal Base

The first of Tapihritsa's teachings is to introduce the "natural state" (*gnas lugs*). (334) The ordinary mind is characterized by mind-wandering, distractibility, being lost in conceptual thought, and deluded, dualistic, localized perception of the ordinary world. From the vantage point of the ordinary mind it is nearly impossible to recognize awakened awareness as always right here. Always right here is a limitless field of bright awakened awareness shining forth. However, most sentient beings fail to recognize it because of being caught up in the clouds of conceptual thought and dualistic perception, like failing to recognize the sun that is always shining because it is covered by clouds. Therefore, the teachings begin with a description of the natural state so that the practitioner knows how to set up the view for the realization of awakened mind. The natural state entails direct experience of a timeless, limitless, non-dual field of awareness, wherein whatever arises in this expanse is immediately and automatically known as empty upon arising. Automatic emptiness of whatever arises immediately upon arising is important because automatic emptiness serves as a clearing agent for all residual instances of doing anything during meditation, and all residual attempts to conceptualize about state or outcome. As a result of automatic emptiness the mind returns to its natural state of simplicity (absent of all doing) and freshness (absent of all conceptualization. Once all residual conceptual thought settles down, the lucidity and brightness of the field of timeless, boundless awareness becomes apparent. This natural state is also referred to as "non-meditation meditation" (*sgom med*).

With this natural state as a foundation in meditation, it is possible to set up the view in just the right way to shift the basis of operation out of ordinary mind to operating out of awakened mind. The view—sometimes referred to as "lion's gaze"—entails taking the limitless, timeless field of awareness itself as the object of meditation, holding the view of the non-dual unbounded wholeness uninterruptedly, moment-by-moment, without looking at anything in particular. In this way, any tendency of the mind to pick out anything particular is viewed as the activity of the unbounded wholeness itself, in such a way that the view no longer interferes with the direct recognition of the unbounded wholeness that is always right here. However, the practitioner must use his or her metacognitive awareness to recognize this unbounded wholeness of awakened awareness through one or another of two pathways of recognition. First, is the pathway of recognizing non-localization. At some point the meditator realizes that he or she is no longer operating out of localized, individual consciousness, but instead is operating out of being the unbounded wholeness—a place that is no place and has no reference point. Alternatively, at some point the meditator realizes that there is something evidently distinct about the field of awakened awareness as compared to ordinary awareness in its "brightness" (*dwangs pa*), "intensity" (*ngar*), "sacredness" (*dam pa*), and "awakeness" (*hrig ge*). Either way, the practitioner comes to recognize awakened awareness as always right here. Recognition of this limitless expanse constitutes a direct realization of the limitless expanse of the *dharmakāya*, which literally means "the embodiment of all the teachings."

Once having recognized awakened awareness using these precious instructions, the practitioner's spiritual duty is to repeatedly settle into the natural state, set up the lion's gaze view, and shift his or her basis of operation during formal meditation sessions from ordinary mind to awakened mind frequently, for longer duration, and more immediately. Each time the meditator shifts the basis of operation to awakened mind, he or she dismantles more and more of the residuals of the ordinary mind. Over time, the practitioner remains in the awakened mind most of the time in formal meditation sessions. Then, the practitioner learns to "mix" (*'dres ba*) awakened awareness into a variety of daily activities, outside of formal meditation, until attaining the confidence that he or she can maintain awakened awareness at all times and in all situations.

As the practitioner frequently shifts the basis of operation from the ordinary mind to awakened mind, the view naturally shifts from the ground aspect of awakening to the expressive aspect of awakened mind. In other words, the view becomes seeing whatever arises moment-by-moment—every thought, emotion, sight, sound, special meditation state, etc.—as none other than the liveliness of awakened awareness, such that the view becomes a continuous, uninterrupted flow of liveliness. Once stabilizing the experience of liveliness, the practitioner then takes the view of the inseparable pair, simultaneously the limitless vast expanse of awareness-space and the uninterrupted liveliness of awakened awareness of whatever arises in that expanse. As part of that view, but not as a strategy of *doing* something, the practitioner no longer mentally engages whatever arises moment-by-moment. Because mental engagement—also called "accepting and rejecting" for processing (*blangdor*)—is necessary to form new karmic memory traces, non-mental engagement results in no longer forming new karmic memory traces, and therefore initiates an automatic process of releasing the ripening of all previously stored karmic memory traces. Through practicing non-mental engagement all the time, all immediately arising karmic memory traces run their course and immediately disappear, leaving no trace, like writing on water, and all previously stored karmic memory traces are automatically released. This automatic process is called "self-arising/self-liberated" (*rang snang rang 'grol*), and is also called the "path of liberation" (*'grol ba'i lam*), and the end point over time is referred to as "*dharmadhātu* exhaustion" (*chos nyid zad pa*) because the entire storehouse of karmic memory traces is exhausted. The endpoint is "complete purification and the flourishing of all positive states" (*sang rgyas*). Since negative states of mind obscure the experience of the positive states, after sufficient purification the eighty-three Bon "positive states" (*yon tan*) become manifest or flourish.

Self arising/self-liberated as a practice is the thoroughly cutting through Great Completion prerequisite for the by-passing Six Lamps practice. The teaching on the first lamp is essentially an introduction to the "universal basis" or "groundless-ground" of existence (*kun gzhi*). This refers to the limitless expanse of awakened awareness like a limitless expanse of space. Like space, it has no substance and is groundless. Unlike space, this limitless awareness/space has the capacity to know, so it is sometimes referred to as "knowing-awareness" (*shes rig*).

In ordinary experience, this limitless expanse is rarely recognized because the universal basis has an overlay of millions of karmic memory traces. It has become the reservoir for all these karmic memory traces. The "universal basis" (*kun gzhi*) has become the "ordinary storehouse mind" (*kun gzhi rnam shes*). However, the Great Completion practitioner has now developed a stable practice of automatic self-arising/self-liberated to the point where the matrix of existence (*kun gzhi*) has been cleaned up of the majority of karmic memory traces, such that it is now possible to directly realize this universal basis or matrix of existence, no longer obscured by the overlay of millions of memory traces.

Development of self-arising/self-liberated practice is the starting point of Six Lamps practice. The first lamp teaching essentially extends the view of non-engagement of whatever arises in the expanse, herein specifically applied to ordinary perception—sights, sounds, smells, tastes, and body sensations—instead of to the spontaneous ripening karmic memory traces and emotions in thoroughly cutting through practice. The path of liberation has three parallel tracks, each of which addresses a different type of ordinary experience to purify: (1) Thoroughly cutting through self-arising/self liberated Great Completion practice purifies karmic memory traces and afflictive emotions. (2) By-passing inner fire practice purifies the residual substantiality of the physical body. (3) By-passing visions practice purifies ordinary perception. It mainly emphasizes purification of ordinary perception and conceptual thought into the three pure visions, with ultimate sound reflecting the purified sound of the liveliness of awakened awareness, pure light reflecting purified visual forms, and light-rays (because of directionality) reflecting purified conceptual thought. The Six Lamps is a major teaching on the Bon by-passing Great Completion practice of refining ordinary perception and developing the four levels of visionary experience. Such by-passing practice on the visions is the most effective way to develop a stable perception of the pure *Buddha* realms of the *mandala* of the *sambhogakāya* as always right here. This is a necessary stage in the development of the direct manifestation of the three-fold embodiment of enlightenment and fruition *Buddhahood*.

The Six Lamps practice begins with special pith instructions designed for direct realization of the *dharmakāya*, i.e., the limitless expanse of non-dual awakened awareness space. This limitless expanse is the groundless-ground of existence within which everything arises as the liveliness of awakened awareness. If the purpose of practice is to set up the view for direct realization of the universal base—the limitless expanse of empty awareness/space—the term used is *dharmakāya*.

If the purpose of practice is to realize everything that arises within this expanse as liveliness, the term used for the matrix within which everything arises is *dharmadhātu*. These respective terms refer to the ground aspect and the appearance aspects of awakening. Ordinary individuals are highly unlikely to directly recognize the ground aspect of the universal basis (*kun gzhi*) because such direct realization has become obscured by an overlay of millions of karmic memory traces. They mainly experience the very active ripening of karmic memory traces in the form of spontaneously emerging, largely negative states of mind coming from the ordinary storehouse mind (*kun gzhi rnam shes*). However, Great Completion practitioners who have practiced self-arising/self-liberated for some time have largely cleaned out karmic memory traces, such that direct realization of the universal basis or groundless-ground becomes quite possible. For this reason, the teaching of the first lamp points out the nature of the universal basis or groundless-ground. As the *Ultimate Meaning* commentary says, "These instructions explain the essence of universal ground just as it is." (397)

The root text introduces the essential point of the teaching. It says, "The universal ground, *bodhicitta* itself, is empty clear-light and it is unconstructed and unadulterated. It is the great original purity of the *dharmakāya*. It is free of any stains whatsoever. It is awareness untouched [by any limits or extremes]." (334) The limitless lucid field of awakened awareness is never covered by mental constructions or stained by ordinary states. Yet this universal ground is the container for all of both the positive states of *nirvāṇa* and the suffering of *saṁsāra*. Therefore, stable realization of the universal ground entails liberation from all ordinary states of mind, such as those based on dualistic constructs such as "existence/non-existence, appearance/emptiness, eternalism/nihilism, birth/death, and accepting/rejecting," as the Sun-Light commentary says.

The pith instructions next introduce the Enlightened Form-bodies—pure realms of the *sambhogakāya*—and the aspiration to serve the welfare of sentient beings stuck in cyclic existence by manifesting enlightened intention in the form of immeasurable emanations or *nirmāṇakāyas*, impartially serving sentient beings throughout cyclic existence, that are also spontaneously present in the universal ground. Having implanted the view of the three-fold embodiment of enlightenment, the root text returns to a more detailed description of the universal ground. It adds, "It is the same lucid space that pervades everything—lucid space without partiality." (335) This means that the *dharmakāya* is genuinely limitless space, free of edges or boundaries, and of any kind of articulation of this limitless awareness/space, such as top/bottom, front/back/, cardinal or intermediate directions. This universal ground is the "domain" (*klong*) of infinite space, the matrix within which everything exists, everything arises, and everything is interconnected.

Next the root text introduces this as the ground of awakened awareness. It says, "From the domain of space [awakened awareness] arises like the sun rising in the sky." (335) Here what is emphasized is the lucidity pathway of recognizing awakened awareness. It adds that awakened awareness "is lucid. Its nature is empty. Its aspect is non-conceptual knowing-awareness." (335) From the mind-perspective or ground aspect, this limitless awareness space is "knowing-awareness." From the event perspective or appearance aspect, this same awakened awareness is dynamic, expressing its "liveliness" (*rtsal*) in a pure form, namely as the visions of ultimate sound, light, and light-rays, and in an impure form as ordinary visual forms, sounds, thoughts, and emotions. The root text continues, "From that [lucid, empty, knowing-awareness] three types of liveliness appear, and the three are ultimate sound, light, light-rays." (335) However, the text makes it very clear that visions must be seen in the non-dual field, and not through the lens of ordinary dualistic perception. It says, "Object and awakened awareness [that knows the object] are without distinction." (335) Another way of emphasizing non-dual perception of the visions is to describe them as "self-arising" (*rang shar*).

Next the teachings address ordinary conceptual thought. For sentient beings, conceptual thought used to interpret ordinary perceptual events leads to "deluded" (*'khrul ba*) perception. However, for the Great Completion practitioner familiar with self-arising/self-liberated meditation, the view of conceptual thought arising from the universal ground allows the practitioner to see conceptual thoughts in their purest form, as light-rays. Ordinary thought has the properties of moving in the field of awareness and of having directionality. We can direct our thoughts along certain lines or themes. Seen in its original purity, conceptual thought still moves in the field of awareness, as a property of liveliness, and thought still has directionality. However, seen correctly, thoughts are empty and insubstantial, and express the speed and directionality of enlightened intention, like rays of light that streak in various directions from the sun, their single source. Ultimately, conceptual thought in its original purity is discriminating primordial wisdom utilized by a *Buddha* to discern the best match of an approach or skillful means to a given individual, and many specific approaches for each sentient being served. The root text says, "Although the king of knowing-awareness is free from conceptual thought, all the diverse types of reflective thoughts...arise from the universal ground, like light-rays...from the liveliness of awakened awareness...the six sense-consciousnesses and the six sense-objects also arise from liveliness."(336) In other words, the by-passing Great Completion practitioner is instructed to view all thought and conceptual interpretation of perceptual events as none other than the liveliness of awakened awareness.

Tapihritsa summarizes this teaching on the first lamp on the inseparable pair of the universal ground and awakened awareness and on the liveliness of conceptual thought that arises within it as follows. He says, "Universal ground is sort of like an open portal of space. Awakened awareness is sort of like the heart of the sun. Ordinary conceptual thought is sort of like the rays of the sun. Ultimate sound arises as self-occurring liveliness. Light is sort of like rainbow light. Light-rays are like a matrix of sun rays. [This defines] the natural state whose disposition is primordially unconditioned." (336) The objective of by-passing practice of the first lamp is to establish the universal ground as a stable basis of operation, and every moment to view whatever arises within this expanse as none other than the liveliness of awakened awareness, letting everything run its own course without mental engagement, and through that perpetuate the process of automatic self-arising/self-liberated.

Tapihritsa adds a teaching on how the pathway of deluded perception develops. He says, "Sentient beings [who wander through *saṁsāra* by virtue of their] karma do not have the realization." The difference between *Buddhas* and sentient beings is that *Buddhas* have realized the universal ground and awakened awareness and perceive the pure visions, and sentient beings have not realized the universal ground nor recognized awakened awareness and perceive the impure ordinary seemingly existing world." (336) He adds, "Failing to know these as self-appearing illusions, you see them as real external appearances. The ultimate truth of awakened awareness becomes obscured by ordinary conceptual thought, seeing it as something other." (337) This failure of accurate recognition leads to dualistic perception, then to the causal elements, which create the impression of substantiality, and finally to the creation of the ordinary sense-systems and sense-objects. The "mind consciousness" (*yid shes*) utilizes conceptual thought to appraise and interpret perceptual objects, and, in so doing, conceptualization instead of direct perception defines the pathway of deluded perception. Tapihritsa defines the path of delusion. He says, "Through the influence of not recognizing [awakened awareness] and becoming totally conceptualized, grasping the duality of self and other arises. Through grasping the duality of self and other, afflictive emotions like the five poisons occur.... Under the influence of the five poisons, the karmic activity of the formative aggregate occurs. Under the influence of [both] afflictive emotions and karmic activity, habitual karmic propensities accumulate in the storehouse. Universal ground…becomes the storehouse for the accumulation of karmic traces…. Through the accumulation of karmic propensities associated with the six sense-consciousnesses, there comes delusions of the six classes of beings… the known ordinary world arises." (338) However, the precious pith instructions define the pathway out of delusion to the complete purification of perception, through which direct perception of the Enlightened Form-bodies becomes likely, and, through that, attainment of the realization of the three-fold embodiment of enlightenment.

THE LAMP OF THE FLESHY HEART-MIND

The next precious secret teaching is on how to enhance the recognition of awakened awareness by focusing the view on the center of the thumb-sized space in the center of the physical heart. While it is certainly true that awakened awareness is non-localized, and its limitless unbounded wholeness pervades everywhere, it is also true that focusing the view in a localized manner on the center of the space within the physical heart space enhances the recognition of awakened awareness. The reason is that upon conception the indestructible essence of individualized consciousness is seated in the center of the heart and held there by a series of *chakra* knots. Therefore, focus that is localized at this site, as compared to anywhere else, increases the likelihood of direct recognition of awakened awareness, and of continuous recognition of the full measure of awakened awareness. As the *Ultimate Meaning* commentary says, "In the midst of groundless-ground the center of the [fleshy] heart is where stainless, completely pure awakened awareness stays and arises in-and-by-itself.... This is the lamp wherein [awakened awareness] stays as great self-lucidity and is not obscured by anything whatsoever." (415) The root text adds that awakened awareness is easier to recognize at the site of the heart lamp because the lucidity pathway of recognition is enhanced there. Tapihritsa says, "Although the universal ground pervades the body, filling everything like space, it is generally obscured by the clouds of delusion and lacks lucidity. Within the center of the heart-mind, primordial wisdom stays on the inside as immense yet pervasive clarity, like a cloudless sky. Although awakened awareness stays and saturates everything like the sun, it is generally obscured by the darkness of conceptual thought and lacks clarity. In the center of this heart-mind, self-awakened awareness resides and shines forth immensely from within, like the [dawning] sun in a cloudless sky." (341) Emphasis is given to the pathway of recognition of the bright, lucid, awakened awareness at the site of the heart. There awakened awareness is said to shine forth in its full radiance like the dawning of the first morning sun. Yet this immense light is not perceived dualistically, as bright light out there, but is recognized as self-arising, immense brightness of knowing-awareness.

Although awakened awareness is non-localized and pervades everywhere as the "mother" consciousness, it is also packaged in the heart of each sentient being as the "son" consciousness. Practicing at the site of the heart lamp collapses the boundary between mother and son consciousness, which is also the dissolution of packaging awakened mind-itself in the physical body or anywhere. Tapihritsa uses a number of metaphors to illustrate the release of awakened awareness: like a bird in a cage when the cage disappears, like a person riding a horse on the ground where the ground disappears, and like a fin caught in a net where the net is taken away.

Introduction

The Lamp of the Soft White Channels

The next step in by-passing practice is to delineate the channel from the heart to the fluid eye lamps. This is not an ordinary wind channel. It is called the *kati* tube channel or soft white channel, which consists of a short horizontal pathway, the golden tube channel, which extends from the center of the heart and connects to the upper half of the central channel, then connects the upper central channel to the throat, and then splits into two channels that go up the back side of the head under the skull, and loop down connecting to each of the two fluid eye lamps. The root text says:

> Then, in the center of this heart-mind [space], from the liveliness of the light and awakened awareness, the wind of the space element arises. From that, the door of the heart-mind opens to the channels. [This is the great golden channel that goes from the heart to the central channel]. From that, by means of the upwardly moving winds, the interior of the central channel opens upwards. This [wind] courses up the central channel and extends through the throat *chakra*, and emerges from the center of the [throat *chakra*]. It penetrates the *chakra* of great bliss at the top of the crown. At the crown protuberance is a gateway that is a completely open hole. This is the pathway to pass beyond [all] suffering [i.e., the path of *nirvāṇa*]. [It is also called the channel of threads of white silk]. (342)

However, as an advanced by-passing Great Completion practice, it is not necessary to visualize the channel. Rather, the channel pathway defines itself-to-itself-by-itself. Once awakened awareness arises in its full radiance in the heart lamp, it spontaneously ignites. The meditator perceives considerable activity of dancing energy drops at the heart-mind site. Next, these activated energy drops begin to flow and define their own pathway, first flowing backwards and horizontally defining the golden tube channel, then flowing upwards in the upper central channel to the Adam's apple, then flowing along two side channels around the outside of the brain under the skull, and then turning down to enter the eye lamps. Each time the practitioner focuses on the site of the eye lamp, awakened awareness brightens, the energy drops again become activated, the energy drops again flow through the soft white channel and pour into the fluid eyes lamps, and each time the channel pathway becomes more and more clear until the energy drops flow easily from the heart lamp to the fluid eye lamps without the slightest obscuration.

This is the point along the path where it becomes obvious to the practitioner that the unfolding path has its own intelligence and shows itself-to-itself-by-itself. Therefore, the language shifts from talking about awakened awareness to talking about primordial wisdom manifesting itself. As the root text says, "Here regarding the Lamp of the Soft White Channels is the essential point on how to draw forth the transparency of primordial wisdom from whatever occurs on the path." (342) Transparent here means that the self-arising intelligence of the path becomes obvious. The root text adds, "This central channel is like a cloudless sky, wherein primordial wisdom shines forth with complete transparency." (344)

The Fluid Eye Lamps of the Extensive Lasso

The fluid eye lamps refer to the fluid eye balls, which are like crystal balls within which the pure visions arise and are directly perceived. Setting up the gaze in the right way at this site enables the practitioner to observe the moment-by-moment dance of the pure visions as an expression of the liveliness of primordial wisdom showing itself-to-itself-by-itself. As the root text says, "Here is what is called 'the essential point of the Fluid Eye Lamp of the Extensive Lasso,' to see awakened awareness nakedly in whatever has arisen from the [sense] gateway [of the eyes]." (344) The practitioner sets up the gaze looking out from the universal ground, and looks up at an angle just below the lower boundary of the eyebrows—the eyebrow fence. The angle of looking up is sometimes referred to as the "bolt-mountain" gaze. As the root text says, "The gateway for seeing awakened awareness projects out [just below the eyebrow fence]." (345) The distance of the gaze is to look as far as the outer surface of each fluid eye lamp, much like looking at a film projected onto a movie screen or like looking at images appearing on the surface of two crystal balls. After setting up the gaze, the practitioner watches the dance of visions on the surface of the viewing screen, the fluid eye lamps.

It is important that the practitioner not see the visions dualistically as out there, but rather sees them as self-arising and generated inside the eye lamps. This essential point is implied in the metaphor of an extensive lasso. The metaphor implies that ordinary visual perception seems to project out from the eyes to perceive visual forms out there. In other words, ordinary perception is like a lasso that extends out to capture visual forms as if they were out there to catch. However, the metaphor also implies roping something in. The practitioner must overcome the habit of seeing the visions as out there, but must come to see them as internally generated. This argument is similar to the Mind Only school in Buddhism. The objective of seeing into the emptiness of visual forms as being substantial and out there is to adopt an inward orientation, such that all seemingly out there visual forms are viewed as in the field of the mind's non-dual awareness. Roping in visual forms in Great Completion practice is comparable to adopting an inward orientation in Mind Only practice.

The Condensed Style; All Four Lamps at Once

Before developing the visions the practitioner meditates on all four lamps simultaneously. As the root text says, "...the universal ground stays primordially as it is, and awakened awareness stays in the heart.... [Primordial wisdom] is drawn forth on the pathway of the [upper central] channel, and then arises in the lamp of the fluid gateway [of the eyes]....The gateway for seeing awakened awareness projects [just below the eyebrow fence]." (345) First, the meditator establishes the universal ground of limitless, non-dual, non-localized awakened awareness as his or her basis of operation. Having established this as the basis of operation, at the same time the practitioner focuses on the heart lamp until awakened awareness arises like the dawning of the first morning sun, and then until the energy drops become ignited. Now, by practicing both lamps simultaneously the practitioner lets the soft white channel define itself until the pathway is free of all obscuration and the energy drops flow freely from the heart to the eyes. Then, by setting up the view and gaze correctly, the energy drops are expressed as the visions on the surface of the fluid eye lamps. In other words, the practitioner opens all four lamps at once. Operating out of the universal ground corrects for seeing the visions as out there. Opening the heart lamp guarantees a continuous flow of the liveliness of awakened awareness to fuel the incessant display of visions on the surface of the fluid eye lamps. Defining and opening the soft white channel, free of obscuration, insures a continuous flow of energy drops from the heart lamp to the fluid eye lamps to fuel the visions. Setting up the gaze allows for viewing the appearance of the internally-generated visions on the outer surface of the fluid eye lamps, as if watching a movie projected onto a movie screen.

THE DEVELOPMENT OF THE VISIONS; THE LAMP OF THE *BUDDHA*-FIELDS

Once firmly setting up the view and gaze and practicing over time, there are five levels in the development of visions. Tapihritsa summarizes these levels:

> First, appearances seem to proliferate. They are seen like concentrated and scattered mercury. Second, visions multiply like a wildfire, like the sun or moon shining forth in the space beyond. Awakened awareness is seen as a *maṇḍala* of light. The energy drops are seen like tents of light. Third, the visions become quite extensive. The *maṇḍala* of the *sambhogakāya* and the five enlightened families are seen. Fourth, the visions become complete. The *maṇḍala* of the gesture [*mudra*] of spontaneous presence is seen. The [pure] visions are seen as the *Buddha*-fields of light. Seeing becomes an unshakable miraculous display.
> Finally, the ultimate state of the visions shines forth. Light is the naturally arising light of awakened awareness, the way a rainbow arises by itself in empty space. Ultimate sound is the naturally occurring sound of awakened awareness, the way an echo occurs by itself in empty space. Light-rays are the natu-

rally emitting rays of awakened awareness, the way the miraculous display of reflections appears in space. The Enlightened Form-bodies are the naturally-occurring form of awakened awareness, the way the form of the reflection of the moon arises over water. (349-350)

Ultimately, all visual forms, smells, tastes, and body sensations directly manifest as light. Ordinary thought and emotions, because they have the characteristic of directionality, directly manifest as light-rays, also having directionality. Ordinary sound directly manifests as ultimate sound, namely the sound of the liveliness of awakened awareness expressing itself. These are referred to as the "three visions" (*snang gsum*). Ultimately, the experienced by-passing practitioner lives in a world of lively awakened awareness and sacred light.

Even when meditating on all four lamps simultaneously, the initial visions are still sometimes hard to get started. Seeing the visions at first is often enhanced by sun gazing. The practitioner meditates outside at times when the sun is not too strong—early morning up to mid-morning, or late afternoon after mid-afternoon. The practitioner meditates either with the sun behind him or her or directly looks at the sun with the eyes covered by a silk cloth. The practitioner never looks directly at the sun. Practicing in the presence of sunlight activates the energy drops and the visions. Energy drops dance on the surface of the eye lamps. Patterns of ever changing colors like looking into a kaleidoscope.

The root text says, "Once staying in bare [awareness] without grasping, open, and free of conceptual thought, then all seeming appearances of sense-objects become like reflections in a crystal ball, and shine forth." (347) The visions are more likely to appear once direct perception is purified of conceptualization about perception. The first level of visions is expressed as moving energy drops, filaments, and splashes of some colors appearing usually in the periphery of the visual field. The practitioner is instructed to hold the gaze "until you see a miraculous display, the matrix of light-rays, like a web or filigree: light-rays right within the obscurity of darkness. Come to see the immeasurable light of the clear appearance, like a rainbow in the sky." (349) The *Ultimate Meaning* commentary adds:

You encounter many of these—encountering two, encountering three, encountering many that appear, the heart-essence of awakened awareness, mere grains of energy drops, like filaments of energy drops, or silver-white threads, or filaments of white silk. They stay like a string of very small grains. In the midst of these energy drops the coarse types of enlightened *Buddha*-bodies are just projections and there they reside in a subtle way. At that time these visions are like a waterfall gushing from a mountain, or like drops of water not staying but scattering or coming together. They arise and cease, scatter and come together, move and become agitated. (448-449)

At the second level, simple geometric shapes appear; splashes of brightly colored lights of all colors cascade. The root text says, "Second, visions multiply like a wildfire, like the sun or moon shining forth in the space beyond. Awakened awareness is seen as a *mandala* of light. The energy drops are seen like tents of light." (350) The *Ultimate Meaning* commentary adds:

At that time, the lucid self-radiance of the *mandala* of light, the essence of self-awakened awareness, is made clear, having a brilliance that is never obstructed. The external and internal body is made clear—the flesh, blood, muscles, wind channels, sense-organs, sense-supports, become the unobstructed vessel of truth [as a light-body]. These visions of clear-light arise externally everywhere in all directions and internally without obscuration. In these fields the visions of white energy drops arise; the chain of energy drops surrounded by the offering tent of five [wisdom] lights; lucid, clear, and bright light-rays emanate; a chain of three energy drops about the size of a bronze dish; an offering tent of energy drops like peacock eggs and so forth. They arise more slowly and gently than before, and appear more stable for a moment. In the midst of this, a very subtle enlightened *Buddha*-body just the size of a very small grain emerges for a little bit with just the slightest clarity. A white chain of energy drops and various colored energy drops also arise like light-rays. Internally, through the strength of the clarity of the practitioner's realization these do not proliferate but become liberated in-and-by-themselves. (449-450)

There is a remarkable shift between the second and third level of visions. The meditator is likely to get previews of third level visions. At times the ordinary world will seem to fade and instead the meditator directly perceives the sacred *Buddha*-fields of the *mandala* as being always right here. In fact, the sacred realms of the mandala are indeed always right here. They are not to be found by travelling to some remote *Buddha*-field. The essential point is that the conceptual interpretation of perception by the mind consciousness (*yid shes*) obscures the direct perception of the sacred realms of the mandala as being always right here. However, the practice of self-arising/self-liberated, followed by practice with respect to the direct perception of the first levels of visions has purified perception sufficiently that at some point the *Buddha* realms become obvious as always right here.

In order to insure the correct realization of these *Buddha*-fields and of the three-fold embodiment of enlightenment, the root text includes a teaching on recognizing them. The root text utilizes two kinds of teachings, an initial pointing out instruction, followed by a teaching to develop a more refined realization, called a "close-to-the-heart instruction." The pointing out instruction begins with a review of how to recognize the *dharmakāya*. Tapihritsa says,

> Here are the first, the pointing out instructions. Oh! Children of the Lineage! The natural state, universal ground, stays as [ultimate] *bodhicitta*, that which entirely pervades everything and is without boundaries or divisions. This is the expanse of the *dharmadhātu*. When this stays, only this stays and nothing else, as the immense original purity of self-awakened awareness. This is the self-arising *dharmakāya,* wherein the *Buddha*-fields of the *dharmadhātu* abide in their own way. Even though it accompanies you perpetually across the three times it remains unrecognized. (346)

Next, Tapihritsa gives the pith instruction for recognizing the pure realms of the *sambhogakāya* as always right here.

> Herein are the unsurpassable highest *Buddha*-fields of 'Og Min...
> Here the *sambhogakāya* shines forth in-and-by-itself, and the *Buddha*-fields of the *sambhogakāya* also remain in-and-by-themselves. If there is no direct realization, only deluded realms come forth. (346)

At a certain point in the purification process the practitioner sees the sacred realms everywhere: looking into each individual energy drop, looking into the heart lamp, looking into the visual field of the eye lamps, or looking into the seed-syllables in the chakras and at points in the channels within the sacred landscape of the body.

As direct realization of the *sambhogakāya* becomes constant and stable a genuine aspiration begins to grow that all sentient beings throughout cyclic existence who fail to realize this sacred world come to the realization of the *Buddha*-fields. As the contrast between the sacred world and the ordinary world deepens through meditation, the aspiration grows stronger and stronger. At some point the aspiration explodes into immeasurable enlightened intentions, each specific to immeasurable sentient beings. These become manifest as immeasurable emanations each with the intention to serve the welfare of a specific sentient being, subduing their mind-stream and guiding them through teaching out of cyclic existence. The ordinary activities of the three gateways—body, speech, and mind—manifest as enlightened body, enlightened speech, and enlightened heart-mind in the form of immeasurable enlightened activities serving the welfare of sentient beings. Tapihritsa gives the essential pith instruction for the practitioner recognizing him- or herself as innumerable emanation bodies. He says once the sense-systems are purified this becomes obvious:

> ...then the six sense systems and six sense-objects arise as the liveliness [of awakened awareness]. The seemingly ordinary various activities of the three [doors]—body, speech, and mind—are the *nirmāṇakāyas* arising in-and-by-themselves, yet staying in-and-by-themselves as the *Buddha*-fields of the *nirmāṇakāyas*. If

there is no direct realization, only the six classes of ordinary beings seem to arise. (346)

[The root text] gives the pith instructions for the third level of visions: "Then [third] the visions become quite extensive. The *mandala* of the *sambhogakāya* and the five enlightened *Buddha* families are seen." (350) According to the *Ultimate Meaning* commentary, the sign that signals a shift to the third level of visions is that the energy drops stop moving and become stable. Then it becomes obvious that each individual energy drop is like a computer chip that contains the entire world of the sacred mandala. All that is required is for the practitioner to open right into any energy drop. The commentary says:

> Even though there are many energy drops, they become differentiated into each of the five *Buddha* families. Within each of the energy drops each of the respective five *Buddha* families shines forth. The essence of awakened awareness is a single thread of compassion [extending throughout all existence]. The energy drops stay [stationary] like a string of pearls, and from inside of each of these, each of the five enlightened *Buddha*-bodies shines forth. (450)

The fourth level of visions is when the visions become complete and the two Enlightened Form-bodies—*sambhogakāya* and the *nirmāṇakāyas*—manifest in a stable way. The root text says, "The visions become complete. The *mandala* of the gesture [*mudra*] of spontaneous presence is seen. The [pure] visions are seen as the *Buddha*-fields of light. Seeing becomes an unshakable miraculous display." (350) The *Ultimate Meaning* commentary explains in more detail:

> Thus, the pure visions arise. Being purified by the liveliness of primordial wisdom's awakened awareness, the impure five aggregates become pure by leaving them in their own way and arise as the five deities. Having separated the pure elements from the dregs, seemingly real external appearances, when left in their own way, become pure, and become directly manifest

as the three-fold embodiment of enlightenment and all the *Buddha*-fields existing in themselves as spontaneously present. Internally, these pure visions appearing by themselves arise impartially in three ways—externally, internally, and secretly—in the immeasurable *mandala* along with their thrones and their mansions. Externally, internally, and secretly, emanating from the five principal *Buddha* families, many visions arise. Whatever arises, the *sambhogakāya* and the *nirmāṇakāyas*, everything—the ornaments, the throne, the major characteristics, the minor characteristics, possessed with the three certainties, emanating light-rays in the ten directions with immovable clarity, seeing immovably, and internally the occurrence of mere arising without meditation, without distraction wherein the movement of the mind toward effortful thought of an object of meditation and an act of meditation—is liberated. (451)

The fifth and final level is when the visions become exhausted and cease, and what remains is merely the unobstructed liveliness of awakened awareness, manifesting as the fruition of the three-fold embodiment of enlightenment directly, wherein *Buddhahood* becomes manifest in a stable way. The root text says, "Finally, the ultimate state of the visions shines forth. Light is the naturally arising light of awakened awareness, the way a rainbow arises by itself in empty space."(350) The *Ultimate Meaning* commentary explains:

> Thus, the aggregates [of the physical body] having outflows and the enlightened *Buddha*-bodies and *Buddha*-fields without outflows arise. They arise as the liveliness of primordial wisdom's self-awakened awareness. Know this pure miraculous display of self-appearance. The light is self-light like a rainbow. The sound is the self-sound like an echo. The light-rays are self-rays like the rays of the sun. Form is self-form like reflections arising in a mirror. This brings the three visions to their ultimate end. This ends the close-to-the-heart instructions. What is to be purified has been purified. What is to be realized has been realized. There is liberation from the ordinary body and mind as the primordial wisdom of the enlightened body of the deity [of the *mandala*]. (451-452)

The close-to-the-heart instructions introduce the same points for a deeper, more refined realization of the three-fold embodiment of enlightenment using passages from scripture, metaphors, and signs drawn from actual meditation experiences. Tapihritsa introduced six metaphors to guide the practice. Each metaphor addresses a certain stage of the overall by-passing Great Completion practice. The realization that awakened awareness is always right here is illustrated by a butter lamp that is always lit. The effects of purification based on the practice of self-arising/self-liberated is illustrated by a pure lotus arising from the mud. The immense brightness of awakened awareness in the heart lamp is illustrated by the heart of the sun. The direct perception of the initial visions is illustrated by the metaphor of a spotless mirror. The direct, non-conceptual experience of the magical display of the visions on the surface of the fluid eye lamps at the eyebrow fence is illustrated by images appearing in two crystal balls. The exhaustion of all the visions is illustrated by the metaphor of pouring space into space.

The Lamp of the After-Death States

Tapihritsa adds a supplemental teaching on how to use the dying process and after-death states as a vehicle for realization. During the dying process the mind separates from the body, conceptual thought ceases, perception of sense-objects ceases, and the five elements dissolve and become absorbed into each other. What remains at a certain point in the dying process is only the clear-light of death. The metacognitive recognition of, or failure to recognize, the clear-light of dying is very similar to recognizing, or failing to recognize, awakened awareness during one's lifetime. Therefore, recognition of the clear-light of dying becomes an opportunity to attain *Buddhahood* through accurate recognition. Furthermore, even if failing to recognize the clear-light of dying at the right time during the dying process, it is still very possible to recognize the true nature of the visions during the next after-death state of the *bardo* of the *dharmadhātu* because the visions in that *bardo* are comparable to the levels of visions in by-passing Great Completion practice, such that the by-passing practitioner is likely to find the after-death visions of the *bardo* of the *dharmadhātu* to be familiar ground.

Tapihritsa offers individualized teachings according to the practitioner's capacity. The practitioner of highest capacity is capable of recognizing the clear-light of dying at the point of physical death when the subtle mind separates from the body. The root text says, "At the right moment, as the mind separates from its close association with the body, it is possible to distinguish the brightness from the dregs…. In the expanse of universal ground, like infinite space without boundaries, primordial wisdom's awakened awareness arises, pervades and spreads everywhere like the sun." (351)Those of middling capacity are unlikely to recognize the clear-light of dying during the dying process, but if they have practiced by-passing during their life they are likely to find the visions of the *dharmadhātu* to be quite familiar, and therefore, have the opportunity for realization of *Buddhahood* during the *bardo* of the *dharmadhātu*. The root text says, "The appearance of the three—ultimate sound, light, and light-rays—shines forth…awakened awareness remains, unsupported and naked [the realization becomes possible]…having developed familiarity with it…these visions become self-liberated as illusions." (352) Those of lesser capacity, even if given the pith instructions during their lifetimes, "have less realization…[and] they remain deluded in the after-death state. Through the influence of these pith instructions, however, they may attain a body associated with a favorable rebirth [next lifetime]," according to the root text. (353)

According to the root text, after Tapihritsa appeared in the sky and conveyed the root text teachings, he disappeared like a rainbow fading in the sky. His final instruction was, "Be guided by this oral transmission free of the stains of ordinary words." (354)

THE SIX LAMPS
ACCORDING TO THE ZHANG ZHUNG ORAL TRANSMISSION LINEAGE OF BON DZOGCHEN

ROOT TEXT BY TAPIHRITSA
AND
GYERPUNG NANGZHER LOPO

Explanatory Commentaries:
A. THE ORNAMENTATION OF SUNLIGHT COMMENTARY
BY URI

B. THE INTENTION AND ULTIMATE MEANING COMMENTARY
BY DRUGOM GYALWA YUNGDRUNG

TRANSLATED UNDER THE GUIDANCE OF
HIS HOLINESS THE THIRTY-THIRD
MENRI TRIZIN

BY GESHE SONAM GURUNG
AND DANIEL P. BROWN, PH.D.

FOR MUSTANG BON FOUNDATION

Reader's Note:

The root text is in **bold Franklin Gothic**.

Each section of the root text is followed by one or both explanatory commentaries, which are labeled **Commentary A** and **Commentary B**.

(Page numbers for the commentary are in parentheses.)

The two practice-related commentaries, *The Six Essential Points of Bodhicitta*, and *The Six Energy Drops* are included at the end. Both explanatory commentaries and both practice-related commentaries are from the same volume (vol. 27) of the Bon Dialectical School texts.

(331) Here are the teachings on the Six Lamps from the *Zhang Zhung snyan rgyud* lineage of the Great Completion.

Commentary A:

(319) Here is the Ornamentation of Sunlight Commentary on the [Six] Lamps according to the *Zhang Zhung* Oral Transmission Lineage of Great Perfection.

(332) Homage to Kun tu bZang po, omniscient self-awakened awareness.

Commentary A:

The root text says, "Homage to Kun tu bZang po, omniscient self-awakened awareness." Here are the teachings for seeing awakened awareness nakedly, and the pith instructions on the essential points for reaching the final state of Great Completion.

There are three divisions to opening up the pith instructions regarding what is referred to as the "Six Essential Points of *Bodhicitta*:"

(1) the meaning of the previous described preliminaries,

(2) making a determination of the meaning of the essence of the main practices, and

(3) a brief conclusion.

A.1.0 The Meaning of the Previous Described Preliminaries

The meaning of the previous described preliminaries has three parts:

(1) the homage,
(2) the actual teachings on the preliminaries, and
(3) a brief summary.

Commentary B:

B.1.0 The Overall Meaning

"Homage to Kun tu bZang po, omniscient self-awakened awareness." These instructions are the epitome of the oral and pith instructions of this lineage. They are the quintessence of everything for the gateway of this [Great] Vehicle. They are the vital essence of the heart-mind of Kun tu bZang po. They are the pith instructions of the nine victors of the Mind-to-Mind Transmission Lineage, the instructions of the Ear-Whispering Lineage of the twenty-four awareness-holders. These instructions are the attainment of Master sNang bzher Lod po. They are the six essential points of *bodhicitta*. These instructions have three parts:

(1) the overall meaning,

(2) the main explanation, and

(3) a brief summary.

First, has three parts:

(1) the homage,

(2) a description of the instructions, and

(3) explaining the way it really is and extolling its greatness.

Commentary A:

A.1.1 The Homage

[The root text says, "Homage to Kun tu bZang po, omniscient self-awakened awareness." There are two parts to this passage:

(1) expounding on compassion, and

(2) explaining how this is connected to self-awakened awareness.

A.1.1.1 Expounding on Compassion

Expounding on compassion has two parts:

(1) the object of the homage, and

(2) explaining the purpose of the homage.

A.1.1.1.1 The Object of Homage

With respect to the object, *kun tu* ("everything") refers specifically to the act of subduing [all negative states of mind] with nothing whatsoever left out. *bzang po* ("good") (320) refers to equal, impartial compassion [toward all beings]. *rang rig* ("self-awakened awareness") refers to [the fact that awakened awareness] arises by-itself-to-itself and cannot be taught to anyone. Omniscience is to know everything just the way it is, and to refine the way of seeing everything that there is, with nothing at all left out.

A.1.1.1.2 Explaining the Necessity of Homage

Explaining the necessity of homage has two parts:

(1) explaining the necessity of homage, and

(2) the actual meaning of the homage.

A.1.1.1.2.1 Explaining the Necessity of Homage

The lively expressivity of the three [gates] generally conforms with ultimate truth: the arms and hands of the body actually bow [with respect]; you do not engage in unnecessary speech; and you make the mind also conform to ultimate truth. The purpose of the homage is to purify the obscurations of the three [gates]—body, speech, and mind. This is necessary for the direct manifestation of the fruition as enlightened body, speech, and mind.

A.1.1.1.2.2 The Actual Meaning of the Homage

The actual meaning has two parts:

(1) explaining how to connect with the teachings about awakened awareness manifesting itself-to-itself, and

(2) the object of the homage.

The object of the homage refers to *kun tu* ("everything"), referring to all seemingly external and internal appearances of the container and contained of all *saṁsāra* and *nirvāṇa*, with nothing left out. *bzang po* ("good") refers to the victorious sublime wisdom of self-awakened awareness, the intention of awakening [that expresses itself] impartially and thoroughly pervades all of *saṁsāra* and *nirvāṇa* without distinctions such as good/bad, large/small, or above/below. *Rang rig* ("self-awakened awareness") refers to the fact that awakened awareness is primordially present and arises by-itself-to-itself. "Omniscience" refers to the lucidity and brightness, without any obscuration whatsoever, of all seemingly external and internal phenomena of the container and contained of all *saṁsāra* and *nirvāṇa*, as the intention of awakening. Understanding this becomes more clear through the examples, meaning, and signs. It becomes especially clear when you nail the meaning of this commentary.

With respect to the teachings on the purpose of the homage, this refers to paying homage to the intention of *bodhicitta*, and then establishing concentrated evenness and non-duality over and over again, until you clear away all obscurations of *saṁsāra*, arrive at *Buddhahood*, and directly manifest this enlightened intention as omniscience.

Commentary B:
B.1.1 **Homage**

First, [Homage]. *kun tu* ("everything") [refers to] unwavering from the real nature of primordial *Buddha* [Kun tu bZang po]. *bzang po* ("good") [refers to] the *Buddha* realm of those fortunate ones who, without remainder, become objects of compassion. All are the [field of] play for the primordial wisdom body. The innate positive qualities arise without [the mental engagement of] being accepted or rejected. Because of that, there is refuge, without any tendency or partiality toward self. With respect to self-awakened awareness arising, the mind is self-occurring primordial wisdom just as it is. It arises in-and-by-itself, (392) and manifests as the ultimate truth of what has arisen. As much as can be known in its own power becomes omniscience. The object of the homage can neither be shown nor designated. The homage refers to engaging in different activities of the [three] gateways such that the activities of body, speech, and mind [are done with] one-pointedness and continuously encounter [ultimate reality].

(332) When the great master, Gyer spungs sNang bzher Lod po was at a solitary hermitage at [the site of] "deer-faced rock" in [the region] West of Dra 'Bye, at some point the enlightened emanation body of Lord Tapihritsa appeared to him, following which his prideful arrogance was overcome. He [Taphiritsa] showed him the natural state of self-awakened awareness. Once freed from the burden

of all the fetters that bound him, he was able to extend the value of an equanimous state until he was able to let awakened awareness stay in its own way.

Commentary A:

A.1.2 The Actual Teachings on the Preliminaries

The actual teachings on the preliminaries have four parts:

(1) the way to establish the pith instructions in your mind-stream,

(2) explaining the greatness of the pith instructions,

(3) explaining the enumeration of the pith instructions, and

(4) the container/contained for the pith instructions.

A.1.2.1 The Way to Establish the Pith Instructions in Your Mind-Stream

[The root text] explains [the way to] establish the pith instructions in your mind-stream. It says, "The great master sNang bzher Lod po was at a solitary hermitage at deer-faced rock in Western Dra 'Bye. At some point the enlightened emanation body (*nirmāṇakāya*) of Lord Tapihritsa appeared to him, following which his prideful arrogance was overcome. He gained the benefit of [realizing] the natural state of self-awakened awareness. Once freed from the burden of all the fetters that bound him, he was able to extend the value of an equanimous state until he was able to let awakened awareness stay in its own way." According to this passage, this was the occasion in which he was given the instructions to cut [through the ordinary mind] and [establish] only awakened awareness.

(332) After about five years had come to pass, the one who had accumulated wisdom [sNang bzher Lod po] still practiced and remained in residence on a solitary island [at a nearby] lake. Around noon of the fifteenth day of the first summer month, while sNang bzher Lod po remained in a [state of single-minded] enlightened intention, the enlightened emanation body of the great [master] Tapihritsa simply appeared to him in the sky in front of him. His enlightened body was stainless, crystal-white in color. This self-originated body was unadorned. The body was seen naked, without any

obscurations covering it, seated [in a meditative posture]. [sNang gzher Lod po] was stricken with a deep faith. He circumambulated and made prostrations [and requested that blessings be bestowed upon him]. Then, [directly] from the mouth of [Tapihritsa came these words], "Oh, fortunate child of the lineage! You have a karmic connection [to these teachings] left over from practice in previous lifetimes. (333) Listen with [your best] mental faculties to the teachings on ultimate truth. I give you three profound words from the heart in order to teach the future generations of fortunate ones about this unmistaken pathway.

Commentary A:

[The root text] says, "After about five years had come to pass, the one who had accumulated wisdom [sNang bzher Lod Po] still practiced and remained in residence on a solitary island [at a nearby] lake. Around noon of the fifteenth day of the first summer month, while sNang bzher Lod po remained in a [state of single-minded] enlightened intention, the enlightened emanation body of the great Tapihritsa simply appeared to him in the sky in front of him. His enlightened body was stainless, crystal-white in color. This self-originating body was unadorned. The body was seen naked, without any obscurations covering it, seated [in a meditative posture]. [sNang gzher Lod po] was stricken with deep faith. (322) He circumambulated and made prostrations [and requested that the blessings be bestowed upon him]. Then, [directly] from the mouth of [Tapihritsa came these words], 'Oh, fortunate child of the lineage! You have a karmic connection [to these teachings] left over from practice in previous lifetimes. Listen with [your best] mental faculties to the teachings on ultimate truth. I give you three profound words from the heart in order to teach the future generations of fortunate ones about the unmistaken pathway." According to this passage, this was the occasion in which the instructions for seeking awakened awareness nakedly came to his mind-stream.

A.1.2.2 Explaining the Greatness of the Pith Instructions

Explaining the greatness of the pith instructions has three parts:

(1) explaining the instructions for reaching the final state of everything about Bon;

(2) explaining how these instructions enable making a determination about awakened awareness without which you will not come to the gateway to nothing more profound than the vehicle of Bon; and

(3) explaining how to directly draw forth [the realization].

Commentary B:
B.1.2 The Way the Instructions are Described

B.1.2.1 The First Meeting

The second has two parts, namely the first and second time each met, and how the teachings were explained. With respect to the first meeting, Tapihritsa's reply has four parts [to whom it was said, where it was said, by whom it was said, and why it was said]. First, with respect to whom it was said, it was to the great master sNang bzher Lod po [on account of him being] a great suitable vessel. With respect to where it was said, it is said to have taken place at a solitary hermitage at deer-faced rock in the Western Dra 'Bye region. There he stayed in solitude to increase his virtue. With respect to who said it, the text says that an emanation of Tapihritsa appeared at that time to subdue [his mind-stream] and to teach him. With respect to why it was said, it was to overcome his prideful arrogance through explaining the natural state of awakened awareness. Because of the arrogance of the great master, in order to eliminate the obscurations to supreme truth, he was directly taught the stark [truth of] the natural state. As the root text says, "Once freed from the burden of all the fetters that bound him, he was able to extend the value of an equanimous state." He became liberated from filling up his mind with philosophical tenets overlaying groundless-ground, and took up having the intent of a non-dual equanimous state. [The root text adds], "…until he was able to let awakened awareness stay in its own way." Stories composed like this are plentiful.

B.1.2.2 The Second Meeting

With respect to the second meeting (393) there are six parts. The first pertains to the time of the teachings. It was "about five years later." Master sPungs chen po "remained in residence on a solitary island [at a nearby] lake.... [It was] around noon of the fifteenth day of the first summer month," in the year of the earth-moon that he gave voice to these teachings. Second, with respect to whom this was spoken, [the root text says], "sNang bzher Lod po remained in a [state of single-minded] enlightened intention." Third, with respect to by whom it was spoken, [the root text says], "The enlightened emanation body of the great Tapihritsa simply appeared to him in the sky in front of him. His enlightened body was stainless, crystal in color," with a view that was pure and transparent. [The root text says], "This self-originating body was unadorned. The body was seen naked, without any obscurations covering it, seated [in a meditative posture]." This is the intermediate state that is explained as bare self-clarity. Fourth, with respect to why it was said, it was so that afterwards he could make a connection to the practice. [The root text says], "[sNang gzher Lod po] was stricken with a deep faith. He circumambulated and made prostrations [and requested that blessings be bestowed upon him]. Then, [directly] from the mouth of [Tapihritsa came these words], "Oh, fortunate child of the lineage!" as he transmitted from that intermediate state. [The root text continues], "You have a karmic connection [to these teachings] left over from practice in previous lifetimes," as transmitted from the intermediate state. [The root text continues], "Listen with [your best] mental faculties to the definitive teachings on ultimate truth." This refers to the special vessel [for the transmission], and with respect to these teachings, [that person] being a proponent of listening. Fifth, to whom this great ultimate truth is said, [the root text says], "I give you three profound words from the heart in order to teach the future generations of fortunate ones about the unmistaken pathway." These sayings are the root of all the gateways and means to enter the path. (394) Sixth, with respect to what is said, [the root text says], "I give you three profound words from the heart in order to teach the future generations of fortunate ones about the unmistaken pathway." Internally, these sayings are secret. What is explained are the essential points of the profound meaning of this secret and its limitlessness.

(333) **This is the quintessence of the Bon Great Completion teachings about the ultimate realization of the eighty-four thousand teachings, the nine lineages of mind-to-mind [transmission] of the *Sugatas*, and the oral transmission of the twenty-four human root masters.**

Commentary A:

A.1.2.2.1 **Explaining the Instructions for Reaching the Final State of Everything About Bon**

[The root text] says, "This is the quintessence of the Great Bon Completion teachings about the ultimate realization of the eighty-four thousand teachings, the nine lineages of mind-to-mind [transmission] of the *Sugatas*, and the oral transmission of the twenty-four other root masters." According to this passage, these teachings enable you to reach the final state of everything about Bon.

(333) **If you do not know these teachings on the so-called "six essential points of *bodhicitta*," even if you have a lama who gives you pith instructions, it is like showing something material to a blind person. If you are without these pith instructions, however many oral instructions [*lung*] and *tantras* on the Great Completion Lineage you are given, it is like a body without a heart [to realize], or the sense faculties without eyes [to see the truth]. However the eighty-four thousand teachings on the essence and emptiness of Bon are explained, they only result in conventional truth, which can only explain so much. Without these [pith instructions] you will never come to the ultimate truth, of which nothing is more profound.**

Commentary A:

A.1.2.2.2 **Explaining How These Instructions Enable Making a Determination about Awakened Awareness Without Which you will Not come to the Gateway of Nothing More Profound than the Vehicle of Bon**

[The root text] says, "If you do not know these teachings [on awakened awareness], even if you have a lama who gives you pith instructions, it is like showing something substantial to a blind person. If you are without these pith instructions, however many oral instructions [*lung*] or *tantras* of the Great Completion Lineage you are given, this is like a body without a heart [to realize] or the sense faculties without eyes [to see the truth]. However the eighty-four thousand teachings on the essence and emptiness of Bon are explained, they only result in conventional truth, which can only explain so much. Without these [pith instructions on awakening] you will never come to the epitome of these teachings." This passage means that [without this explanation of awakened awareness] you will never come to the ultimate truth, of which nothing is more profound. (323)

Commentary B:

B.1.3 Explaining the Way it Really is and Extolling its Greatness

Third, extolling the greatness [of these teachings] and the way it really is has three parts:

(1) the extraordinary instructions, the teachings for reaching the ultimate end of everything;

(2) numerous ordinary instructions, the teachings on the concealed meaning; and

(3) extolling the greatness, the precious qualities of these teachings.

B.1.3.1 The Extraordinary Instructions, the Teachings for Reaching the Ultimate End of Everything

First [the extraordinary instructions]. If you happen to come across these [teachings] for reaching the ultimate end of everything about the "eighty-four thousand teachings," then "this is the quintessence of the Great Bon Completion Teachings," as the root text says. These teachings are like what is already inside butter. This is the fat that is refined into its essence, and so, as the root text says, "the nine lineages of mind-to-mind [transmission] of the *Sugatas*." What is subsumed yet concealed in this primordial empty condition is the real nature of its enlightened intention, such that it self-arises as a transmission [teaching], and as the root text says, "the ear-whispered transmission of the other twenty-four root masters." This oral transmission is from ear-to-ear, [originating] from gShen lha ['Od dkar], then passed through skillful means and magical display to all those along the lineage having the banner of the victorious moon, entering the mind-stream of those in deep *samādhi*. Proximity to this transmission comes from Tapihritsa, an emanation of Kun tu bZang po, who is said to have passed it to Gyer spungs. Then, it was transmitted along a succession of those pure [enough to receive it]. The ultimate meaning of this transmission is that the awakened mind-itself of every [sentient being] is inseparable from [enlightened] Kun tu bZang po. Kun tu bZang po gave these teachings to guide the mind-streams [of all sentient beings] without exception to take up [the path to the point that] the need to purify [the mind-stream] is primordially non-existent.

B.1.3.2 Numerous Ordinary Instructions, the Teachings on the Concealed Meaning

Second [the ordinary instructions], has five parts:

(1) If whatever has been taught is not known, as the root text says, "If you do not know (395) these so-called six essential points of *bodhicitta*,"

(2) by whom they are taught, as the root text says, "even if you have a lama who gives you the pith instructions," then

(3) the metaphor used is that "it is like showing something substantial to a blind person," so that there is no ability to establish the certainty [of these teachings].

(4) The reason is that "if you are without these pith instructions, however [many]...oral readings...from the Great Completion Lineage are given, this is like a body without a heart [to realize] or the sense faculties without eyes [to see the truth]." Being without a heart is also explained as being without realization of ultimate truth.

(5) As for the way to practice, the root text says, "However the eighty-four thousand teachings on the essence and emptiness of Bon are explained, they only result in conventional truth, which can only explain so much. Without these [pith instructions] you will never come to the ultimate truth, of which nothing is more profound." The entire arrangement of the phrases [of the instructions] shows the hidden meaning in the provisional truth, enables you to come to the highest truth, and [enables] the integration of this into your mind-stream.

(333) Oh! Children of the Lineage! These teachings are the mirror by which the universal ground is recognized, the lamp which reveals the secret of primordial wisdom, the pith instructions which extract awakened awareness nakedly [i.e., free of conceptualization]. These instructions cut through delusion. These instructions are close-to-the-heart and point the finger to the natural state.

Commentary A:

A.1.2.2.3 **Explaining How to Directly Draw Forth [the Realization]**

When you utter the expression, "Oh! Children of the Lineage" [as found in the root text], this most excellent Bon speech comes from the universal ground itself. It emanates from the pure state of those holding the lineage. Accordingly, these instructions are said to be the gateway and vehicle than which there is nothing more profound. These are the teachings that enable you to make the determination about awakened awareness. [The root text] says, "…the mirror by which universal ground is recognized." Just like when shown a mirror you see a beautiful face, when shown these instructions on universal ground you come to see directly what was not seen before. [When the root text] then says, "…the lamp which reveals the secret of primordial wisdom," it means it is like holding a lamp in the midst of darkness, so that whatever exists is seen directly and obviously without anything concealed. In this very instance, through these instructions you come to see every way that primordial wisdom has been hidden and has remained that way. [When the root text] says, "Extract awakened awareness nakedly," it means that these instructions are like seeing a person's body directly and nakedly without any clothing, in that awakened awareness is drawn forth nakedly and its three manifestations are revealed nakedly. [When the root text] says, "These instructions cut through delusion," it means that just as water does not descend from a waterfall when it is too dry, these instructions enable you to make a determination [of awakened awareness] that remains above the very foundation of delusion, so that delusion is shown to not exist at all. [When the root text] says, "These instructions are close-to-the-heart and point the finger to the natural state," it means that these instructions enable you to determine the natural state [of the mind] and to develop a belief in that because whatever exists is pointed out in such a way (324) that it is obvious what to believe.

Commentary B:
B.1.3.3 Extolling the Greatness, the Precious Qualities of These Teachings

Third, [extolling the greatness] has three parts:

(1) explaining the unique positive qualities of these instructions,

(2) explaining the numerous designations, and

(3) explaining who should be accepted or rejected [regarding these teachings].

B.1.3.3.1 Explaining the Unique Positive Qualities of These Instructions

First, [explaining the unique positive qualities], the root text says, "Oh! Children of the Lineage! These teachings are the mirror by which universal ground is pointed out." Like looking at your face in a mirror and having something become clear, these instructions enable you to see what has not been seen—universal ground. Where the root text says, "the lamp which reveals the secret of primordial wisdom," [it means that] it enables you to discover directly the secret of primordial wisdom, much like holding up a mirror to see something clearly. The root text says, "...the pith instructions which extract awakened awareness nakedly [i.e., free of conceptualization]." This refers to seeing the transparency of awakened awareness without obscuration, like an individual whose body has been stripped bare without clothing. The root text says, "These instructions cut through delusion." [These instructions] are like channeling water into an irrigation ditch [so it flows in the right direction], (396) and cut through all delusion in a way that it is impossible ever to fall into delusion anymore. The root text says, "These instructions are close-to-the-heart and point the finger to the natural state." Explaining the substance of the finger-pointing instructions is like seeing [the real nature of the mind] nakedly. By making a connection to the natural state via these finger-pointing instructions, you are able to see awakened awareness nakedly.

These six teachings include:

(1) **The Lamp of the Basis that Stays**, the essential point of identifying what kind of essence stays as the universal ground;

(2) **The Lamp of the Fleshy Heart-Mind**, the essential point on how self-awakened awareness shines forth from within, where it resides in the basis;

(3) **The Lamp of the Soft White Channels**, (334) the essential point on how the transparency of primordial wisdom is drawn forth from whatever occurs in the channels;

(4) **The Lamp of the Far-Reaching Lasso of the Fluid Eye Lamp**, the essential point on seeing awakened awareness nakedly in whatever has arisen through the [eye sense gateways];

(5) **The Lamp of the *Buddha*-Fields**, the essential point of making a close-to-the-heart determination of the three-fold embodiment of enlightenment through whatever occurs along the path in the meditation practice; and

(6) **The Lamp of the After-Death Bardos**, the essential point about the way to separate *samsāra* and *nirvāna* and to encounter the [seeming] boundary between realization and delusion.

Commentary A:

A.1.2.3 **Explaining the Enumeration of the Pith Instructions**

Explaining the enumeration of the pith instructions is as follows: These teachings enable you to make a determination as to each of the six essential points for each of the Six Lamps until the thread [of meaning is completely] clear. The instructions pertaining to [building the] vessel have two parts:

(1) the teachings are secret for those four types of individuals without a [proper] vessel, and

(2) the instructions [given to those] with a [proper] vessel.

Commentary B:

B.1.3.3.2 **Explaining the Numerous Designations**

Second, [explaining the numerous designations]. There are six [lamps], namely the lamp of the basis that stays, and so forth. If something is obscure, it becomes clear [like a lamp illuminating it].

(334) Oh, Children of the Lineage, here are the instructions. However, these instructions are not appropriate for those individuals:

(1) who lack faith,

(2) who have wrong views,

(3) who lack confidence, and

(4) who are easily distracted, spiritually immature, or who practice the lower vehicles. Not even a word of these teachings should be spoken to such individuals.

Commentary A:

A.1.2.3.1 **The Teachings are Secret for Those Without a Vessel**

First, [the root text] says, "Oh! Children of the Lineage, here are the instructions. However, these instructions are not appropriate for those individuals who lack faith, those who have wrong views, those who lack confidence…and those spiritually immature, or those practicing the lower vehicles. Not even a word of these teachings should be spoken to such individuals." This passage refers to keeping the teachings secret for those without [the proper] vessel.

(334) Now, for those individuals who fear the cycling of re-birth and death and who seek enlightenment from the bottom of their hearts; for those who have tireless faith; for those who carry their lama on their crown [in Guru Yoga]; and for all those who abandon worldly activities and are seeking this profound truth, these teachings are given to all those who have become the most excellent vessels for such instructions.

Commentary A:

A.1.2.3.2 **The Instructions [for Those Who Have Built the] Vessel**

The root text says, "Now, for those individuals who fear the cycling of rebirth and death and who seek enlightenment from the bottom of their hearts, for those who have tireless faith, for those who carry their lama on their crown [in Guru Yoga], for all those who abandon worldly activities and are [capable] of finding this profound truth, these are the teachings given to all those who have become the most excellent vessels for such instructions." Here are the pith instructions on the *Six Lamps* and the teachings on the six essential points of *bodhicitta*." This passage explains giving the instructions to [those who have the proper] vessel.

Commentary B:
B.1.3.3.3 Explaining Who Should be Accepted or Rejected Regarding these Teachings

Third, [explaining who should be accepted or rejected regarding these teachings] has two parts:

(1) the necessity of who should be accepted or rejected, and

(2) a brief summary.

B.1.3.3.3.1 The Necessity of Who Should be Accepted or Rejected

First, [with respect to who should be accepted or rejected], the root text says, "Oh, Children of the Lineage." The root text continues, "[those for whom the teachings] are not appropriate." The primary meaning of this passage is that [these teachings remain] secret for those [who did not build a proper] vessel. The reason is that [if given to such individuals] the potency of the instructions would slip away, and the gift-waves of influence in one's mind-stream would fade away. For those whose spiritual duties are discarded these instructions are kept especially secret. The root text says, "Now, for those individuals who fear the cycling of rebirth and death…" These teachings are shown to those having a karmic connection [to them]. The reason is that these [instructions] are suitable to be shown to those likely to master them, for accomplished beings, and are especially needed by those for whom the root of the instructions has become unceasing.

(334) Having spoken accordingly, [Tapihritsa] taught him the instructions on the Six Lamps [pertaining to] the teachings on the six

essential points of *bodhicitta*. **May this teaching serve the benefit of all sentient beings, and may they never diminish from now until the end of time!** *Samaya!*

Commentary A:

A.1.3 A Brief Conclusion

[The root text] says, "May this teaching serve the benefit of all sentient beings, and never diminish from now until the end of time!" This passage conveys the aspiration that [the teachings] be firmly established, be propagated, and flourish. [Next, the root text] says, "*Samaya!*" (325) This is for those not yet with a proper vessel. They must seal the authority of the instructions and be sincere [in their practice].

Commentary B:

B.1.3.3.3.2 A Brief Summary

Second [a brief summary]. The pith instructions on the Six Lamps, in the root text are called "the teachings on the six essential points of *bodhicitta*." Your main spiritual duty, as the text says, is to "never let it diminish from now until the end of time." With respect to your devotion the root text says, "*Samaya!*" [which means to seal] these words as secret.

B.2 An Explanation of the Meaning of the Six

1. The Lamp of the Basis that Stays

Commentary A:

A.2.0 Making a Determination of the Meaning of the Essence of the Main Practices

Making a determination of the essential basic meaning of each of the Six Lamps. Regarding the first lamp, here is an explanation of the essential point for recognizing the essence of the Lamp of the Basis that Stays, namely that universal ground stays just as it is. There are three parts [to this section]:

(1) the homage,

(2) elucidating the meaning, and

(3) a brief conclusion.

Commentary B:
B.2.1 The Lamp of the Basis that Stays

Second, regarding an explanation of the meaning of the six, first is the Lamp of the Basis that Stays. (397) It has three parts:

(1) a brief explanation,

(2) an extensive explanation, and

(3) a summary.

(334) Homage to Kun tu bZang po, the primordial *Buddha* of self-awakened awareness.

Commentary A:
A.2.1 Homage

[The root text] says, "Homage to Kun tu bZang po, the primordial *Buddha* of self-awakened awareness." According to this passage, Kun tu bZang po is said to be the primordial *Buddha*. There is nothing more profound. There is no delusion about the enlightened intention of *bodhicitta* of the Victorious One whose awakened awareness knows itself-by-itself. [In this primordial condition] there is no falling into *saṁsāra*. There is no need to purify the two accumulations.[1] There is no need to gather the two accumulations [of merit and wisdom]. Awakened awareness arises primordially in-and-by-itself as *Buddhahood*, and cannot be explained by the masters. Thus, the homage is made according to what is the best [of realizations].

A.2.2 Elucidating the Meaning

There are two parts to elucidating the meaning:

(1) the synopsis, and

(2) the extensive explanation.

(334) Oh, Children of the Lineage! Here is what is called "the Lamp of the Basis that Stays."

---

[1]. *sgrib pa gnyis*: "two obscurations, i.e., "emotional" (*nyon mongs pa'i srib pa*) and "cognitive obscurations" (*shes bya'i sgrib pa*).

Commentary A:

A.2.2.1 The Synopsis

[The root text] says, "Oh, Children of the Lineage! Here...is the Lamp of the Basis that Stays...and the teachings on the natural state, which is the essence-itself of the universal ground." [The text continues], "...[and] the teachings on the way *saṁsāra* and *nirvāṇa* become divided in two." This refers to the teachings on the way the universal ground stays primordially, and the teachings on the way the duality between *saṁsāra* and *nirvāṇa* becomes purified.

Commentary B:

B.2.1.1 A Brief Explanation

First, as before, with respect to the homage to Kun tu bZang po, primordial wisdom's self-awakened awareness, *Buddhahood* is such that *Buddhahood* stays primordially wherein the ultimate truth of primordial wisdom's awakened awareness is self-occurring. The root text says, "Oh, Children of the Lineage! ...the Lamp of the Basis that Stays." These instructions explain the essence of universal ground just as it is.

(334) First, the teachings on the natural state, which is the essence-itself of the universal ground. Second, the teachings on the way *saṁsāra* and *nirvāṇa* become divided into two [as a duality]

Commentary A:

A.2.2.2 The Extensive Explanation

The extensive explanation has two parts:

(1) the teachings on the natural state, the basis, the essence-itself, and

(2) the teachings on the way *saṁsāra* and *nirvāṇa* become divided into two.

Commentary B:

B.2.1.2 An Extensive Explanation

Second, the detailed explanation in this system has two parts, as the root text says, "the natural state, which is the essence-itself of universal ground," and "the way *saṁsāra* and *nirvāṇa* become divided into two [as a duality]."

(334) Now, with respect to the teachings on the natural state of the basis, whose essence is [the universal ground], you should know that there are three aspects, the three being:

(1) the universal ground,

(2) awakened awareness, and

(3) the ordinary conceptual mind.

Commentary A:

A.2.2.2.1 The Teachings on the Natural State, the Basis, the Essence-Itself

The teachings on the natural state, the basis, the essence-itself has three parts:

(1) the brief explanation,

(2) the extensive explanation, and

(3) the summary and conclusion.

A.2.2.2.1.1 The Brief Explanation

The teachings on the natural state of the basis include the three—universal ground, awakened awareness, and [ordinary] conceptual thought. Here, [the root text] says, "What is known is that there are three aspects, the three being universal ground, awakened awareness, and ordinary [conceptual] thought." This is the brief explanation.

Commentary B:

B.2.1.2.1 The Explanation of the Natural State of Universal Ground.

The first, the explanation of the natural state of universal ground, as the root text says, "What is made known is that there are three aspects, the three being:

(1) universal ground,

(2) awakened awareness, and

(3) conceptual thought." There are three parts to this explanation.

Commentary A:

A.2.2.2.1.2 **The Extensive Explanation**

The extensive explanation has three parts:

(1) explaining the natural state of groundless-ground,

(2) explaining the natural state of awakened awareness, and

(3) explaining the natural state of [ordinary] conceptual thought.

Commentary B:

B.2.1.2.1.1 **Universal Ground**

First, the explanation of universal ground has three parts:

(1) a brief explanation,

(2) an extensive explanation, and

(3) a brief summary.

(334) First, the universal ground, bodhicitta itself, is empty clear-light and it is unconstructed and unadulterated.

Commentary A:

A.2.2.2.1.2.1 **Explaining the Natural State of Groundless-ground**

Explaining the natural state of groundless-ground has two parts:

(1) explaining the essence of groundless-ground, and

(2) explaining the natural state of groundless-ground.

A.2.2.2.1.2.1.1 **Explaining the Essence of Groundless-ground**

[The root text] says, "groundless-ground, *bodhicitta* itself." According to this passage, these teachings enable you to determine in general about groundless-ground [as the basis of] *saṁsāra* and *nirvāṇa*, that this is the great basis of *Buddhahood* for all sentient beings, and that this is also the so-called "expanse of *dharmadhātu*," the great pervasive display of everything that arises from groundless-ground. [The root text] continues, "empty clear-light unconstructed and unadulterated." This means that the clear-light of *bodhicitta* is never covered by any obscurations, and is without substantiality or characteristics. "Unconstructed" means that it is never contaminated by anything whatsoever.

A.2.2.2.1.2.1.2 Explaining the Natural State of Groundless-ground

Explaining the natural state of groundless-ground has four parts:

(1) explaining the natural state as original purity,

(2) explaining the natural state as spontaneously present,

(3) explaining the natural state as neutral, and

(4) explaining the natural state as a single interconnected sphere of ultimate reality.[2]

Commentary B:

B.2.1.2.1.1.1 A Brief Explanation

[First, the brief explanation]. The root text says, "First, groundless-ground, *bodhicitta*." Groundless-ground is shown to be the root and basis of [all] *saṁsāra* and *nirvāṇa*. It is the basis [of everything that] occurs. It is the ultimate truth shown by [all] the great predecessors [of this lineage].

(334) It is the great original purity of the *dharmakāya*. It is free of any stains whatsoever. It is awareness untouched [by any limits or extremes].

Commentary A:

A.2.2.2.1.2.1.2.1 Explaining the Natural State as Original Purity

[The root text] says, "...the great original purity of the *dharmakāya*" because the essence of universal ground stays primordially as original purity. [The term], "*dharmakāya*" refers to everything being completely pure from the beginning and [remaining] just as it is. [The text] says, "Awakened awareness is free of any stains whatsoever." This means that [in universal ground] there is no distinction between *saṁsāra* and *nirvāṇa;* (327) *Buddhahood* and sentient beings; suffering and compassion; ordinary thought and primordial wisdom; vice and virtue; happiness and misery; faults and positive qualities; higher and lower birth realm; self and other; container and contained; object of knowledge and knowing that object;

---

2. *thig le nyag gcig tu*: "single interconnected sphere" of ultimate reality.

or cause and effect, and so forth. Furthermore, there is no distinction whatsoever between stain and stainless. Additionally, there is no distinction whatsoever between existence/non-existence; appearance/emptiness; eternalism/nihilism; birth and death; or rejecting and accepting.

(334) ...whose self-nature is spontaneously present as the *sambhogakāya*. It completes everything [in *samsāra*], completes everything [in *nirvāna*], and completes everything [in both].

Commentary A:

A.2.2.2.1.2.1.2.2 **Explaining the Natural State as Spontaneously Present**

Explaining the natural state as spontaneously present is as follows: [The root text] says, "...whose self-nature is spontaneously present as the *sambhogakāya*." Buddhahood cannot be brought about by a meditator in this essence of universal ground. It is not constructed by any sentient being. It is not affected by causes or conditions. It cannot be affected by any person's conceptual thought. It cannot be accomplished by human effort. It is primordial, spontaneously present, self-occurring, and self-arising. When the text says, "*sambhogakāya*," if you were to ask why it is complete just the way it is, it is because, as the text says, "It completes everything [in *samsāra*], completes everything [in *nirvāna*], and completes everything [in both]." This means that it completes all kinds of phenomena in *samsāra*, thoroughly completes the kinds of phenomena in *nirvāna*, completes the compassionate activities of a *Buddha* and the suffering of sentient beings, and completes these without the need of any further explanation and without remainder.

(335) It is the indeterminate *nirmānakāyas* [i.e., it can take any form] and is neutral [pertaining to virtuous, non-virtuous, or neutral conditions]. Its miraculous display impartially can arise as anything whatsoever.

Commentary A:

A.2.2.2.1.2.1.2.3 **Explaining the Natural State as Not Prophesied**

[The root text says,] "It is the indeterminate *nirmānakāyas* [enlightened emanation bodies [i.e., it can take any form] and is neutral [with regard to virtuous, non-virtuous, or neutral conditions]." The essence of universal ground as explained before encompasses all of *saṁsāra* and *nirvāṇa*. How is it neutral? Whatever it is cannot be explained extensively. Whatever it is, it arises as suitable [to the situation]. [The root text continues], "Indeterminate *nirmāṇakāya* [enlightened emanation body." Why does this arise indeterminately, just the way it is? [The root text] says, "Without bias, its miraculous display can arise as anything whatsoever." As explained previously, it arises from the supporting conditions for realization or non-realization; it arises as *saṁsāra* and *nirvāṇa*, likewise, as a *Buddha* or a sentient being.

A.2.2.2.1.2.1.2.4 Explaining the Natural State as a Single Thread of Energy

Fourth, explaining the natural state as a single thread of energy has two parts—the brief and the extensive explanation.

(335) These three [the three-fold embodiment of enlightenment] have no separate distinction between them. [First], like space-itself, universal ground saturates all of the [seemingly] appearing world, and completely pervades and saturates all of *samsāra* and *nirvāna*.

Commentary A:
A.2.2.2.1.2.1.2.4.1 Brief Explanation

First, [the root text] says, "[These three enlightened bodies] have no separate distinction between them." This expanse of universal ground is the pervasiveness in which all *Buddhas* and sentient beings are the same. If you were to think that these seem as if each of these is not the same, they are [simply] the pervasiveness of a single interconnected sphere of ultimate reality [that appears variously]. [The root text continues], "Like space-itself…it completely saturates all of *saṁsāra* and *nirvāṇa*." For example, the characteristics of the seemingly appearing world seem to appear as not the same and as various, but there is no difference between each of [these seeming appearances] as space-itself, as it is completely saturated by the same interconnected sphere. [The root text continues], "…completely pervades and saturates all of *saṁsāra* and *nirvāṇa*." Even for those knowledgeable of lesser teachings, when awakened awareness and universal ground are established within one's mind-stream, it may not seem as if *Buddhahood* can arise mixed into the mind-stream of sentient beings, but in the essence of universal ground there is no difference between each [*Buddhas* and sentient beings], and both *Buddhas* and sentient beings alike are completely saturated by the same single interconnected sphere of ultimate reality.

A.2.2.2.1.2.1.2.4.2 Extensive Explanation

The extensive explanation has two parts:

(1) explaining the three—space, sphere, and expanse—as the same interconnected sphere; and

(2) explaining the three—example, meaning, and sign—as the same single interconnected sphere. (329)

(335) It is the same lucid space that pervades everything—lucid space without partiality.

[Second,] everything arises from that same great domain of space—the domain of space of emptiness, groundlessness. Everything stays in the same great expanse. This is the same expanse without highs or lows. This is what is called "the universal ground bodhicitta."

Commentary A:

A.2.2.2.1.2.1.2.4.2.1 Explaining the Three—Space, Sphere, and Expanse—as the Same Single Thread of Energy

[The root text] says, "It is the same lucid space that pervades everything." This means that the essence of universal ground is clear-light that is never covered by any obscurations. "Lucid space" in the root text means the great display of pervasiveness that is thoroughly saturated by the same single interconnected sphere of ultimate reality. "Lucid space…without partiality" means that the essence of universal ground is great lucid space itself, with nothing higher or lower than it, without direction or characteristics, without center or edges, without outside or inside, without opening or depth, without beginning or end, the seeming display of the existing world, and that of all *saṁsāra* and *nirvāṇa* stays and pervades everywhere without partiality. [The root text continues], "From that same interconnected sphere everything arises." Because the essence of universal ground is empty and selfless, this is known as the "sphere of great emptiness." From this very sphere everything [contained within] *saṁsāra* and *nirvāṇa* arises, the entirety of all phenomena. There is nothing that does not occur from it. [The root text] says, "This sphere of emptiness is without being spacious or confined." It means that from this sphere of universal ground everything that exists within the phenomena of *saṁsāra* and *nirvāṇa* occurs. Everything that there is arises. Everything that there is stays. Because nothing whatsoever is contained within it, comes together within it, or contradicts it, it is said to be "not confined." [The root text] says, "In this same vast emptiness everything abides." It means that because this essence of universal ground stays as non-dual clarity/emptiness, it is said to be "the expanse of great sameness." [The root text] says, "This expanse of sameness is without highs or lows." It means that in this expanse of universal ground (330) is everything—all *Buddhas*, all sentient beings, all *saṁsāra* and *nirvāṇa*, all the seemingly external container and the internal contained, all good/bad, great/small, high/low, near/far—in a way that never diminishes. Because universal ground stays completely the same and does not change it is said to be "without highs and lows." In this expanse wherein the three—space, sphere, and expanse—manifest the same single interconnected sphere of ultimate reality, if you were to give this a name it would be [what the root text refers to as] "universal ground *bodhicitta*." It is also known as the "universal ground wherein ultimate truth resides," or "universal ground wherein great pervasiveness arises," or "the expanse of *dharmadhātu*."

(335) With respect to how conventional truth is explained, there seem to be three [ways to describe it—example, meaning, and sign], but with respect to ultimate truth, there is no distinction [between the three], and everything abides as a single great interconnected sphere of light.[3] *Samaya!*

---

3. *thig le chen po gcig*: "single great interconnected sphere" of ultimate reality.

Commentary A:

A.2.2.2.1.2.1.2.4.2.2 **Explaining the Three—Example, Meaning, and Sign—as the Same Single Thread of Energy**

Explaining the three—example, meaning, and sign—as the same single interconnected sphere of ultimate reality is as follows. [The root text continues], "Where with respect to conventional truth there seem to be three [example, meaning, and sign]…" This means that with respect to provisional truth there is nothing to be realized within the expanse of universal ground. Through the example or metaphor of space, you establish the signs of [awakened] mind-itself. The meaning of *dharmadhātu* comes from making a determination of the natural state. This is the explanation of the three—example, meaning, and sign. [The root text continues], "…but with respect to ultimate truth, there is no distinction [between the three], and everything abides as a single great interconnected sphere of light." This means that the thought that these are to be subdued is unnecessary when the three are shown to be in essence the same. With respect to ultimate truth, each of these has no distinction, but stays as the single interconnected sphere of ultimate reality. Furthermore, what is called [the expanse of] "space" is the expanse of universal ground within which everything seemingly external occurs and arises within this pervasiveness, and what is called "awakened mind-itself" is the expanse within which everything seemingly internal occurs within this pervasiveness. What is called "*dharmadhātu*" is where everything seemingly external or internal arises as non-dual. You eradicate doubt in the following manner. When [your experience] of everything seemingly external and internal is in accordance with the example of [the expanse of] "space," (331) you clear away doubt. You also clear away doubt with the example of water and reflections in that water. Both of these examples are said to clear away doubt. [The root text] says, "*Samaya!*" This means practitioners must seal the authority of the instructions.

(335) Second, with respect to what is known as "primordial wisdom's awakened awareness," from the domain of space [awakened awareness] arises like the sun rising in the sky.

Commentary A:

A.2.2.2.1.2.2 Explaining the Natural State of Awakened Awareness

Explaining the natural state of awakened awareness has six parts:

(1) explaining the basis of arising[4] of primordial wisdom's awakened awareness;

(2) explaining the essence;

(3) explaining liveliness;

(4) explaining the enumeration of the names;

(5) explaining the way it arises[5] in anyone's mind-stream; and

(6) the way it exists as the foundation of all *saṃsāra* and *nirvāṇa*.

Commentary B:

B.2.1.2.1.1.2 An Extensive Explanation

Second, [an extensive explanation]. Primordial universal ground stays, as the three-fold embodiment of enlightenment, as the great identitylessness. Its clear-light is never covered by any obscurations. Being without any substantiality or [definable] characteristics, it is empty. Its original purity is unmodified by any causes or conditions. It is the *dharmakāya* that stays, primordially and bare, not covered or obscured by anything whatsoever. "It is free of any stains whatsoever," without any [distinctions] like happiness/suffering, fault/positive quality, virtue/sin, *saṃsāra/nirvāṇa*, object/knowing the object, etc. "Untouched by boundaries," pure, and transparent, "whose self-nature is spontaneously present." This condition is without any [distinctions] of *saṃsāra* and *nirvāṇa*, (398) suffering, afflictive emotions, primordial wisdom, etc. [Everything] arises as spontaneously present, without purposeful action. Everything arises as self-occurring, without making any effort. This is the *sambhogakāya*. Everything is completed in that. All [seemingly] external and internal objects, and the knowing of those objects, are completed within that, with nothing left out. "Completes everything" is everything in *saṃsāra*

---

4. *'char gzhi*: "basis of arising."

5. *rgyud la shar tshul*: "the way it arises in the mind-stream."

and *nirvāṇa*, such that it opens to the first [taste] of complete understanding inclusive of everything to be known, with nothing left out, nothing remaining. The root text says, "It is the indeterminate *nirmāṇakāya*...and is neutral [with regard to virtuous, non-virtuous, or neutral conditions]. Regarding its essence, nothing whatsoever is made to happen as various miraculous displays become active, however what arises functions. Whatever its characteristics, they are ineffable. The root text says, "Without bias, its miraculous display arises." This refers to its real nature that stays as the great sameness impartially, and does not have any aspects either. [Great] variety arises in the expanse of *dharmadhātu*—happiness and suffering etc.—whether there is realization or deluded appearance by non-realization. The root text says, "These [three-fold embodiments of enlightenment] have no separate distinction between them. Like space itself...[that] saturates all of the seemingly appearing world." This refers to one and the same universal ground that completely pervades [all] *saṃsāra* and *nirvāṇa*. You might think it is not the same and stays in each one individually, yet everything is completely pervaded by the same interconnected sphere. The real nature of the seemingly appearing world stays in each individually, but as space, it is not as if there are many individual spaces. The root text says, "It completely pervades and saturates all of *saṃsāra* and *nirvāṇa*." A knowing-awareness in each individual mind-stream arises in-and-by-itself in universal ground, and *Buddhahood* arises as unadulterated and primordially present in the mind-stream of each sentient being, yet everything displayed is completely pervaded by the same essence-itself of groundless-ground. The three—space, domain, and expanse—are explained as follows. With respect to space, it is the same lucid space (399) that pervades everything. Because it is never covered by obscurations, from that comes its great clear-light. It pervades all of *saṃsāra* and *nirvāṇa* as the way it is, without [distinctions] like great/small, most/least, subtle/coarse, thick/thin, like sesame oil [that pervades] the sesame seed. Thus, the root text says, "It is the same lucid space that pervades everything without partiality." This means that it stays as the great sameness, completely without directions and divisions, throughout the seemingly appearing world, and all *saṃsāra* and *nirvāṇa*, such that it is without [distinctions such as] direction/borders, above/below, middle/end, outer/inner, surface/depth, or beginning/end. With respect to the interconnected domain [within which everything arises], the root text says, "Everything arises from that same great interconnected sphere." This refers to the domain of great emptiness and identitylessness. Yet, in Bon there is no non-occurrence, no non-existence, no non-arising from that for everything throughout *saṃsāra* and *nirvāṇa* that can be known. This is referred to as "the domain of emptiness, groundlessness," in that it is not compatible with the condition of an "I." There is nothing composed, contradicted, confined, or diminished. With respect to the expanse, the root text says, "Everything stays in the same great expanse." In that expanse of non-dual great sameness, everything that can be known throughout *saṃsāra* and *nirvāṇa* stays such that there are no distinctions like letting go, separating from, connecting to, partializing, or near/far. The root text says, "This same vast expanse is without highs and lows." With respect to staying like that, it stays as the great coming-together-all-at-once, without distinctions such as good/bad, great/small, higher/lower, and without anything being diminished or taken from it. Thus, the root text says, "This is what is called 'universal ground *bodhicitta*.'" This is just a name given to it. Universal ground is also called "primordial ultimate truth." It is also called "the general ground of *saṃsāra* and *nirvāṇa*." It is also called "the ground which is the essence-itself."

B.2.1.2.1.1.3 **A Brief Summary**

Third, a brief summary. The root text says, "With respect to how conventional truth is explained, there seem to be three [example, meaning, and sign]." If you were to illustrate [this truth] by saying something in words, there would be the three—space, awakened mind-itself, (400) and *dharmadhātu*. There are also the terms—example, meaning, and sign—that imply a progression. The root text says, "But with respect to ultimate truth, there is no distinction," because ultimate truth goes beyond all expressions, thoughts, and words. The root text says, "Everything abides in the one great interconnected sphere of ultimate reality." This means ultimate truth is without even the subtlest of enumerations and beyond any object of expression or illustration. Yet, having pointed this out and integrated the example, meaning, and sign into the mind-stream as inseparable and as the same taste, no such distinctions develop regarding definitive knowledge. [Lastly], "*Samaya!*" [in the root text] refers to sealing [these teachings] as secret.

Commentary A:

A.2.2.2.1.2.2.1 **Explaining the Basis of Arising of Primordial Wisdom's Awakened Awareness**

First, [the root text] says, "The primordial wisdom's awakened awareness." This means that the universal ground and the knowing-awareness that arises within the universal ground that abides within the mind-stream of each and every individual arise simultaneously[6] by themselves. [The root text continues], "From the domain of space [awakened awareness] arises like the sun." For example, from the single domain of space the heart of the sun does not arise differently to each and every individual. [The text continues], "Awakened awareness arises from the sphere of universal ground." [This means] that the universal ground is the ultimate truth that stays. Just as the heart of the sun arises in the single domain of space, likewise, knowing-awareness arises in this same universal ground, so therefore, also in the mind-stream of each and every individual within this same universal ground.

(335) Its essence is lucid. Its nature is empty. Its aspect is non-conceptual knowing-awareness.

Commentary A:

A.2.2.2.1.2.2.2 **Explaining the Essence of Primordial Wisdom's Awakened Awareness**

Regarding explaining the essence [the root text] says, "Its essence is lucid; its self-nature is empty." This means that awakened awareness is bright and clear, and never covered by any obscurations. Being empty it is free of all grasping. [When the root text says, "Its aspect is a knowing-awareness that is non-conceptual," it means that while being mindful of awakened awareness along with all the various events that seem to

---

6. *lhan skyes*: "arise together" or "simultaneously," or "co-emergent."

arise from universal ground, in this essence, there is no grasping, (332) and knowing-awareness stays [completely] non-conceptually.

(335) From that [lucid, empty knowing-awareness] three types of liveliness appear, and the three are ultimate sound, light, and light-rays. From this lucid space, light arises. From this empty domain of space, ultimate sound occurs by itself. From this non-duality, light-rays of awakened awareness emanate.

This is called "knowing the appearing object." Object and awakened awareness [that knows the object] are without any distinction. They are unified and cannot be differentiated.

Commentary A:

A.2.2.2.1.2.2.3 **Explaining Liveliness**

[The root text] explains the liveliness of primordial wisdom's awakened awareness by saying, "From that [lucid, empty, knowing-awareness] three types of liveliness appear." This passage means that, in that the foundation of universal ground and awakened awareness is non-duality, these three are the three great appearances, the manifestations of unobstructed liveliness that arise primordially and arise by themselves. As the text says, "In whatever arises, the three are ultimate sound, light, and light-rays." Ultimate sound is the self-manifesting sound of awakened awareness. Light is the self-manifesting light of awakened awareness. Light-rays are the self-manifesting rays of awakened awareness. [The text continues], "From this lucid space light arises." When awakened awareness arises as the light of its own liveliness, it is not covered by any obscurations. [The text continues], "From this empty sphere, ultimate sound occurs by itself." When awakened awareness occurs as the sound of its own liveliness, it is empty and selfless. [The text continues], "From this non-duality, light-rays of awakened awareness emanate." This means that light-rays emanate from the liveliness of knowing awakened awareness as non-dual emptiness/clarity. [As the text continues], "Thus, what is called 'knowing the appearing object' means that [both] what seems to appear as an object and the seeming 'knower' of that object [are both] primordial wisdom's awakened awareness. [As the text continues], "...[they] are without any distinction" between the object and the awakened awareness that knows the object. This means that there is absolutely no difference between the object known and knowing that object. The object known arises from the liveliness of awakened awareness and awakened awareness arises from the expanse also in which the object arises. [The root text continues], "They are unified and cannot be differentiated," meaning that the object known and the awakened awareness that knows it cannot be differentiated. Having mixed together what was heretofore distinct, what remains is the inseparable [non-dual] pair.

(335) Thus, it is called "primordial wisdom's awakened awareness." It is also called "knowing-awareness active within the mind-stream within universal ground." Primordial wisdom is like a mirror, which is the basis of all positive qualities. [Ordinary] storehouse consciousness is the basis of habitual karmic propensities.

Commentary A:
A.2.2.2.1.2.2.4 **Explaining the Enumeration of the Names**

[The root text] explains the enumeration of the names of primordial wisdom's awakened awareness by saying, "This is called primordial wisdom's awakened awareness." This means that awakened awareness stays primordially, and is simultaneously arising with the primordial wisdom that stays. (333) It is also called "the knowing-awareness active in the mind-stream within universal ground." This passage means that knowing-awareness knows whatever changes in the universal ground and arises as seemingly various [events], while the essence remains uninterrupted within seeming conventional time within the mind-stream. In the root text it is also called "mirror-like primordial wisdom of positive qualities" because when mirror-like primordial wisdom is realized, all the embodiments of enlightenment and primordial wisdoms manifest from the universal ground. When not realized, the universal ground manifests as the storehouse of all habitual karmic propensities, and all karma [ripens] and afflictive emotional states manifest from the storehouse.

(335) It is unmixed and absolutely complete [in itself]. Awakened awareness arises in the mind-stream of each individual sentient being. The expanse of universal ground is like space.

Commentary A:

A.2.2.2.1.2.2.5 Explaining the Way it Arises[7] in Anyone's Mind-stream

[The root text] says, "It is unmixed and absolutely complete [in itself]. Awakened awareness arises in the mind-stream of each individual sentient being. The expanse of universal ground, like space," is the great single interconnected sphere of ultimate reality, wherein everything pervades [this space]. Primordial wisdom's awakened awareness, like the center of the sun, arises in the mind-stream of each individual sentient being yet is unmixed [into the ordinary mind-stream]. While it arises in each and every [sentient being], nevertheless it is [absolutely] complete as the single interconnected sphere of ultimate reality. To eliminate any doubt, it is said that you can either use the metaphor of water and water-moon, or the metaphor of a doorway into the space of the victorious ones.[8]

(336) The universal ground is non-conceptual and neutral. Its essence is originally pure and stainless. It is the foundation for both the faults of *samsara* and the positive qualities of *nirvāna*. Furthermore, when the light becomes connected to awakened awareness, it becomes the basis for transforming the ordinary body into the enlightened body [of a *Buddha*]. When sound becomes connected to awakened awareness, it is the basis for transforming ordinary speech into the enlightened speech [of a *Buddha*]. When light-rays become connected to awakened awareness, it is the basis for transforming the ordinary mind into the enlightened heart-mind [of a *Buddha*]. Samaya!

---

7. *rgyud la shar tshul*: "the way it arises in the mind-stream."

8. *rgyal mkhar dang sgo mo*: "doorway into the space of the victorious ones."

Commentary A:

A.2.2.2.1.2.2.6 **The Way it Exists as the Foundation of all** *Saṁsāra* **and** *Nirvāṇa*

Primordial wisdom's awakened awareness is explained as the foundation of all *saṁsāra* and *nirvāṇa*. [The root text continues], "Universal ground is non-conceptual and neutral. Its essence is originally pure and stainless. It is the foundation for both the faults of *saṁsāra* and the positive qualities of *nirvāṇa*." What is the essence of this primordial wisdom's awakened awareness? It is neutral.[9] It is intangible yet stays as original purity. Once realized, it is the basis for the arising of positive qualities. (334) If not realized, it becomes the basis for the arising of all the faults of *saṁsāra*. [The root text continues], "When light becomes connected to awakened awareness, it becomes the basis for transforming the ordinary body into the enlightened body [of a *Buddha*]. This means that if you realize the liveliness [of awakened awareness manifesting as light] then the Enlightened *Buddha*-body and all its manifestations occur. If not realized, however, the ordinary body of sentient beings and all its manifestations seem to occur. [The root text continues], "When sound becomes connected to awakened awareness, it is the basis for transforming ordinary speech into Enlightened Speech." This means that if you realize the liveliness [of awakened awareness manifesting as ultimate sound] then the Enlightened Speech [of a *Buddha*] and all its manifestations occur. If not realized, however, the ordinary speech of a sentient being and all its manifestations seem to occur. [The root text continues], "When light-rays become connected to awakened awareness, it becomes the basis for transforming the ordinary mind into the Enlightened Heart-Mind [of a *Buddha*]." This means that if you realize the liveliness of awakened awareness manifesting as light-rays, then all the omniscience wisdom energies of a *Buddha* manifest. If not realized, however, all the ordinary recollections and thoughts of a sentient being seem to occur. Then the root says, "*Samaya!*" the meaning of which has been described previously.

---

9. *lung du ma bstan*: "neutral."

Commentary B:

B.2.1.2.1.2 Primordial Wisdom's Awakened Awareness

Second, primordial wisdom's awakened awareness has five parts:

(1) the subject, the natural state of primordial wisdom's awakened awareness,

(2) the object; how ultimate sound, light, and light-rays arise,

(3) explaining the inseparable non-dual pair of subject/object,

(4) explaining the enumerations and distinctions regarding awakened awareness, and

(5) how *saṁsāra* and *nirvana* arise from making a connection with the non-dual inseparable pair.

B.2.1.2.1.2.1 The Subject, the Natural State of Primordial Wisdom's Awakened Awareness

First, [with respect to the subject, the natural state of primordial wisdom's awakened awareness] the root text says, "With respect to primordial wisdom's awakened awareness," it arises as simultaneously born in-itself from groundless-ground and thus is called "knowing-awareness in the mind-stream from groundless-ground." The root text says, "In the sphere of [this same] space [awakened awareness] arises like [the heart of] the sun [the same way in the mind-stream of each and every of many individuals. It stays in the mind-stream of each and every individual being. [It arises] like the sun from the domain of space, and so the root text says, "Awakened awareness arises from the domain of groundless-ground." Groundless-ground is the ultimate truth of what stays, and from the domain of this same space, within groundless-ground a knowing-awareness arises in the mind-stream, like the heart of the sun. Primordial wisdom's awakened awareness arises in each and every individual being's mind-stream. The root text continues, "Its essence is lucid; its self-nature is empty; its aspect is a knowing-awareness that is non-conceptual." (401) This awakened awareness, moreover, is never covered by obscurations. The real nature of its lucidity is empty and selfless, beyond any activity or object of thought, and beyond ordinary consciousness. The king of awakened awareness stays free of all conceptual thought.

B.2.1.2.1.2.2 The Object, How Ultimate Sound, Light, and Light-rays Arise

Second, [the object, how ultimate sound, light, and light-rays arise]. The root text says, "From that three types of liveliness appear." With respect to what arises in-and-by-itself, these arise as elemental wind and unobstructedness from the non-duality of groundless-ground and awakened awareness. These three arise as the great visions. With respect to whatever arises, the root text says, "The three are ultimate sound, light, and light-rays." Furthermore, because awakened awareness is without obscuration, the root text says, "From this lucid space, light arises. From this empty domain, ultimate sound occurs by itself." Sound arises from the liveliness of emptiness and selflessness. The root text continues, "From this non-duality, light-rays of awakened awareness emanate." From the liveliness of the non-duality of emptiness/lucidity, light-rays arise. Thus, the objects of the appearing visions are the three—ultimate sound, light, and light-rays. As the root text says, "What are called [seemingly] arising objects," arise in-and-by-themselves. Everything that seems to be an external object [of appearance] arises from these [visions]. This is called "knowing the appearing object with respect to primordial wisdom's awakened awareness."

B.2.1.2.1.2.3 Explaining the Inseparable Non-dual Pair of Subject/Object

Third, with respect to explaining the inseparable non-dual pair of subject/object, when the root text says, "Object and awakened awareness are without any distinction," it means that there is no difference between the two, or that they are not something that you either unite with or become separated from. When the root text says, "They are unified and cannot be differentiated," it means that seeming objects arise from the liveliness of awakened awareness, and awakened awareness arises from the expanse of these [seeming] objects. There is no difference. Through their integration, they stay unadulterated, inseparable, and a non-dual pair.

B.2.1.2.1.2.4 Explaining the Enumerations and Distinctions Regarding Awakened Awareness

Fourth, explaining the enumerations and distinctions regarding awakened awareness, the root text says, "Thus, it is called [the light-rays of] primordial wisdom's awakened awareness." From the domain of groundless-ground, awakened awareness arises lucid in-and-by-itself, without conceptual thought, without obscuration, bare. It arises from primordial wisdom's awakened awareness. As the root text continues, "It is also called knowing-awareness (402) active within the mind-stream within groundless-ground." All reflections and recollections become knowing-awareness in groundless-ground, and its essence remains uninterrupted across the three times. The root text says, "Primordial wisdom is like a mirror, which is the basis of all positive qualities." The essence, lucidity, is without its own nature; its activity is the arising of all the *Buddha*-bodies and primordial wisdom energies; and it becomes the basis of liberation. The root text continues, "Ordinary storehouse consciousness is the basis of habitual karmic propensities." Regarding this activity, the essence is neutral; all afflictive emotions arise from the basis. The root text says, "It is unmixed and absolutely complete [in itself]." The [seeming] characteristics of the appearing world arise individually yet unmixed (unadulterated). Yet everything is absolutely complete in the condition of basic space, and as such everything is absolutely complete in the one [great] sphere of ultimate reality. Primordial wisdom's awakened awareness arises in the mind-stream in each and every mind. In the condition of [absolute] *bodhicitta*, awakened awareness arises in each and every individual's mind-stream the same, complete in each and everyone, throughout all *saṁsāra* and *nirvāṇa*.

B.2.1.2.1.2.5 How *Saṁsāra* and *Nirvāṇa* Arise from Making a Connection with the Non-dual Inseparable Pair

Fifth, how *saṁsāra* and *nirvāṇa* arise from making a connection with the non-dual inseparable pair. The root text says, "Groundless-ground is non-conceptual and neutral [as virtuous, non-virtuous, or neutral]." Its essence stays as the great original purity, its aspects are beyond any object that can be illustrated or described, and whatever its activity it cannot fall into bias and cannot be annihilated [crushed] by bones. When the root text says, "Its essence is originally pure and stainless," it means that it does not contact any kind of limits, but stays as pure, transparent, naked, bare, stainless lucidity-in-itself. The root text says, "It is the foundation for both the faults of *saṁsāra* and the positive qualities of *nirvāṇa*." If there is no realization, it is the basis of the faults of *saṁsāra*, and if there is realization, it is the basis of the positive qualities of *nirvāṇa*. The root text says, "Furthermore, when the light becomes connected to awakened awareness, it becomes the basis (403) for transforming the ordinary body into the Enlightened Body [of a *Buddha*]." If there is realization, all the Enlightened Emanation Bodies of a *Buddha* come forth, and if there is no realization, all the aggregates of the ordinary body of a sentient being come forth. The root text says, "When sound becomes connected to awakened awareness, it is the basis for transforming ordinary speech into the Enlightened Speech [of a *Buddha*]." From the liveliness of this come the emanations of enlightened speech, and [without realization] these become the ordinary spoken speech of a sentient being. The root text says, "When light-rays become connected to awakened awareness, it is the basis for transforming the ordinary mind into the Enlightened Heart-Mind [of a *Buddha*]." From the liveliness of this comes the primordial wisdom of the omniscience of a *Buddha*, and [without realization] all the conceptual thought and recollections of an ordinary sentient being come forth. The root text says, "*Samaya!*" meaning it is a profound secret.

(336) Third, with respect to the ordinary mind of conceptual thought, although the king of knowing-awareness is free from conceptual thought, all the diverse types of reflective thoughts and ordinary mindful awareness arise from the universal ground, like light-rays from the wind of the sun. They arise as seemingly ordinary thought from the liveliness of awakened awareness.

Commentary A:

A.2.2.2.1.2.3 **Explaining the Natural State of Ordinary [Conceptual] Thought**

The explanation of the natural state of ordinary conceptual thought[10] has three parts:

---

10. *blo*: "ordinary conceptual thought."

(1) explaining the basis of arising of ordinary thought;

(2) explaining the essence of ordinary thought; and

(3) the enumeration of ordinary thought.

A.2.2.2.1.2.3.1 Explaining the Basis of Arising of Ordinary Thought

First, with respect to [what the root text describes as] "the intention of ordinary...conceptual thought," [it goes on to say], "Although the king of knowing-awareness is non-conceptual, all the diverse types of reflective thoughts and ordinary mindful awareness arise from groundless-ground, like light-rays from the wind of the sun. They arise as seemingly ordinary thought from the liveliness of awakened awareness." Whatever seemingly ordinary thought arises, it can only arise from groundless-ground. As explained before, the activity of awakened awareness stays as groundless-ground. This king of knowing-awareness once realized is non-conceptual. [Yet, its liveliness], like (335) light-rays when they arise, arises from the liveliness of the sun itself.

(336) Ordinary conceptual thought arises from the liveliness of awakened awareness, as does ordinary mindful awareness, and various [thought] activities toward sense-objects. The six sense-consciousnesses and the six sense-objects also arise from liveliness. This is known as "reflective thought mind." *Samaya!*

Commentary A:

A.2.2.2.1.2.3.2 Explaining the Basis of Arising of Ordinary Thought

[The root text continues], "The six sense-consciousnesses and the six sense-objects arise as liveliness." This pertains to the activity of the six sense-organs—eyes, ears, nose, tongue, body and sense-mind—and the six sense-objects—form, sound, smell, taste, sensation [and conceptualization].

A.2.2.2.1.2.3.3 Explaining the Enumeration of Ordinary Thought

[The root text says], "This is known as reflective thought mind."

This pertains to the activity of intention of recollection with respect to these sense-objects. Then [the root text] says, "*Samaya!* Seal! Seal! Seal!" as before.

Commentary B:

B.2.1.2.1.3 The Explanation About Ordinary Conceptual Thought

Third, the explanation about ordinary conceptual thought has two parts:

(1) how four kinds of conceptual thought arise in the basis, and

(2) an enumeration of the kinds of thought that arise.

B.2.1.2.1.3.1 How Four Kinds of Conceptual Thought Arise in the Basis

First, how four kinds of ordinary conceptual thought arise is as follows: The root text says, "with respect to conceptual thought...." In essence, there isn't even the slightest particle of grasping, yet it is called reflective thought. The root text says, "Although the king of knowing-awareness is non-conceptual, all the diverse types of reflective thought and mindful thoughts arise from groundless-ground, like light-rays from the wind of the sun. They arise as seemingly ordinary thought from the liveliness of awakened awareness." This is like light-rays arising from the liveliness of the sun. From primordial wisdom's awakened awareness, various reflective thoughts and mindful thoughts arise. The root text says, "...as does mindful awareness, various [thought] activity toward sense-objects." This refers to the six sense-systems, six sense-objects, and six sense-consciousnesses, and the respective visual forms, sounds, smells, tastes, and touch sensations arising from Bon [itself].

B.2.1.2.1.3.2 An Enumeration of the Kinds of Thought That Arise

Second, an enumeration of the kinds of thought that arise (404) is as follows: The root text says, "This is known as 'reflective thought mind.'" What is called "reflective thought mind" is called so because it acts to reflect on its object. What is called "mindful" is mindful because it is aware. "Mindful reflection" is called that because it reflects with awareness. What is called "thought activity toward sense-objects" is called that because it is the activity of mindfulness that makes the sense-object an object of thought.

(336) If one were to make a condensed summary, it would be like this: These three—universal ground, awakened awareness, and ordinary conceptual thought; these three—the foundation, the heart, and the magic show; and these three—the mother, the child, and the liveliness—are known [by the distinction of] ordinary mind [in contrast to awakened] mind-itself.

Commentary A:
A.2.2.2.1.3 A Brief Conclusion

This conclusion includes a summary of the teachings on the natural state and teachings on the way this stays every moment in an individual's mind-stream.

A.2.2.2.1.3.1 Summary Regarding the Natural State

First, [the root text] says, "This is a condensed summary." This refers to it being a condensed summary of the pith instructions. The text continues, "These three—groundless-ground, awakened awareness, and ordinary conceptual thought." These three pertain to groundless-ground being the expanse of the *dharmadhātu*, awakened awareness being the primordial wisdom of the awakened mind-itself, and seemingly ordinary conceptual thought being how this mind-itself arises as various [events], respectively. [When the root text] says, "The three—the foundation, the heart, and the magic show," it refers to the foundation being [ultimate] *bodhicitta*, the heart being primordial wisdom's awakened awareness, and seemingly ordinary thought being the magic show, respectively. [When the root text] says, "The three—the mother, the child, and the liveliness," it refers to the mother as empty, selfless groundless-ground in the expanse of the *dharmadhātu*; the child as awakened awareness, lucid in-and-of-itself without grasping as the primordial wisdom of the awakened mind-itself; and the liveliness of seemingly ordinary thought as the inseparable pair of mother and child, respectively. [When the root text] says, "These are known as ordinary mind and awakened mind," the "ordinary mind" refers to ordinary mindfulness, thought, and conceptual thought, (336) and "awakened mind-itself" refers to *bodhicitta*, the essence which thoroughly pervades everything. Primordial wisdom's awakened awareness is simultaneously-born, and arises in-and-by-itself in the awakened mind-itself. Regarding the three—groundless-ground, awakened awareness, and seemingly ordinary conceptual thought — it is taught that these are [the same within the single sphere of ultimate reality].

(336) The way it stays within the mind-stream of each individual every moment is such that you are never uniting to it to or separating from it. Universal ground is sort of like an open portal of space. Awakened awareness is sort of like the heart of the sun. Ordinary conceptual thought is sort of like the rays of the sun. Ultimate sound arises as self-occurring liveliness. Light is sort of like rainbow light. Light-rays are like a matrix of sun rays. [This defines] the natural state whose disposition is primordially unconditioned. *Samaya!*

Commentary A:

A.2.2.2.1.3.2 Explaining the Way this Stays Every Moment in an Individual's Mind-stream

[The root text continues], "The way it stays within the mind-stream of each individual every moment, never being separated from it…" This means that within groundless-ground, mother and child stay as inseparable. In staying like this, [the root text] says, "Groundless-ground is sort of like the openness of space," and within this open space are the rays [of the enlightened intention] of *bodhicitta*. [The root text continues], "Awakened awareness is sort of like the heart of the sun." In primordial wisdom's awakened awareness are the rays. [It continues], "Ordinary conceptual thought is sort of like the rays of the sun." Just as [light-]rays come from the sun, [the rays of mental events come from primordial wisdom's awakened awareness. From the liveliness of awakened awareness, all the various thoughts occur. [The root text] says, "Ultimate sound arises as self-occurring liveliness." This means that in the sphere of groundless-ground sound occurs in-and-by-itself as the empty [liveliness] of awakened awareness, coming forth like thunder. [The root text] adds, "Light is sort of like rainbow light." Light is housed in the sun, and a rainbow is its expression. [The text adds], "Light-rays are like a matrix of sun rays." "Light-rays" refers to the matrix like [a display] of light-rays. [The root text adds], "The natural state whose disposition is unconditioned from the beginning." This means that primordial wisdom stays just as it is in groundless-ground.

[The root text closes with], "*Samaya!*"

Commentary B:
B.2.1.3 **A Condensed Summary**

Second, the brief summary has two parts:

(1) an enumeration of the three—subject, mother and son, and liveliness, and

(2) how [awakened awareness] stays in the mind-stream of any individual being.

B.2.1.3.1 **An Enumeration of the Three—Subject, Mother and Son, and Liveliness**

First, the root text says, "This is a condensed summary." It summarizes the pith instructions like this, "These three—groundless-ground, awakened awareness, and ordinary conceptual thought," are explained. The third— conceptual thought and ordinary mindfulness—arises as *bodhicitta's* [enlightened intention], as primordial wisdom's awakened awareness. "These three—the basis [conceptual thought], the heart, and the magic show" are called that because *bodhicitta* is the basis. "These three—the mother and son, and the liveliness," are called that because *bodhicitta*, (the mother), primordial wisdom's awakened awareness (the son), and conceptual thought, are liveliness as mother and son inseparable. As the root text says, "These refer to the ordinary mind and [awakened] mind-itself." Mindful awareness pertains to ordinary mind. *Bodhicitta*, wherein the essence thoroughly pervades everything, pertains to [awakened] mind-itself. Primordial wisdom's awakened awareness pertains to mind-itself that stays in-itself simultaneously born.

B.2.1.3.2 How [Awakened Awareness] Stays in the Mind-stream of Any Individual Being

Second, how [awakened awareness] stays in the mind-stream of any individual being. The root text says, "The way it stays within the mind-stream of each individual every moment, never being separated from it." These three are in the mind-stream of each individual. (405) They stay just as they are. Groundless-ground, mother, and son, are inseparable. The natural state stays as the ultimate truth of *Buddhahood*. The mother—groundless-ground—stays as empty space. The son—primordial wisdom's awakened awareness—stays like the heart of the sun. Both [mother and son] stay as non-dual lucidity/emptiness like the sun arising in empty space. All mindful and reflective thought is self-arisen and self-liberated and stays like light-rays of the sun. From that condition, the clear-light of [seeming] objects arise like self-appearing illusions in the empty expanse. Ultimate sound arises as the liveliness of awakened awareness, like the self-occurring echo of awakened awareness. Light arises like swirling rainbows in space, the self-arisen light of awakened awareness. Light-rays arise like the rays of the sun, the self-emission of awakened awareness. Thus, both objects known and the knower of the objects are non-dual and inseparable. The great clear-light, the embodiment of enlightenment, and the primordial wisdoms stay primordially in their own real nature within the *Buddha*-fields of the *mandala* in one's own mind-stream. Basis clear-light [of enlightenment] is primordial *Buddhahood* staying. Path clear-light is the ultimate truth of this arising in one's mind-stream and directly becoming evident. This is the direct manifestation of *Buddhahood*. The absolute completion of this and reaching the final state is Fruition clear-light, wherein [stable] completion [of *Buddhahood*] is reached.

(336) How does *samsāra* and *nirvāna* become divided into a duality? How is Kun tu bZang Po the primordial *Buddha*? How does the karma of sentient beings lead to *samsāra*? [The answer is that] Kun tu bZang po is the primordial *Buddha* who has the realization. Sentient beings [who wander through *samsāra*] by virtue of their karma do not have the realization. The basis of [either] realization or delu-

sion is universal ground and awakened awareness. The conditions that differentiate between realization and delusion pertain to the three visions—[ultimate sound, light, and light-rays]. The causes of realization and delusion are knowing-awareness and ordinary mindful awareness, respectively. With respect to universal ground and awakened awareness, there is neither realization nor delusion, and there is no division of *saṃsāra* into duality. Yet, with respect to ordinary conceptual thought and ordinary mindful awareness, either realization or delusion will ensue [and from this lack of realization] *saṃsāra* and *nirvāṇa* become a duality.

Commentary A:

A.2.2.2.2 The Teachings on How *Saṃsāra* and *Nirvāṇa* Become Divided in a Duality

The teachings on the way *saṃsāra* and *nirvāṇa* become divided in two has three parts:

(1) a brief summary of how *saṃsāra* and *nirvāṇa* become divided,

(2) a detailed explanation, (337) and

(3) a conclusion.

A.2.2.2.2.1 A Brief Summary of How *Saṃsāra* and *Nirvāṇa* Become Divided

[The text begins], "How *saṃsāra* and *nirvāṇa* become separated into a duality." This describes the root phrase. Following that, a question is set forth [in the root text], "How is Kun tu bZang po a primordial *Buddha*? How does the karma of sentient beings lead to *saṃsāra*?" If not even a whisker of virtue is done by Kun tu bZang po and he is a *Buddha*, and not even a whisker of sin is done by sentient beings in the three realms, and they are in the realms of *saṃsāra*, the answer follows [in the root text], saying, "Primordial *Buddhas* like Kun tu bZang po have realization, while sentient beings [who wander through *saṃsāra* by virtue of their] karma do not have realization." Kun tu bZang po is a *Buddha* because the realization appears in-and-by-itself. Sentient beings across the three realms remain in the realms of *saṃsāra* because the realization has not arisen in-and-by-itself. Following that is a description of the three—the basis, conditions, and essence of realization and delusion. [The root text continues], "The basis of [either] realization or delusion is groundless-ground and awakened awareness. The conditions [that differentiate between] realization or delusion pertain to the three—ultimate sound, light, and light-rays. The cause [that differentiates between] realization or delusion pertains to knowing-awareness and ordinary mindfulness, respectively." This means that the pair, groundless-ground and awakened awareness, is the basis for [both] realization and delusion [alike]. The conditions of both realization and delusion are the three—sound, light, and light-rays. The essence of both realization and delusion is [either] knowing awakened awareness or [ordinary] conceptual thought and mindfulness. Moreover, whatever realization comes is not from ordinary conceptual thought or mindfulness but from [directly] knowing awakened awareness. Whatever conditions are brought about, the realization comes from [establishing all appearance] as the three—ultimate sound, light, and light-rays. If there is any delusion whatsoever, this delusion comes from failing to realize the natural state of groundless-ground and awakened awareness. If there is any delusion about any conditions, this delusion comes from not bringing about the condition [of establishing all appearance] as the three—sound, light, and light-rays. (338) Next comes recognition of the essence [of either] realization or delusion. Either realization or delusion can occur with respect to groundless-ground, or awakened awareness, or seemingly ordinary conceptual thought. [The root text continues], "With respect to groundless-ground or awakened awareness, there is neither realization nor delusion, and there is no division of *saṃsāra* and *nirvāṇa* into duality. Yet, with respect to ordinary conceptual thought that reflects on this, either realization or delusion will ensue, and *saṃsāra* and *nirvāṇa* arise as a duality." With respect to groundless-ground and awakened awareness, the realization arises in the three times no longer covered by the stains of delusion, and through this realization, there is no division of *saṃsāra* and *nirvāṇa* into a duality. Yet, lacking this realization and remaining deluded, *saṃsāra* arises.

A.2.2.2.2.2 **An Extensive Explanation**

There are two parts to the extensive explanation regarding the way *saṁsāra* and *nirvāṇa* become divided:

(1) the way of the primordial *Buddha*, Kun tu bZang po, and

(2) the way delusion arises from the karma of sentient beings of the three realms.

A.2.2.2.2.2.1 The Way of the Primordial *Buddha*, Kun tu bZang po

The way of the primordial *Buddha*, Kun tu bZang po, has three parts:

(1) explaining the way primordial wisdom's awakened awareness arises;

(2) explaining the way to attain the self-influence of awakened awareness; and

(3) explaining the way the emanations of *nirvāṇa* arise.

Commentary B:

B.2.1.2.2 The Way *Saṁsāra* and *Nirvāṇa* Become Divided into Two [as a Duality]

Second, "the teachings on how *saṁsāra* and *nirvāṇa* become divided into a duality" has three parts:

(1) the teachings,

(2) the extensive explanation, and

(3) the conclusion.

B.2.1.2.2.1 The Teachings

First, [the teachings] as the root text says, "How is Kun tu bZang po a primordial *Buddha*? Primordial *Buddhas* like Kun tu bZang po have realization. How does the karma of sentient beings lead to *saṁsāra*? (406) While sentient beings [who wander through *saṁsāra* by virtue of their] karma do not have realization, the basis of [either] realization or delusion is groundless-ground and awakened awareness." In essence, any realization or delusion is stainless, because both realization and delusion come from the basis [groundless-ground]. The root text says, "The conditions that differentiate between realization and delusion pertain to the three visions [sound, light, and light-rays]. By not knowing the three—

sound, light, and light-rays—as self-arising, these conditions make the realization become deluded. The root text says, "The cause of realization and delusion are ordinary mindfulness and knowing-awareness, respectively." With respect to conceptual thought, it can occur as either realization or non-realization. As the root text says, "With respect to groundless-ground and awakened awareness, there is neither realization nor delusion, and there is no division of *saṁsāra* and *nirvāṇa* into duality. Yet, with respect to ordinary conceptual thought and mindfulness, either realization or delusion will ensue." Groundless-ground and awakened awareness come from the basis as either realization or delusion, yet whichever of these two occurs is stainless. The root text says, "*Saṁsāra* and *nirvāṇa* arise without being split into a duality." This is the natural state of the basis, which is never split into duality, yet, "with respect to conceptual thought and mindfulness, it can occur as realization or delusion." Mindfulness occurs just as it is, and from wrong mindfulness duality occurs. As the root text says, "*Saṁsāra* and *nirvāṇa* arise as a duality." *Nirvāṇa* comes from realization and *saṁsāra* from non-realization.

What is the reasoning for how realization comes? Through the arising of the liveliness of the three appearing sense-objects, and by knowing through ordinary conceptual thought or ordinary mindful awareness, (337) these [appearances] are clearly seen as self-appearing illusions. Through bringing about the conditions by which seeming sense-objects [are realized to be] self-appearing, awakened awareness arises naked and bare. The universal ground free of obscuration is vividly and distinctly realized.

Commentary A:

A.2.2.2.2.2.1.1 **Explaining the Way Primordial Wisdom's Awakened Awareness Arises**

[The root text continues], "What is the reasoning for how realization comes?" If there were to be such a realization of Kun tu bZang po, [as the root text says], it would be because "the three visions have arisen as liveliness." [This means that realization occurs whenever appearance] directly manifests itself as [the liveliness of] sound, light, and light-rays. [The text continues], "Knowing through ordinary conceptual thought or mindful awareness is clearly seen as a self-appearing illusion." (339) [The expanded explanation means] seeing the light of seemingly ordinary conceptual thought and its mindfulness like self-appearing rainbow light, perceiving self-occurring sound like an echo, and seeing self-appearing light-rays like an illusion. [The root text continues], "Through bringing about the conditions by which seeming sense-objects [are realized to be] self-appearing." This means that [by establishing] the conditions by which [seeming] sense-objects are seen as awakened awareness's [liveliness] as the three [sound, light, and light-rays], it is like seeing one's own face reflected in a mirror. [When the root text says], "Awakened awareness arises naked and bare," it means that when this happens it is not covered by the animal hide of seemingly ordinary conceptual thought. "There is realization of groundless-ground vividly and distinctly," which means naked, not covered by habitual karmic propensities or by obscurations, no longer clouded.

(337) Through this realization, awakened awareness is held in its own way. Without chasing after [seeming] external objects of appearance, at that time they directly manifest under their own self-influence.

Commentary A:

A.2.2.2.2.2.1.2 Explaining the Way to Attain the Self-influence of Awakened Awareness

The way to establish influence-in-and-of itself is as follows. [The root text continues], "Through this realization awakened awareness knows itself by itself." This means that you apprehend the basis of what makes Kun tu bZang po a victorious one. It is like a victor who seizes victory. [The root text continues], "…without chasing after [seeming] external objects of appearance." This means that through apprehending the basis of awakened awareness, you do not need to chase after common [everyday] appearances. [The root text continues], "At that time they manifest themselves under their own self-influence." This means that by knowing [awakened awareness], you no longer chase after [seeming] external sense-objects, and instead realize awakened awareness through its own self-influence.

(337) ...these manifestations of *nirvāna*, cannot be made to happen and arise of their own wind. From connecting light with awakened awareness, all the emanations of the enlightened body arise. From connecting [ultimate] sound with awakened awareness, all the manifestations of enlightened speech arise. From connecting light-rays with awakened awareness, all the emanations of the enlightened heart-mind arise. From the activity of the three livelinesses—enlightened body, speech, and heart-mind—the positive qualities and enlightened activity arise spontaneously. There is no need for the accumulation of the two accumulations [of merit and wisdom] because these occur through the strength of the realization itself. *Samaya!*

Commentary A:

A.2.2.2.2.2.1.3 **Explaining the Way the Emanations of *Nirvāṇa* Arise**

[The text begins], "These manifestations of *nirvāṇa*...." [This pertains to] the embodiment of enlightenment, the primordial wisdoms, etc., and the accumulation of positive qualities that manifest at the time of realization. These arise for no reason other than the strength of the realization. Thus, [the root text] says, "...cannot be made to happen, and arise of their own wind." The five Enlightened *Buddha*-bodies, the five [*Buddha*] families, and five *Buddhas* [all] arise from the immeasurable strength of the liveliness of this, and "from the activity of connecting light with awakened awareness." [The root text continues], "All the emanations of the embodiment of enlightenment arise." (340) [This refers to] the *Buddha*-fields, the ornaments of the *mandala*, the clear-light bodies, their colors and ornaments like scepters, etc. [of the *mandala* deities], all of which arise as none other than reflections [in a mirror]. [The root text continues], "From the activity of connecting [ultimate] sound [of liveliness] with awakened awareness, all the manifestations of enlightened speech arise." The melodious enlightened speech of the sages, and the truths imparted into the mind-streams [of practitioners] of this [Great] Vehicle, [all] arise from none other than the liveliness of this. [The root text continues], "From the activity of connecting light-rays with awakened awareness, all the emanations of the enlightened heart-mind arise." The five omniscient wisdom energies arise, transform, and divide into twenty-four, four thousand, ten thousand, and one hundred thousand manifestations, as the strength of positive qualities and enlightened activities, all arising from none other than the liveliness of this. [The root text continues], "From the activity of the three livelinesses of enlightened body, speech, and heart-mind." This means that by making a connection with the liveliness of all three [ultimate sound, light, and light-rays], all the positive qualities and enlightened activity and depth [for the benefit of others] arise from the strength of this state effortlessly. [The root text continues], "There is no need for the accumulation of the two accumulations [of merit and wisdom]." Merit pertains to the lower vehicle. With respect to the primordial wisdoms, there is no need for accumulation of merit because [as the root text adds], "these occur through the strength of the realization itself." They arise as spontaneously present, effortlessly, from the strength of the realization.

Commentary B:
B.2.1.2.2.2 The Extensive Explanation.

Second, the extensive explanation has two parts:

(1) how *nirvāṇa* gets separated, and

(2) how *saṁsāra* gets separated.

B.2.1.2.2.2.1 How *Nirvāṇa* Gets Separated

The first, how *nirvāṇa* gets separated, also has two parts:

(1) how the realization comes from the natural state just as it is, and

(2) how *nirvāṇa* is attained through realization.

B.2.1.2.2.2.1.1 How the Realization Comes From the Natural State Just As It Is

First, [how the realization comes from the natural state just as it is], the root text says, "What is the argument for realization?" If you were to have the realization of Kun tu bZang po just as it is, it would be that "the three visions have arisen as liveliness." This means that at the very moment something arises it directly arises as the three—sound, light, and light-rays. The root text says, "Knowing through ordinary conceptual thought or mindfulness is clearly seen as self-appearing illusion." (407) Mindful thought is light, light-itself, like a rainbow. Sound is self-sound, like an echo. Light-rays are self-light-rays, like seeing reflections in a mirror. The root text says, "Through bringing about the conditions by which seeming sense-objects [are realized to be] self-appearing." By looking into the mirror, you see the seeming thing through whatever conditions [support seeing] the object, yet you are seeing awakened awareness. At that time, you do not experience putting on the skin of conceptual thought in that, as the root text says, "awakened awareness arises naked and bare. There is realization of stainless groundless-ground vividly and distinctly." There is the realization of groundless-ground vividly and distinctly, not experienced as covered by habitual karmic propensities or obscurations. As the root text says, "Through this realization awakened awareness knows-itself-by-itself." This ends with the highest seat of [the realization of] Kun tu bZang po. The root text continues, "...without chasing after [seeming] external objects of appearance." This means that awakened awareness ends as the highest seat, and there is no chasing after ordinary appearance [anymore]. The root text says, "At that time [internally] they manifest themselves under their own self-influence." Awakened awareness of objects is attained by its own influence. Knowing that, there is no chasing after [seeming] objects.

B.2.1.2.2.2.1.2 How *Nirvāṇa* is Attained Through Realization

Second, [how *nirvāṇa* is attained through realization] is as follows: The root text says, "These manifestations of *nirvāṇa* cannot be made to happen, and arise of their own wind." When the realization happens, it arises from its own force, in that it is not necessary for the purpose of the assembly of positive qualities, such as the *Buddha*-bodies and the wisdom energies. The root text continues, "From the activity of connecting light with awakened awareness, all the emanations of the Enlightened *Buddha*-bodies arise." From the liveliness of this, the three *Buddha*-bodies, the five *Buddha* families, the immeasurable abodes of the deities of the *mandala*, the *Buddha*-fields and realms, the ornaments, the color of the body [of the deities], the hand instruments, all arise as reflections wherein the body is a body of light-rays. As the root text says, "From the activity of connecting [ultimate] sound (408) with awakened awareness, all the manifestations of enlightened speech arise." From the liveliness of this, what arises are the many words and sounds of the truth of the gateway of Bon and *tantric* vehicle spoken in the tones of sacred speech. The root text says, "From the activity of connecting light-rays with awakened awareness, all the emanations of the enlightened heart-mind arise." This means that from the liveliness of this, what arises are the five primordial omniscient wisdoms and all the ways to divide the teachings into sixty-one, eighty-four thousand, and one-hundred thousand. The root text continues, "From the activity of the three livelinesses—enlightened body, speech, and heart-mind—the positive qualities and enlightened activity arise from its strength." This means that from the liveliness of unifying the three of these, all the great positive qualities and the various enlightened deeds arise from its state or from its strength in such a way that does not require any effort on the path. The root text continues, "There is no accumulation of the two accumulations [of merit and wisdom] because these occur through the strength of the realization itself." This means that while there is accumulation of merit in the lower vehicles, [in this vehicle] there is no accumulation of wisdom or merit because through the force of the realization these occur effortlessly as spontaneously present.

(337) What is the reasoning on how sentient beings become deluded? Whenever the three objects become manifest, ordinary mindfulness and conceptual knowing becomes deluded with respect to these sense-appearances. Failing to know these as self-appearing illusions, you see them as real external appearances. The ultimate truth of awakened awareness becomes obscured by ordinary conceptual thought, seeing it as something other. Failing to recognize self-awakened awareness, there is no realization of the ultimate truth of the universal ground. This is co-emergent non-recognition.

Commentary A:

A.2.2.2.2.2.2 The Way Delusion Arises from the Karma of Sentient Beings of the Three Realms

The way delusion arises from the karma of sentient beings of the three realms has two parts:

(1) explaining the way delusion arises from not recognizing awakened awareness, and

(2) explaining the way *saṁsāra* arises.

A.2.2.2.2.2.2.1 Explaining the Way Delusion Arises from Not Recognizing Awakened Awareness

First, [The root text continues], "What is the argument regarding how the delusion of sentient beings comes forth?" This sets out the [main] question. [The root text continues], "Whenever the three visions become manifest." This means that the three—[ultimate] sound, light, and light-rays—arise as objects of ordinary conceptual thought. [The text then says], "[Ordinary] mindfulness and conceptual knowing becomes deluded with respect to sense-objects." This refers to not knowing the way sense-objects actually exist. [The root text continues], "Failing to know these as self-appearing illusions, you see them as external, real appearances." This means that you do not know the three—[ultimate] sound, light, and light-rays—as the liveliness of awakened awareness, and do not see beyond the appearance in your own mind-stream. For example, it is like a form itself appearing inside water, and not seeing it as the form itself, but seeing it instead as the form of something else. [The text continues], "The ultimate truth of awakened awareness becomes obscured by ordinary conceptual thought seeing it as something else." Ordinary conceptual thought covers over naked awakened awareness. For example, it is like the sun being covered over by clouds. [The root text continues], "Failing to recognize awakened awareness in-and-by-itself, there is no realization of the ultimate truth of groundless-ground." Failing to recognize awakened awareness-in-and-by-itself is like failing to recognize the sun, and instead there is no awakened awareness,[11] like the sun obscured and shrouded in darkness. Likewise, the ultimate truth of groundless-ground, like space, becomes covered over, just as if the sun had disappeared, covered by the darkness of space. [The root text con-

---

11. *ma rig pa*: "not recognizing awakened awareness."

tinues], "This is co-emergent non-recognition." This refers to failing to recognize the natural state of groundless-ground and awakened awareness just as it is. If you want to affix a name to this, it is "co-emergent non-recognition."

Commentary B:
B.2.1.2.2.2.2 How *Saṁsāra* Gets Separated

Second, how *saṁsāra* gets separated, has three parts:

(1) with respect to ultimate truth, in what way delusion arises;

(2) through delusion, how one wanders in *saṁsāra*; and

(3) a brief summary about the meaning of this.

B.2.1.2.2.2.2.1 With Respect to Ultimate Truth, in What Way Delusion Arises

First, [with respect to ultimate truth, in what way delusion arises] has four parts: (1) how non-recognition of awakened awareness and simultaneousness [of appearance] occurs; (2) how non-recognition of groundless-ground occurs; (3) how the self-grasping and afflictive emotions of the ordinary sense-mind occurs; and (4) how habitual karmic propensities accumulate in the basis.

B.2.1.2.2.2.2.1.1 How Non-recognition of Awakened Awareness and Simultaneousness [of Appearance] Occurs

First, [how non-recognition of awakened awareness and simultaneousness occurs]. The root text says, "Whenever the visions become manifest." This refers to the time when the three—sound, light, and light-rays—become directly evident. (409) The text then says, "Ordinary mindfulness and conceptual knowing become deluded with respect to sense-objects." One does not know the [true] way of the six sense-objects. The root text continues, "Failing to know these as self-appearing illusions, you see them as external, real appearances." You no longer know the three—sound, light, and light-rays—as the liveliness of awakened awareness, but see them in your own mind-stream as if seeing something on the outside. For example, a form arises within [a pool of] water, itself the water, yet you see it as if that form is not the water-itself but as an external form. The root text continues, "The ultimate truth of awakened awareness becomes obscured by ordinary conceptual thought, seeing it as something other." Naked awakened awareness becomes covered by the clothing of ordinary conceptual thought. For example, it is like the sun becoming covered by clouds. The root text then says, "Failing to recognize awakened awareness in-and-by-itself, there is no realization of the ultimate truth of groundless-ground." By failing to recognize that awakened awareness in-and-by-itself is like the sun, such non-recognition is like a darkness that obscures and envelops [everything], obscuring the ultimate truth of groundless-ground like [clear] space. For example, it is like the sun setting [on the horizon] and becoming obscured by darkness. The root text continues, "This is co-emergent non-recognition." The natural state is left by itself and there is no recognition of it.

(337) The [way of] knowing under the influence of this non-recognition becomes movement toward [seemingly real external] objects, through which these [specific] objects of perception are perceived and discriminated. This is called "mind-consciousness." Because the mind [dualistically] moves toward sense-objects, [the mind] stops settling in its own way. Because the mind stops being in its own way, the three objects of appearance become disturbed. Because the three objects of appearance have become disturbed, the five kinds of causal elements arise. By the five types of causal elements arising, the five sense-objects appear. By the five sense-objects appearing, [conscious] knowing via the five sense-doors arises. There are so many different and various kinds of discursive thoughts with respect to these six sense-consciousnesses.

Commentary A:
A.2.2.2.2.2.2.2 **Explaining the Way Saṁsāra Arises**

Explaining the way saṁsāra arises has two parts:

(1) a general explanation of the way saṁsāra arises, and

(2) a specific explanation.

A.2.2.2.2.2.2.2.1 A General Explanation of the Way *Saṁsāra* Arises

The general explanation of the way *saṁsāra* arises has three parts:

(1) the way sense-objects and ordinary knowing arise,

(2) the way the habitual karmic propensities accumulate, and

(3) the way the three realms and the body arise. (342)

A.2.2.2.2.2.2.2.1.1 The Way Sense-objects and Ordinary Knowing Arise

[The root text] says, "The [way of] knowing under the influence of this ignorance becomes movement toward [seemingly real external] sense-objects." This means that under the influence of not knowing the natural state or awakened awareness as it is, ordinary mindfulness and conceptual knowing move toward [seemingly real external] sense-objects, having all kinds of movement of the mind-consciousness. [The root text continues], "…through which these objects are perceived and discriminated." This means that because [the kind of] knowing that is from the mind-consciousness[12] moves toward these sense-objects, it is not left in its own way,[13] like clouds blown around by the wind. [The text] says, "Because the mind stops being in its own way, the three objects of appearance become disturbed." The three objects [in this case] refers to the original condition of [ultimate] sound, light, and light-rays becoming disturbed, much like clouds getting agitated by the wind. [The root text] continues, "Because the three objects of appearance have become disturbed, the five kinds of causal elements arise." From the five kinds of causal elements the five sense-objects arise—sight, sound, smell, taste, and touch sensation. [The root text] continues, "By the five sense-objects appearing, knowing via the five sense-doors[14] arises." The five sense-objects refers to the sense-objects arising from each of the respective sense-consciousnesses—the eye consciousness, ear-consciousness, taste-consciousness, smell-consciousness, body-sensation-consciousness,

---

12. *yid shes*: the sixth sense-system, the "mind-consciousness."

13. *rang sa*: "in its own way."

14. *sgo lnga*: "five sense-doors."

and mental consciousness. [The root text] continues, "There are so many different and various kinds of discursive thoughts with respect to the six sense-consciousnesses." What are called the six sense-systems include the five sense-consciousnesses and the mental consciousness. This sixth sense-system [the mental consciousness has] the activity of many various kinds of discursive thoughts with respect to the six sense-objects. [The root text then] says, "That becomes not recognizing awakened awareness, i.e., becoming totally conceptualized." This refers to knowing that represents the activity of various [kinds of discursive thoughts]. What is referred to as "not recognizing awakened awareness" means to become totally conceptualized. (343) [The root text] then says, "Through the influence of not recognizing awakened awareness and becoming totally conceptualized, grasping the duality of self and other arises." This means that by not knowing awakened awareness and becoming totally conceptualized, duality develops with respect to [knowing] sense-objects. [The root text] continues, "Through grasping the duality of self and other, afflictive emotions like the five poisons occur." This means that the five poisons occur from the influence of self-grasping.[15] Desire comes from having a sense-object and from the mental consciousness's [interpretation of that sense-object]. Hatred does not pertain to mental consciousness. Ignorance does not pertain to either [sense- or mental consciousness]. Pride depends on the self. Envy depends on others. [The root text] continues, "These are the afflictive emotions [some of which are associated with] mental-consciousness." This means that with respect to [any kind of] knowing associated with a self and with self-grasping, [some of] such activity comes from mental consciousness and [leads to the development of] having afflictive emotions.

Commentary A:

B.2.1.2.2.2.2.1.2 **How Non-recognition of Groundless-ground Occurs**

Second, [how non-recognition of groundless-ground occurs]. How non-recognition that is conceptual labeling occurs is described in the root text where it says, "The [way of] knowing under the influence of

---

15. *bdag 'dzin gyi dbang*: "from the influence of self-grasping."

this non-recognition becomes movement toward [seemingly real external] objects." Through non-recognition, [external sense-objects] occur coming from the movements of the ordinary sense-mind. The root text continues, "...through which these objects of perception are perceived and discriminated." This means that with respect to the three—sound, light, and light-rays—you have become attached to [external sense-objects] as having a kind of reality. The text says, "Because the mind moves toward sense-objects, [the mind remaining] in its own way stops." Yet, there is no stopping of awakened awareness staying in its own way. The text says, "Because the mind stops being in its own way, the three objects of appearance become disturbed." (410) If the wind follows after the clouds, the wind agitates the clouds. The text says, "Because the three objects of appearance have become disturbed, the five kinds of causal elements arise." From the karmic activity of the three—sound, light, and light-rays—the five types of causal elements arise—fire, water, earth, wind, and space. The root text says, "By the five types of causal elements arising, the five sense-objects appear." The vital essence of these five elements becomes the five sense-objects—form, sound, smell, taste, and touch sensation. Through the appearance of these five sense-objects comes the conscious knowing of these through the sense gateways—the sense-consciousness of the eye knowing these [forms], and of the ear, the nose, the tongue, and the sense-consciousness of the body, respectively. The root text continues, "There are so many different and various kinds of discursive thoughts with respect to the six sense-consciousnesses." [What follows] is grasping [and making distinctions] such as good/bad, great/small, top/bottom, self/other, enemy/friend, god/demon, and so forth. This kind of knowing based on making distinctions is called "knowing which makes distinctions."

That becomes not recognizing awakened awareness, i.e., becoming totally conceptualized. Through the influence of not recognizing [awakened awareness] and becoming totally conceptualized, grasping the duality of self and other arises. (338) Through grasping the duality of self and other, afflictive emotions like the five poisons occur. These are the afflictive emotions [associated with] the

mind-consciousness.

Commentary B:

B.2.1.2.2.2.2.1.3 **How the Self-grasping and Afflictive Emotions of the Ordinary Sense-mind Occurs**

Third [how the self-grasping and afflictive emotions of the ordinary sense-mind occurs]. The root text begins, "Through the influence of not recognizing [awakened awareness] and becoming totally conceptualized, grasping the duality of self and other arises." Through such [dualistic] grasping, the agent of grasping, namely the self, grasps dualistically at sense-objects. As the root text says, "Through grasping the duality of self and other, afflictive emotions like the five poisons occur." Attachment and desire occur toward a desirable object. Hatred occurs toward a repulsive object. When there is neither, there is ignorance. Pride regarding an inflated self occurs. Envy of the positive qualities in others occurs. As the root text says, "These are the afflictive emotions [associated with] mental-consciousness." Through grasping the duality of self and other and thinking about such distinctions, (411) knowing associated with the afflictive emotions and the sense-mind becomes deluded.

(338) Under the influence of the five poisons, the karmic activity of the formative aggregate occurs. Under the influence of [both] afflictive emotions and karmic activity, habitual karmic propensities accumulate in the storehouse. Universal ground, essentially free of thought, [then] becomes the storehouse for the accumulation of karmic traces. The agent who knows via the six sense-consciousnesses will accumulate habitual karmic propensities. Karmic activity and afflictive emotions accumulate even more various habitual karmic propensities. The afflictive-emotions-mind holds on to them without letting go.

Commentary A:

A.2.2.2.2.2.2.2.1.2 **The Way the Habitual Karmic Propensities Accumulate**

The way the habitual karmic propensities accumulate in the storehouse[16] is as follows. [As the root text] says, "Under the influence of the five poisons the karmic activity of the formative aggregate occurs." This means that under the influence of afflictive emotions like the five poisons, various kinds of non-virtuous or virtuous karmic or neutral activity occur. [According to the root text], "Under the influence of [both] afflictive emotions and karmic activity, habitual karmic propensities accumulate in the storehouse." This means that through making a connection between and unifying karmic activity and afflictive emotions, various habitual karmic propensities accumulate in the storehouse. With respect to whatever has accumulated, [the root text] says, "Groundless-ground, essentially free of thought, [then] becomes the storehouse for the accumulation of karmic traces." These habitual karmic propensities are accumulated in ordinary storehouse mind.[17] With respect to whatever karmic propensities have accumulated, [as the root text] says, "The agent who knows via the six sense-consciousnesses will accumulate habitual karmic propensities." Knowing by means of the six sense-consciousnesses is what causes the accumulation of karmic propensities. With respect to whatever karmic propensities have accumulated, [the root text] says, "Karmic activity and afflictive emotions accumulate even more various habitual karmic propensities." The karmic activity and afflictive emotions that are associated with grasping after anything whatsoever is what causes the accumulation of various [additional] karmic propensities. (344) [The root text] continues, "The mind of afflictive emotions holds on to them without letting go." This means that because of the [operation of] mental [consciousness] and afflictive emotions, the mind holds on without letting go, and thus, [additional] habitual karmic propensities accumulate. Through the integration [of the operations] of the eight consciousnesses [five sense-consciousnesses, mind-consciousness, sense of self, and personal memory system] comes the accumulation of [additional] habitual karmic propensities. As has been described, there is no doubt that habitual karmic propensities will accumulate in the storehouse.

---

16. *gzhi* = *kun gzhi rnam shes*: "storehouse consciousness," i.e., groundless-ground seen through the eyes of not knowing awakened awareness becomes the storehouse for accumulating and ripening habitual karmic propensities.

17. *kun gzhi'i rnam par shes pa*: "ordinary storehouse mind."

Commentary B:

B.2.1.2.2.2.2.1.4 **How Habitual Karmic Propensities [Accumulate in the Basis]**

Fourth, how habitual karmic propensities [accumulate in the basis]. The root text begins, "Under the influence of the five poisons, the karmic activity of the formative aggregate occurs." This occurs through all the various exertions and efforts. The text says, "Under the influence of [both] afflictive emotions and karmic activity, habitual karmic propensities accumulate in the storehouse." This means that the habitual karmic propensities of karmic activity and afflictive emotions accumulate in groundless-ground, and through such accumulation of habitual karmic propensities, "groundless-ground, essentially free of thought, [then] becomes the storehouse for the accumulation of karmic traces." Through such accumulation as this, "the agent who knows via the six sense-consciousnesses will accumulate habitual karmic propensities," and because of this grasper, "karmic activity and afflictive emotions accumulate even more various habitual karmic propensities," as the root text says. Whatever is grasped by the grasper, as the root text says, "…the mind of afflictive emotions holds on to them without letting go."

(338) As the force of these strong habitual karmic propensities increases, ordinary thought [as the expression of the] mind-consciousness manifests as the ordinary physical body. Through the influence of ignorance, those so deluded [are re-born in] the formless realms. As the force of these habitual karmic propensities becomes coarse and increases, the light manifests as the appearance of the seemingly ordinary body. Through the influence of hatred, those so deluded [are re-born in] the form realms. As the force of these habitual karmic propensities greatly increases, the materiality [of the body] manifests as flesh and blood. Through [the influence of attachment], those so deluded [are reborn in] the desire realms. Through making a connection between awakened awareness and the three—ultimate sound, light, and light-rays—the [ordinary] body, speech, and mind, [respectively] become manifest as three [seemingly distinct entities: the body from light, speech from ultimate sound, and the

mind from light-rays]. Through the accumulation of karmic propensities associated with the six sense-consciousnesses, there come delusions of the six classes of beings. Through the influence of the afflictive emotions like the five poisons, those so deluded wander on the five paths of *samsāra*, [i.e., the five non-human realms]. The four great causal elements become the primary cause for the four types of births [womb, egg, heat, and spontaneous birth]. From these four elements—flesh, blood, warmth, and breath—there come the four constituents [wind, bile, blood, and phlegm].

Commentary A:

A.2.2.2.2.2.2.2.1.3 **The Way the Three Realms and the Body Arise**

Third, the way the three realms and the body arise: [The root text] continues, "As the force of these strong habitual karmic propensities increases...." [This passage refers to] the complete accumulation of all habitual karmic propensities. [The text] continues, "...ordinary thought [as an expression of the] mind-consciousness manifests as the ordinary body." Now the movement of the mind-consciousness occurs as activity of the ordinary body. [The root text] continues, "Through the influence of ignorance, those so deluded [are reborn in] the formless realms. This means that ignorance is the cause of being reborn in the empty formless realms [in the future]. [The root text] continues, "As the force of these... habitual karmic propensities increases..." This means that these habitual karmic propensities greatly increase [through ignorance]. [The root text] continues, "...the light manifests as the appearance of the seemingly ordinary body." This means that [primordial] light now seems to appear as the ordinary body. [The root text] continues, "Through the influence of hatred, those so confused [are reborn in] the form realms of *saṁsāra*." This means that the cause of being reborn in the form realms is the influence of hatred [and its karmic ripening]. [The root text] continues, "As the force of these karmic propensities greatly increases..." This means that because of that, habitual karmic traces greatly increase resulting in [great] attachment. [The root text] continues, "Through the influence of attachment, those so deluded [are reborn in] the desire realms." This means that the cause of being reborn in the desire realms is attachment. [The root text] continues, "Through making a connection between awakened awareness and the three—[ultimate] sound, light, and light-rays—the [ordinary] body, speech, and mind [respectively] become manifest as three [seemingly distinct entities—body from light, speech from ultimate sound, and mind from the light-rays]." This means that light transforms into the ordinary body, [ultimate] sound transforms into ordinary speech, and light-rays transform into the ordinary mind. [The root text] continues, "Through the accumulation of habitual karmic propensities associated with the six sense-consciousnesses, there comes confusion about the appearance of the six classes of beings." This means that habitual karmic propensities increase with respect to the eyes seeing visual forms, so that delusion manifests as the appearance of hell-beings; habitual karmic propensities increase with respect to the ears hearing sound, so that delusion manifests as the appearance of hungry ghosts; habitual karmic propensities increase with respect to the nose smelling smells, so that delusion manifests as the appearance of gods and demi-gods; habitual karmic propensities increase with respect to the tongue tasting tastes, so that delusion manifests as the appearance of humans; and habitual karmic propensities increase with respect to [touch] sensations of the body, so that delusion manifests as the appearance of animals. [The root text] continues, "Through the influence of the afflictive emotions like the five poisons, those so deluded wander on the five paths of *saṁsāra*." This means that afflictive emotions like the five poisons become delusion manifesting as the causes of the five paths of *saṁsāra*. [The root text] continues, "The four great causal elements become the primary cause of the four types of rebirths [womb, egg, heat, and spontaneous birth]. This refers to miraculous birth from wind, heat birth from fire, egg birth from water, and womb birth from earth. [The root text] continues, "From these four elements—flesh, blood, warmth, and breath—there come the four compositions [wind, bile, blood, and phlegm]. From the breath come illnesses of wind; from warmth, bile; from blood, phlegm; from flesh comes the sickness of the aggregates [i.e., the body].

Commentary B:

B.2.1.2.2.2.2.2 **Through Delusion How One Wanders in *Saṁsāra***

Second, through delusion how one wanders in *saṁsāra* has three parts:

(1) the divisions of *saṁsāra*,

(2) the essence, and

(3) the way *saṁsāra* actually is.

B.2.1.2.2.2.2.2.1 The Divisions of *Saṁsāra*

The first [the divisions of *saṁsāra*] has six parts:

(1) realms,

(2) support,

(3) types of beings,

(4) paths,

(5) opening the gateways of birth, and

(6) the unique kinds of suffering.

B.2.1.2.2.2.2.2.1.1 Realms

First, the root text says, "As the force of these strong habitual karmic propensities increases." This refers to the overall proliferation of each habitual karmic propensity. "Ordinary thought [as the expression of the] mind-consciousness manifests as the ordinary body." This form becomes the support of the sense-mind. "Through the influence of ignorance, those so deluded [are reborn in] the formless realms." The reason they fall into the formless realms (412) is that their habitual karmic tendencies have become very strong. The root text continues, "The light manifests as the appearance of the seemingly ordinary body." Seeming to be the body, it is the light. The root text says, "Through the influence of hatred, those so deluded [are re-born in] the form realms." The reason they fall into the form realms is that "the force of these habitual karmic propensities greatly increases." Moreover, from the habitual karmic propensities of really great attachment, "the materiality [of the body] manifests as flesh and blood." This body of flesh and blood seems to have solidity. The root text says, "Through the influence of attachment, those so deluded [are reborn in] the desire realms." This is the reason they fall into the desire realms.

B.2.1.2.2.2.2.2.1.2 Support
Second, the differentiation of the three—body, speech, and mind—becomes the support.

B.2.1.2.2.2.2.2.1.3 Types of Beings
Third, from the perspective of types of beings, there are six types of beings in [their respective] six realms.

B.2.1.2.2.2.2.2.1.4 Paths
Fourth, the divisions of the path refer to the five causes of the path of *saṁsāra*.

B.2.1.2.2.2.2.2.1.5 Opening the Gateways of Birth
Fifth, the distinctions between the gateways that are the gateways of birth. The four types of birth in *saṁsāra* are miraculous, warmth, egg, and womb birth.

B.2.1.2.2.2.2.2.1.6 The Unique Kinds of Suffering
Sixth, the unique kinds of suffering pertain to illnesses of wind from the breath, of bile from heat, of phlegm from blood, and of the aggregates from flesh.

(338) Through the association between awakened awareness and light, the body and mind—both the container and contents—arise.

Commentary A:
A.2.2.2.2.2.2.2.2 A Specific Explanation of the Way *Saṁsāra* Arises
The specific explanation has two parts—the brief and extensive explanation.

A.2.2.2.2.2.2.2.2.1 Brief Explanation
[The root text] says, "Through the association of awakened awareness and light, body and mind, container and contents, arise." These

arise from making a connection between and uniting primordial wisdom's awakened awareness and the five lights. The seemingly external container arises as the known ordinary world. The internal contained contents arise as the [mind of] a sentient being. An illusion arises as the seeming physical body. Mindfulness arises as the seeming ordinary mind. (345) Then, the interconnectedness of *saṁsāra* arises in its various forms.

The way the external container, the known ordinary world, arises in the mind is through awakened awareness making a connection between light and space; a continuously flowing wind arises, and through the wind of its agitation the embers of fire burn. The fire and wind burn and through this agitation, water arises.

From the vital essence of this water, (339) earth becomes the ground and from this the container of everything in the known external world that brings attachment is formed. From the vital essence of the five causal elements, the five sense-objects arise. In the [seeming] external container, the known external world arises like this in the mind.

Commentary A:

A.2.2.2.2.2.2.2.2.2 **The Extended Explanation**

The extended explanation has three parts: (1) an explanation of the way the external container, the known ordinary world, arises from mind; (2) an explanation of the way the internal contained contents, the mind of sentient beings, arises from mind; and (3) an explanation of the way *saṁsāra* arises from not knowing awakened awareness.

A.2.2.2.2.2.2.2.2.2.1 **An Explanation of the Way the External Container, the Known Ordinary World, Arises from Mind**

[The root text] says, "The way the external container, the known ordinary world, arises in the mind…." This means that the external container, the known ordinary world, is a way of becoming attached. How does such attachment occur? [As the root text] says, "Through awakened awareness making a connection between light and space, a continuously flowing wind arises, and through the wind of its agitation the embers of fire burn. The fire and wind burn, and through this agitation, water arises. From the vital essence of this water, generative earth becomes the ground, and from this the container of everything in the known external world that brings attachment is formed." From the liveliness of making a connection between the pair—the five lights and awakened awareness—the causal five elements occur. One element supports the next and because of that the external container and everything in the known ordinary world occurs. [The root text] says, "From the contents of the five causal elements the five sense-objects arise." This means that from the contents of these five causal elements, the activity of the sense-objects—form, sound, smell, taste, and touch—occur. [The root text] continues, "In the seemingly external container, the known external world arises like this in the mind." This means that the seemingly external container, the known ordinary world, arises like this.

Commentary B:
B.2.1.2.2.2.2.2.2 **The Essence**

Second, the root text says, "Through making a connection between awakened awareness and light,...both container and contents...arise." There are two parts: external, "the way the external container...arises in the mind," and internal, "the way the internal contents of the mind arise."

B.2.1.2.2.2.2.2.2.1 **The Way the External Container Arises**

First, the way the external container arises, as the root text says, is "from making a connection between space and light." From within this space a continuously flowing wind occurs. In the midst of this, wind is produced and grows full, "and through the wind of its agitation the embers of fire burn." (413) In the midst of this, fire is produced and grows full, and through fire and wind, the struggle between heat and cold, the moisture produces water. In the midst of this, water is produced and grows full. "From the vital essence of this water, earth becomes the ground. In the midst of this, earth is produced and grows full. From the vital essence of these elements, the appearance of the five sense-objects arises."

(339) The way the seeming internal content arises in the mind of sentient beings is from making a connection between the light of space and awakened awareness. It occurs from the recollections of thought and the agitation of the winds. Through the connection of the winds and thought, the movement of the breath occurs. From the strength of the breath there is warmth, coming from the fire element. From bringing together the breath and warmth, there is blood, coming from the water element. From the constituents of the blood, there is flesh, coming from the earth element. From making a connection between the body and mind, the five vital organs come forth, together with the support of the five kinds of elements.

Commentary A:

A.2.2.2.2.2.2.2.2.2.2 An Explanation of the Way the Internal Contained Contents, the Mind of Sentient Beings, Arises from Mind

Second, the explanation of the way the internal contained contents, the mind of sentient beings, arises from mind is as follows. [The root text] continues, "The way that the seeming internal content arises in the mind of sentient beings is as follows:" To explain how the seeming internal content arises in the mind of sentient beings the root text continues, "Through making a connection between awakened awareness and light [appearing in] space, the mindfulness of the [ordinary mind] and the movement of the winds occur." (347) This means that, through liveliness, awakened awareness and light are united into a pair, and from that the mindfulness of the ordinary mind becomes activated, as does the movement of the winds. [The root text] continues, "Through making a connection between the winds and the ordinary mind, the movement of the breath occurs." The movement of the breath comes from liveliness, [once] the winds and the ordinary mind are connected. [The root text] continues, "From the strength of the breath, there is warmth, coming from the domain of the fire [element]." From the wind of the breath, warmth occurs. [The root text] continues, "From bringing together the breath and warmth, there is blood, coming from the domain of the water [element]." From the liveliness of having integrated both the breath and warmth, blood develops. [The root text] continues, "From the constituents of the blood, there is flesh, coming from the domain of the earth [element]." From the blood, fat accumulates and similarly, from that, flesh develops. [The root text] continues, "From making a connection between the body and mind, the five vital organs come forth." The five that develop are the heart, lungs, liver, kidneys, and spleen. [The root text] continues, "…together with support of the five kinds of elements." The heart depends on the space element. The lungs depend on the wind element. The liver depends on the fire element. The kidneys depend on the water element. The spleen depends on the earth element. [The root text] continues, "From the liveliness of the five elements, the five limbs [of the body] arise." From the liveliness of the space element, the head develops. From the liveliness of the wind element, the right leg develops. From the liveliness of the fire element, the right arm develops. From the liveliness of the water element, the left leg develops. From the liveliness of the earth element, the left arm develops. [The root text] continues, "From the constituents of the five elements, the five internal organs develop." From the constituents of space, the womb develops. From the constituents of wind, the small and large intestines develop. From the constituents of fire, the gall bladder develops. From the constituents of water, the urinary bladder develops. From the constituents of earth, (348) the stomach develops. [The root text] continues, "The five sense-organs project from the gateways of the five elements." The gateway of space projects to the eyes. The gateway of wind projects to the nose. The gateway of fire projects to the tongue. The gateway of water projects to the ear. The gateway of earth projects to body sensations. [The root text] continues, "From the liveliness of each of these, the five sense-consciousnesses are generated." Form is generated from the lively activity of the eye-consciousness. Sound is generated from the lively activity of the ear-consciousness. Smell is generated from the lively activity of the nose-consciousness. Taste is generated from the lively activity of the tongue-consciousness. Touch sensation is generated from the lively activity of the body-consciousness. [The root text] continues, "Then comes the activity of and grasping toward each of the five sense-objects." From each of the five sense-consciousnesses the activity of each of the five sense-objects develops. [The root text] continues, "In this way the internal content of the mind of sentient beings arises in the mind." The internal content of the mind of sentient beings arises like this from the mind.

Commentary B:

B.2.1.2.2.2.2.2.2 The Way the Seeming Internal Content Arises in the Mind

Second, "the way the seeming internal content arises in the mind…" is from the liveliness of making a connection between space, light, and awakened awareness. It occurs from mindful thought and the agitation of the winds. "The breath that is from the connection of thought and the winds comes from the wind element. From the strength of the breath there is warmth, coming from the fire element." Blood occurs from the earth element. Regarding this, the root text says, "From making a connection between the body and mind the five vital organs come forth, together with the support of the five kinds of elements." From the full maturation of these, the lamp of the soft white channel develops.

(339) From the liveliness of the five elements, the five limbs [of the body] arise. From the constituents of the five elements, the five internal organs develop. In the five sense-organs the five elements project from the gateways. From the liveliness of each of these respectively, the five sense-consciousnesses are generated. Then comes the activity of and grasping toward the five sense-objects. In this way the internal content of the mind of sentient beings arises like this from the mind.

Through the association between the five causal elements and the ordinary mind, the afflictive emotions and five poisons are generated. Hatred develops from connecting the space element with the ordinary mind. Pride develops from connecting the breath with the ordinary mind. Envy develops from connecting warmth with the ordinary mind. Desire develops by connecting blood with the ordinary mind. Ignorance develops by connecting flesh with the ordinary mind.

Commentary B:

B.2.1.2.2.2.2.2.3 The Way *Saṁsāra* Actually Is

Three, from the perspective of types of beings there are six types of beings in [their respective] six realms. There are three ways that *saṁsāra* actually is:

(1) whatever the causes *saṁsāra* depends on,

(2) whatever the essence of *saṁsāra* is, and

(3) whatever outcome develops.

B.2.1.2.2.2.2.2.3.1 Whatever the Causes *Saṁsāra* Depends On

First, *saṁsāra* supports five [types] of suffering. By connecting the five elements with the ordinary mind, the afflictive emotions and five poisons, etc., are generated that clearly run their course.

B.2.1.2.2.2.2.2.3.2 Whatever the Essence of *Saṁsāra* Is

Second, the essence, *saṁsāra*, with respect to the five aggregates. By connecting suffering with the five elements each of the five aggregates is generated and they run their course.

(339) Through the association of the five elements with the five poisons, the five aggregates are generated. Connecting space with hatred generates the aggregate of consciousness; connecting the breath with pride brings the formative aggregate; connecting warmth with envy generates the cognitive-perceptual aggregate; connecting blood with attachment generates the hedonic tone aggregate; and connecting flesh with ignorance generates the form aggregate. By bringing together these five aggregates and five poisons, various formative patterns, karma, and [karmically influenced] behaviors emerge. By bringing together all the causes and conditions that connect karmic actions to afflictive emotions, all the general and specific types of sufferings of *saṁsāra* will occur.

Commentary B:

B.2.1.2.2.2.2.2.3.3 Whatever Outcome Develops

Third, the root text says, "Through the association of the five elements with the five poisons the five aggregates are generated." Causes and conditions are connected. The root text says, "By bringing together these five aggregates and five poisons, various formative patterns, karma, and [karmically influenced] behaviors emerge." The formative patterns, karma, and behaviors are distinguished as neutral, happy, or suffering. Causing the mind to move toward a sense-object (414) is a karmic activity [resulting in] formative patterns and habitual karmic propensities, etc. Conduct arises from actually engaging in this. The outcome is that if you don't draw it out there is virtue, and if you do draw it out there is suffering, and if you don't do either, it is neutral. The root text says, "By bringing together all the causes and conditions that connect karmic actions to afflictive emotions, all the general and specific types of sufferings of *saṁsāra* will occur." These include, in general, the four types of suffering—suffering of birth, aging, old age, and death—and the six types of suffering of the specific [realms]—the heat and cold of the hell realm beings; the hunger and thirst of hungry ghosts; the dumbness and stupidity of animals; the changeability of humans; the quarrelling of the demi-gods; and the downfall of the gods.

(339) Through the association between the five causal elements and the ordinary mind, the afflictive emotions and five poisons are generated. Hatred develops from connecting the space element with the ordinary mind. Pride develops from connecting the breath with the ordinary mind. Envy develops by connecting warmth with the ordinary mind. Desire develops by connecting blood with the ordinary mind. Ignorance develops by connecting flesh with the ordinary mind. (340) Through the association of the five elements with the five poisons, the five aggregates are generated. Connecting space with hatred generates the aggregate of consciousness; connecting the breath with pride generates the formative aggregate; connecting warmth with envy generates the cognitive-perceptual aggregate; connecting blood with attachment generates the hedonic tone aggregate; and connecting the flesh with ignorance generates the form aggregate. By bringing together the five aggregates

and five poisons, formative patterns, karma, and [karmically influenced] behaviors emerge. By bringing together all the causes and conditions that connect karmic actions to afflictive emotions, all the general and specific types of sufferings of *samsāra* will occur.

Through beginningless time, *samsāra* goes on unhindered. The six causes of suffering open the three realms and cause one to take hold of a body; and through the twelve-fold chain of dependent origination, the Wheel of Life [continues] to turn. Through one's faults, the power of not recognizing awakened awareness gains impetus.

Commentary A:

A.2.2.2.2.2.2.2.2.2.3 **An Explanation of the Way *Saṁsāra* Arises from Not Knowing Awakened Awareness**

[The root text] continues, "Through the association between the five causal elements and the ordinary mind, the afflictive emotions and five poisons are generated." From the liveliness that unites into a pair, the five causal elements and the ordinary sense-consciousnesses, the afflictive emotions and five poisons are generated. [The root text] continues, "Hatred develops from connecting the space element with the ordinary mind. Pride develops from connecting the breath with the ordinary mind. Envy develops by connecting warmth with the ordinary mind. Desire develops by connecting blood with the ordinary mind. Ignorance develops by connecting flesh with the ordinary mind. Through the association of the five elements with the five poisons, the five aggregates are generated." By integrating the five elements with the five poisons (349) the five aggregates are generated. When they are generated like this, [the root text] says, "connecting space with hatred generates the aggregate of consciousness; connecting the breath with pride generates the formative aggregate; connecting warmth with envy generates the cognitive-perceptual aggregate; connecting blood with attachment generates the hedonic tone aggregate; and connecting the flesh with ignorance generates the form aggregate. By bringing together the five aggregates and five poisons, formative patterns, karma, and [karmically influenced] behaviors emerge." The five aggregates are the support for karmic activity, and from them come the inclinations of the five poisons. The behaviors that arise from that are all the various virtuous, non-virtuous, and neutral behaviors. [The root text] continues, "By bringing together all the causes and conditions that connect karmic actions to afflictive emotions, all the general and specific types of sufferings of *saṁsāra* will occur." Karmic action is the cause of afflictive emotions, and, from [the right] conditions, the four stages of life—birth, middle age, old age, and death—occur, as well as the six specific types of suffering of each of the [six classes of beings]. [The root text] continues, "…and through beginingless time *saṁsāra* goes on unhindered. The six causes of suffering open to the three realms and cause one to take hold of a body, and through the twelve-fold chain of dependent origination, the Wheel of Life [continues] to turn." Because of this *saṁsāra* goes on unhindered, and you take up a body as one of the six classes of beings in one of the three realms. From not recognizing awakened awareness, [birth], old age, and death occur as the twelve-fold chain of dependent origination and the Wheel of Life continues to turn. [The root text] continues, "Through one's faults the power of not recognizing awakened awareness gains impetus." With respect to *saṁsāra*, there is no *saṁsāra* other than bad actions and the play of past karma in the three realms. Through the influence of not recognizing awakened awareness (350) these come forth by their own force, much like saliva coming forth of its own force.

(340) And *samsāra* and *nirvāna* arise as a duality. Through realization, and seeing into the [deluded] thoughts [that generate] non-realization, what is perceived is true, and there is no separation between *samsāra* and *nirvāna*. [This realization] abides as the single great sphere [of ultimate reality], the great sameness.

This completes the Lamp of the Basis which Stays. *Samaya!*

Commentary A:
A.2.2.2.2.3 A Brief Summary

Here is a brief summary of the way *saṁsāra* and *nirvāṇa* become separated. [The root text] says, "…and *saṁsāra* and *nirvāṇa* arise as a duality. Through realization and seeing into the [deluded] thoughts [that generate] non-realization, what is perceived is true, and there is no separation between *saṁsāra* and *nirvāṇa*. [This realization] abides as the single great sphere [of ultimate reality], the great sameness." With respect to separating *saṁsāra* and *nirvāṇa* into a duality, this doesn't occur when there is direct seeing and non-conceptual seeing. In ultimate truth, free of duality, the primordial wisdom of great sameness stays. As the root text summarizes, "This completes the lamp of the basis which stays. *Samaya!*"

Commentary B:

B.2.1.2.2.3 A Brief Summary Regarding *Saṁsāra* and *Nirvāṇa*

Third, a brief summary. The root text says, "Through beginningless time, *saṁsāra* goes on unhindered." This means that the wheel of *saṁsāra* turns without beginning and without ending in time. The root text says, "The six causes of suffering open the Three Realms and cause one to take hold of a body." This refers to taking up and remaining in a body of one of the six classes of beings. The root text says, "Through the twelve-fold chain of dependent origination, the Wheel of Life [continues] to turn." It turns without a beginning or ending in time. The root text says, "Through one's faults the power of not recognizing awakened awareness gains impetus." Through this sentient beings wander through *saṁsāra*. Through failure to realize the natural state they wander through *saṁsāra*.

The summary is as follows. The root text says, "Thus, *saṁsāra* and *nirvāṇa* arise as a duality." The root text says, "Through realization and seeing into the [confused] thoughts [that generate] non-realization..." (415) This means that with respect to seeing into this and through realization of this, *nirvāṇa* arises. With respect to not seeing into this and through non-realization, *saṁsāra* arises. The root text says, "What is perceived is true and there is no separation between *saṁsāra* and *nirvāṇa*." With respect to the essence of groundless-ground and awakened awareness, there is no experience of separation between *saṁsāra* and *nirvāṇa*. The root text says, "[This realization] abides as the single great sphere [of ultimate reality], the great sameness." This means that groundless-ground, the mother, and [awakened awareness], the son, stay inseparably.

B.2.1.3 Conclusion

Third, is a brief summary of the way *saṁsāra* and *nirvāṇa* become separated. The root text says, "This completes the Lamp of the Basis which Stays." This refers to the ultimate truth [of these teachings] with nothing left out. "*Samaya!*" means that [these teachings] come with the command to seal them as secret for those who have not built the vessel.

(2) The Lamp of the Fleshy Heart-Mind

(340) Homage to Kun tu bZang po, whose self-awakened awareness shines forth from within [the sphere of the heart]. Oh, Children of the Lineage, here is the essential point on the Lamp of the Fleshy Heart-Mind, wherein universal ground stays as it is, and self- awakened awareness shines forth from within.

Commentary A:
A.2.2.2.3 The Lamp of the Fleshy Heart

Second, the lamp of the fleshy heart has three parts:

(1) homage,

(2) the extensive explanation, and

(3) a brief summary.

A.2.2.2.3.1 Homage

[The root text] says, "Homage to Kun tu bZang po, whose self-awakened awareness shines forth from within [the sphere of the heart]." Here is an explanation of the homage. Kun tu bZang po means that compassion and awakened awareness itself are connected, as explained previously. When the root text says, "Self-awakened awareness shines forth from within [the sphere of the heart]," it means that primordial wisdom's awakened awareness is in the center of the physical heart. It is taught that it stays there and [upon realization] awakened awareness arises by itself from within [this sphere of knowing].

A.2.2.2.3.2 The Extensive Explanation

The more extensive explanation has two parts.

A.2.2.2.3.2.1 A Brief Explanation

First, [the root text] continues, "Oh! Children of the Lineage, here is the essential point on the Lamp of the Fleshy Heart-Mind, wherein universal ground stays as it is, and self-awakened awareness shines forth from within [this sphere of knowing]." This means that awakened awareness arises in-and-by-itself externally from within the physical heart-mind, arises internally from inside the five wisdom lights, and arises secretly from inside groundless-ground.

Commentary B:
B.2.2 The Lamp of the Fleshy Heart-Mind

Second, the teachings on the lamp of the fleshy heart-mind. There are three parts:

(1) a brief introduction,

(2) an extensive explanation, and

(3) a brief summary.

B.2.2.1 A Brief Introduction

First, regarding the brief introduction, the root text begins, "Homage to Kun tu bZang po, whose self-awakened awareness shines forth from within [the sphere of the heart]." This explains the homage. "Kun tu bZang po" refers to the fact that in the midst of groundless-ground in the center of the [fleshy] heart is where stainless, completely pure awakened awareness stays and arises in-and-by-itself. "Homage" refers to these teachings being the object of reverence. The root text says, "Oh! Children of the Lineage. Here is the essential point on the lamp of the fleshy heart-mind, wherein universal ground stays as it is, and self-awakened awareness shines forth from within this sphere [of knowing]. This is the lamp wherein [awakened awareness] stays as great self-lucidity and is not obscured by anything whatsoever."

(340) Due to ordinary thought serving as mindfulness, the duality of realization and delusion arises, and the duality of *samsāra* and *nirvāna* arises. With respect to the universal ground and awakened awareness, they are experienced within the delusion of [conventional] time, the three—past, present, and future—and there is no realization, and *samsāra* and *nirvāna* are divided into a duality.

Commentary A:

A.2.2.2.3.2.2 An Extensive Explanation

Second, the more extensive explanation has five parts:

(1) the explanation that within the domain of groundless-ground and awakened awareness there is no limit to *saṁsāra* and *nirvana*,

(2) explaining how it stays,

(3) explaining how it pervades the body,

(4) explaining how ordinary thought arises in groundless-ground, and

(5) explaining the way to be free from the connection of body and mind.

A.2.2.2.3.2.2.1 Within the Domain of Groundless-ground There is No Limit

[The root text] continues, "Due to ordinary thought serving as mindfulness,[18] the duality of realization and delusion arises," and the duality of *saṁsāra* and *nirvāṇa* arises. With respect to groundless-ground and awakened awareness, they are experienced within the delusion of [conventional] time, the three—past, present, and future—and "there is no realization, and *saṁsāra* and *nirvāṇa* are divided into a duality." This means that with respect to ordinary thought, if the conditions support non-realization instead of realization, then *saṁsāra* and *nirvāṇa* appear as a duality. Also, with respect to groundless-ground and awakened awareness, they remain stainless and beyond all extremes, but appear one way or the other depending on whether there is delusion regarding the three times or realization.

(340) On the other hand, universal ground can never become obscured, and awakened awareness can never become deluded, because the heart-essence stays this way primordially.

---

18. *dran pai' blo*: "ordinary thought serving as mindfulness."

Commentary B:
B.2.2.2 An Extensive Explanation

Second, an extensive explanation has two parts:

(1) explaining how this stays just as it is, and

(2) explaining how the body and mind become connected and become separated.

B.2.2.2.1 Explaining How This Stays Just As it Is

First, (416) explaining how this stays just as it is has three parts:

(1) explaining what stays, the essence of groundless-ground,

(2) explaining what stays, the real nature of the heart-mind, and

(3) the special distinction of primordial wisdom staying just as it is.

B.2.2.2.1.1 Explaining What Stays, the Essence of Groundless-ground

First, [explaining what stays, the essence of groundless-ground]. The root text says, "Due to ordinary thought serving as mindfulness, the duality of realization and delusion arises, and the duality of *saṃsāra* and *nirvāṇa* arises." This means that with respect to ordinary thought as mindfulness, realization becomes non-realization, and *saṃsāra* and *nirvāṇa* become divided. The root text continues, "With respect to groundless-ground and awakened awareness, when experienced within the delusion of [conventional] time, the three—past, present, and future—is such that there is no realization, and *saṃsāra* and nirvana are divided into a duality...." *Saṃsāra* and *nirvāṇa* arise within the domain of groundless-ground and awakened awareness, never covered by any stains whatsoever. They stay as the great original, primordial purity in such a way that groundless-ground is never covered by obscuration. Because groundless-ground is never covered by any obscuration whatsoever, [awakened awareness] stays as lucidity in-and-by-itself. The root text says, "Awakened awareness can never become deluded." This means that awakened awareness stays, stainless, never covered by [either] delusion or realization. As the root text says, "...because the heart-essence stays this way primordially." This means that it stays as the ultimate truth, as the innate, primordial *Buddha*-nature.

(340) Now, where does this basis stay? Hidden in the very center of this spacious clear space. Like an offering tent whose openings are like dark crystals. It abides with crystal-clear appearance, like a canopied tent of light. What is called the "heart-mind channel" resides externally like an eight-sided jewel, internally like an eight-petalled lotus, within the center of which [secretly] the heart essence resides like an erected offering tent of five-colored rainbow lights.

Commentary B:

B.2.2.2.1.2 Explaining What Stays, the Real Nature of the Heart-mind

Second, explaining what stays, the real nature of the heart-mind. The root text says, "Now, where does this basis stay?" It is shown to stay where it becomes full, namely as the root text says, "Hidden in the very center of this spacious clear space." This [awakened awareness] dwells within the heart-essence, in the domain of the space [of groundless-ground]. The root text continues, "Like an offering tent whose openings are like dark crystals." This means that within that space is the crystal-clear heart-essence. The root text continues, "It abides with crystal-clear appearance, like a canopied tent of light." This refers to it being like a canopied tent of the five [rainbow-like primordial wisdom] lights, there inside the heart-essence. (417) In the center of this is where it stays; it is like a butter lamp inside a pot. If you were to ask why it is the case that it stays just the way it is there, it is because, as the root text says, "What is called the 'heart-mind channel' resides externally like an eight-sided jewel." This refers to its seemingly externally appearing shape. The root text continues, "…and internally like an eight-petalled lotus." This refers to the way it appears internally. As the text continues, "…within the center of which, the heart essence resides like an erected offering tent of five-colored rainbow lights." This refers to the form of the five appearing [rainbow wisdom lights] in the heart.

(340) Right in the domain of space of this universal ground, awakened awareness resides stainlessly, not contaminated by anything, in its great original purity.

Commentary A:

A.2.2.2.3.2.2.2 **Explaining How It Stays**

Explaining how the basis, groundless-ground and awakened awareness, stays. [The root text] continues, "On the other hand, groundless-ground can never become obscured, and awakened awareness can never become deluded, because the essence stays this way primordially. Now where does this basis stay?" The essence stays just the way it is—primordial and stainless. [In the root text] the answer follows: "In the very center of this spacious clear space." Primordial wisdom's awakened awareness is said to stay in groundless-ground [from within the] physical heart-mind as a lucid, [clear, awakened awareness]. Yet, it also stays in the center of groundless-ground. [The root text] continues, "Like an offering tent whose openings are dark crystals." (352)

A.2.2.2.3.2.2.3 **Explaining How It Pervades the Body**

Externally, when the text says, "fleshy heart," it means that [the physical body] seems like flesh held up by a tent pole, and the inside of the physical heart-mind area is like an offering tent made of dark crystals. [The root text] continues, "It abides with crystal-clear appearance, like a canopied tent of light." Internally, the so-called "fleshy heart" appears like light, and abides like an open tent whose canopy is the five [wisdom] lights, wherein the natural state stays just as it is. [The root text] continues, "What is called the 'heart-mind channel'[19] resides externally like an eight-sided jewel, and internally like an eight-petalled lotus." Externally, this is said to be the natural state of the fleshy heart-mind. [The root text] continues, "Within the center of which, the heart essence resides like an erected offering tent of five-colored rainbow lights." Internally, this is said to be the natural state of the five wisdom lights. [Thus, the root text] continues, "Right in the center, groundless-ground and awakened awareness reside stainlessly, not contaminated by anything,

---

19. *she thun rta 'dzin*: *Zhang Zhung* for "heart-mind channel."

the great original purity." The secret [perspective] means that groundless-ground and awakened awareness are said to be the natural state.

Although the universal ground pervades the body, filling everything like space, it is generally obscured by the clouds of delusion and lacks lucidity. (341) Within the center of the heart-mind, primordial wisdom stays on the inside as immense yet pervasive clarity, like a cloudless sky. Although awakened awareness stays and saturates everything like the sun, it is generally obscured by the darkness of conceptual thought, and lacks clarity. In the center of this heart-mind, self-awakened-awareness resides and shines forth immensely from within, like the [dawning] sun in a cloudless sky. It resides in the center of the heart-mind in such a way that the infant [of individual consciousness] and the mother [consciousness] of *dharmakāya* are inseparable.

Commentary B:

B.2.2.2.1.3 The Special Distinction of Primordial Wisdom Staying Just As It Is

Third, the special distinction of primordial wisdom staying just as it is has two parts:

(1) explaining how mother, groundless-ground, and son, awakened awareness, are inseparable, and

(2) how ordinary mindful thought arises.

B.2.2.2.1.3.1 Explaining How Mother and Son Groundless-ground are Inseparable.

The root text says, "Right in the sphere, groundless-ground and awakened awareness reside stainlessly, not contaminated by anything, the great original purity." This expanse is non-dual, primordial wisdom, the *dharmakāya*. Here is where the ultimate truth, the stainless original purity of one's *Buddha*-nature resides, never mixed up with deluded conceptual thought, afflictive emotions, etc. With respect to the meaning of this, all sentient beings are said to have innate *Buddha*-nature. These concealed and hidden teachings are orally transmitted to the mind-stream of others. The ultimate meaning is that they are taught about [their own] *Buddha*-nature. The root text says, "Although groundless-ground pervades the body and fills everything like space, it is generally obscured by the clouds of delusion and lacks lucidity." This means that [groundless-ground] stays in such a way as to encompass and pervade everything outside and inside the body, but there is no clarity when it is obscured by delusion. The root text says, "Within the center of the heart-mind, primordial wisdom stays on the inside as immense yet pervasive clarity, like a cloudless sky." (418) Groundless-ground stays like this in the center of the [fleshy] heart-mind. What this ultimately means is that by looking into it, it recognizes itself. It is like looking into a sky free of any clouds or like opening the door to a treasure storehouse. The root text says, "Although awakened awareness stays and saturates everything like the sun, it is generally obscured by the darkness of conceptual thought, and lacks clarity." Awakened awareness stays like this in the body, but because of conceptual thought it has become obscured and is no longer lucid. The root text says, "In the center of this heart-mind self-awakened-awareness resides and shines forth immensely from within, like the [dawning] sun in a cloudless sky." This means that awakened awareness stays like this in the center of the [fleshy] heart-mind. By looking into awakened awareness in its essence, you will come to realize awakened awareness nakedly as the son, like viewing the sun free of clouds, or like the sun arising in a cloudless sky. The root text says, "It resides in the center of the heart-mind in such a way that the infant [of individual consciousness] and the mother [consciousness of the *dharmakāya*] are inseparable." This means that just as empty space and the light-rays of the sun are inseparable, mother—empty groundless-ground—and son—lucid primordial wisdom's awakened awareness—are non-dual as they stay in the center of the [fleshy] heart-mind. By looking into this within, you come to the realization, seeing the essence of the *dharmakāya* nakedly.

(341) Ordinary thought serving as mindfulness is like the rays of the sun. It is drawn along the path of the channels supported by the heart-essence, and then, through the sense-doors, it engages and grasps at sense-objects.

Commentary A:

A.2.2.2.3.2.2.4 Explaining How Ordinary Thought Arises in Groundless-ground

To explain how ordinary thought arises, the root text says, "Ordinary mindful thought is like the rays of the sun." This means that ordinary mindful thought arises recognized as awakened awareness, coming from the liveliness of the inseparable pair—groundless-ground and awakened awareness. This becomes like the rays of the sun arising from the liveliness of the sun's wind. [The root text] continues, "It is drawn along the path of the wind channels supported by the heart essence, and then, through the sense-doors, it engages and grasps at sense-objects." This means that supported by this heart essence, [the liveliness] departs along the path of the wind channels, is propagated through the five sense doors, apprehends each of the respective five sense-objects, and settles on them.

Commentary B:

B.2.2.2.1.3.2 How Ordinary Mindful Thought Arises

Second, how ordinary mindful thought arises. The root text says, "Ordinary thought serving as mindfulness is like the rays of the sun. It is drawn along the path of the wind channels supported by the heart-essence, and then through the sense-doors it engages and grasps at sense-objects." The support of ordinary mindful thought is firmly established in the heart and is drawn out along the path of the channels. Through attachment and aversion, etc., comes grasping at sense-objects through the ordinary sense-doors.

(341) If you were to ask just how both the illusory body and mind either seem to come together or become separated, universal ground seems like all-pervasive space, and awakened awareness stays, sort of like a bird that stays in its own place. The sense-mind is like the wings of the bird that go everywhere. The body is like a cage where the bird is trapped inside. This is how both the bird and the cage come together and also how they become free. In the expanse of space there is no coming together and no separating from, wherein [awakened awareness] stays in what is all-pervading without taking

anything whatsoever as a support.

Universal ground is all-pervading, sort of like the earth, and awakened awareness stays in its own way, sort of like a person [wandering about the earth]. The sense-mind is sort of like a horse being led everywhere, and the body is sort of like the reins where the rider [awakened awareness] with the reins leads the horse everywhere. This vast expanse of groundless-ground is where the body, reins, and rider seem to come together and also where they become free. Within the expanse of universal ground there is no coming together or becoming free within it [awakened awareness] stays in what is all-pervading without taking anything whatsoever as a support.

Universal ground is like a limitless ocean and awakened awareness is like a fish that goes its own way [in that ocean]. The sense-mind is sort of like the fins of a fish that help it to swim everywhere, and the body is sort of like a fish net used to catch the fish in its net. (342) Universal ground is where the fish and its net [seem to] come together and also where they become free. Within the expanse of universal ground there is no coming together or becoming free, wherein [awakened awareness] stays in what is all-pervading without taking anything as a support.

Commentary A:

A.2.2.2.3.2.2.5 Explaining the Way to be Free From the Connection of Body and Mind

Explaining how the body and mind are united and how they are separated is as follows. Three metaphors are used to illustrate the meaning, each of which has the same meaning. The first metaphor is that groundless-ground is like the air. Awakened awareness is like a bird. The sense-mind[20] is like the wings of the bird. The body is like a cage that has trapped a winged creature inside. This is how body and mind are united together. When the cage of a bird is broken open the bird flies away. This is how the body and mind separate from each other. (354) Now, at the

---

20. *yid shes*: "sense-mind."

time that the body and mind seem to become separated, there has never been any separation of body and mind from the expanse of groundless-ground. Like in the metaphor of the bird and the cage, originally [body and mind] stay in the domain of space, then, both seem to come together in the domain of space, and finally, both seem to become free in the condition of this space. Similarly, both the body and mind originally stay in the condition of groundless-ground, then seem to become united within the condition of groundless-ground, and finally, seem to become free within the condition of groundless-ground. The metaphor that groundless-ground is like space means that with respect to both body and mind, at first both are pervaded by, and then are pervaded by, and finally are pervaded by [space-like] groundless-ground, wherein there is never any coming together or any separation of body and mind.

The second metaphor is as follows: groundless-ground is sort of like the ground. Awakened awareness is like the person. The sense-mind is like the horse. The body represents the reins [of the horse].

The third metaphor is as follows: groundless-ground is sort of like the ocean. Awakened awareness is like a fish. The sense-mind represents the fins of the fish. The body is like the net. Thus, both body and mind seem to become united and become free from [each other] within the sphere of groundless-ground. Body and mind seemingly in the three times are [actually] in the expanse of groundless-ground and are beyond being united or separated.

Commentary B:

B.2.2.2.2 Explaining How the Body and Mind Become Connected and Become Separated

Second, explaining how the body and mind become connected and become separated. The root text says, "If you were to ask just how both the illusory body and mind (419) either seem to come together or become separated...." If you were to ask this, the answer would be that space-like groundless-ground is the foundational basis, like an ocean, that stays and completely pervades everything. Awakened awareness is like a bird, a human, or a fish, wherein each respectively stays in-and-by-itself. The sense-mind is like the wings, the horse, [the fins, respectively], wherein everything is activated. The body is like a cage, a trap, or a net, respectively. There is no separation [of body and mind] during the act of grasping, yet body and mind seem connected [under these conditions], even though there is never uniting to or separating from groundless-ground. The root text says, "…wherein it stays in what is all-pervading without taking anything whatsoever as a support." Within groundless-ground there is neither coming together nor separating of body and mind taking it as a support because within groundless-ground the body and mind stay completely pervaded by and saturated by it.

(342) This is what he said.

This completes the Lamp of the Fleshy Heart-Mind! *Samaya!* [Seal what has been pointed out!]

Commentary A:
A.2.2.2.3.3 **A Brief Summary**

The brief summary should be clear from the length [of the extensive explanation]. [The root text concludes], "*Samaya!*" This completes the commentary to the second lamp.

Commentary B:
B.2.2.3 **A Brief Conclusion**

Third, the brief conclusion. This completes the lamp of the fleshy heart-mind. It is the ultimate truth with nothing left out. "*Samaya!*" This means to seal this teaching as secret to those who have not built the vessel.

(3) The Lamp of the Soft White Channels (342)

Homage to Kun tu bZang po, who is the embodiment of transparent primordial wisdom.

Commentary A:
A.2.2.2.4 **The Lamp of the Soft White Channels**

The lamp of the soft white channels has three parts [as explained in the previous sections].

A.2.2.2.4.1 Homage

[The root text] says, "Homage to Kun tu bZang po, who is the embodiment of transparent primordial wisdom." This describes the homage. Kun tu bZang po is explained as it was previously. The enlightened body of transparent primordial wisdom (355) is the Victorious One, namely, awakened awareness knowing itself in the [domain of the] central channel. There primordial wisdom arises as transparent, without outside or inside, without front or back. The homage is the same as has been described previously.

A.2.2.2.4.2 The Extensive Explanation

The extensive explanation has two parts—a brief overview and the extensive explanation.

(342) Oh! Children of the Lineage!

Here regarding the Lamp of the Soft White Channels is the essential point on how to draw forth the transparency of primordial wisdom from whatever occurs on the path.

Commentary B:
B.2.3 The Lamp of the Soft White Channels

Third, the teaching on the lamp of the soft white channels has three parts:

(1) a brief introduction,

(2) an extensive explanation, and,

(3) a brief conclusion.

B.2.3.1 A Brief Introduction

First, the root text says, "Homage to Kun tu bZang po, the embodiment of transparent primordial wisdom." This means that whatever arises along the path in the channels within groundless-ground has a transparent lucidity free of clouds, a transparent emptiness without being an independently existing thing, and without [substantial] characteristics, as the non-duality of lucidity/emptiness. Because whatever arises is non-dual transparency, this transparent primordial wisdom is an object of reverence. The root text continues, "Oh! Children of the Lineage! Here regarding the lamp of the soft white channels." This refers to the [upper] central channel. Within that, originally pure awakened awareness arises (420) thereafter, like the sun arising in a cloudless sky. The root text says, "This is the essential point on how to draw forth the transparency of primordial wisdom from whatever occurs on the path." In general, there is the path of the [upper central] channel. This is also the path wherein transparent primordial wisdom arises, especially in the [upper] central channel.

(342) Universal ground and awakened awareness stay without beginning or end in the heart. Staying is staying in the center of the physical heart-mind, [and the primordial wisdom that] arises is self-occurring in the path of the channel.

Commentary B:

B.2.3.2 The Extended Explanation

Second, the extended explanation has three parts:

(1) whatever arises as the essence,

(2) whatever arises as path, and

(3) the way it arises just as it is.

B.2.3.2.1 Whatever Arises As the Essence

First, with respect to whatever arises as the essence, the root text says, "Universal ground and awakened awareness stay without beginning or end in the heart. Staying is staying in the center of the physical heart-mind [and the primordial wisdom that] arises is self-occurring in the path of the channel."

(342) Here are the instructions regarding the way *bodhicitta* shines forth in the body and mind.

Commentary A:

A.2.2.2.4.2.1 **A Brief Overview**

First, [the root text] says, "Oh! Children of the Lineage! Here regarding the lamp of the soft white channels is the essential point on how to draw forth the transparency of primordial wisdom from whatever occurs on the path." The essential point is that [the liveliness of] primordial wisdom is [most] transparent in the path of the [upper] central channel. [The root text] continues, "Universal ground and awakened awareness stay without beginning or end in the heart. Staying is staying in the center of the physical heart-mind, [and the primordial wisdom that] arises is self-occurring in the path of the channel....Here are the instructions regarding the way *bodhicitta* shines forth in the body and mind." This means that the way *bodhicitta* arises is through the [ordinary] body and mind.

A.2.2.2.4.2.2 **An Extensive Explanation**

There are five parts to the extensive explanation:

(1) explaining the way the body and mind are generated in the mother's womb via the five elements;

(2) explaining the way the three channels and six *chakras* develop;

(3) explaining the way ultimate truth develops in the vessel via the arising of branch channels and further branch channels to the sense-organs;

(4) explaining how the branch channels and further branch channels become differentiated; and

(5) explaining how primordial wisdom arises in the path of the [upper] central channel.

(342) At the time that the body and mind come together in the mother's womb, through the open door of space they become the support for, and are developed by, the earth [element]. When combined with the water [element] as one and the same, they develop further. The body and mind are warmed by the fire [element] and mature. The wind [element] separates what is pure and clears the interior of the channels. The existence of the [seemingly] external body develops at the navel [chakra]. The existence of [seemingly]

internal mind arises from the heart-mind.

Commentary B:

B.2.3.2.2 **Whatever Arises As Path**

Second, whatever arises as path has three parts:

(1) how the body and mind arise as a support;

(2) based on this support, the way the wind currents in the channels develop; and

(3) based on the support, the division of the channels.

B.2.3.2.2.1 **How the Body and Mind Arise as a Support**

First, [how the body and mind arise as a support]. The root text says, "Here are the instructions regarding the way *bodhicitta* shines forth in the body and mind." From making a connection between awakened awareness and light, the body arises, and from making a connection between awakened awareness and light-rays, the mind arises. The root text continues, "At the time that the body and mind come together in the mother's womb…" This refers to the very first point in time that the body and mind come together. The root text continues, "Through the open door of space, they [both body and mind] are supported and developed by the earth [element]. When combined with the water [element] as one and the same, they develop further. The body and mind are warmed by the fire [element] and mature. The wind [element] separates what is pure and clears the interior of the channels." From the four elements, especially the earth element, the body develops and thereafter acts as a source of attachment. The root text continues, "The existence of the [seemingly] external body develops at the navel [*chakra*]." From the liveliness of awakened awareness and light in the channel, the son consciousness comes into existence in the navel *chakra*, and the mother consciousness is linked to the heart some distance away. Yet, the distilled essence, none of which is wasted, (421) is concentrated inside of the navel *chakra*, wherein the ordinary body is generated. The root text continues, "The existence of [seemingly] internal mind-related phenomena shines forth from the heart-mind." Groundless-ground and awakened awareness stay inside the heart-mind. Never being separated from that, much liveliness arises there.

B.2.3.2.2.2 Based on This Support, the Way the Winds in the Channels Develop

Second, based on this support, the way the winds in the channels develop. There are five ways the winds arise in the channels. The way the main channel and the branch wind channels develop, and the way the substance of [both] the dregs and the sacred vessel of ultimate truth develop in the winds of the channels.

(342) At the onset [of seeming existence], the white and red [vital] essences become mixed inside the physical heart-mind space. It is the support of the space element.

Commentary A:

A.2.2.2.4.2.2.1 Explaining the Way the Body and Mind are Generated in the Mother's Womb Via the Five Elements

[The root text] says, "At the time that the body and mind come together in the mother's womb..." This refers to the white essence of the father and the red essence of the mother coming together in the mother's womb, and at the time manifesting as the intention of ordinary mindfulness. [The root text] continues, "...they are supported and developed by the earth element. When combined with the water element as one and the same they develop further. The body and mind are warmed by the fire element and mature. The wind element separates what is pure and (356) clears the interior of the channels." The interval during which [these come together] in the mother's womb is seven days, or between three and thirty-nine days. That is when the body and mind develop. In the first week these [essences] become one. The white and red essences become mixed, and the gelatinous embryo forms in a week. In the next week, the quivering oval develops. In the following week, the oval mass develops. In the next week, the solidifying embryo develops but its formation remains somewhat indefinite. Then, over the next five to thirty-nine weeks, the interior tube of the channels and winds becomes defined, and the [physical] body completes its development. [The root text] continues, "The existence of the [seemingly] external body-related phenomena develops at the navel *chakra*." In the navel chakra, the depths of life of the child and the deepest life of the mother are connected in the wind channels. Utilizing nutrition supplied by the mother, the child's vital essence develops inside the navel *chakra* and then roams free until the child's body develops. [The root text] continues, "The existence of the [seemingly] internal mind-related phenomena shines forth from the heart-mind. At the onset [of seeming existence], the white and red essences become mixed inside the physical heart-mind space." This means that [their mixing and their development] has the support of the space element in the heart-mind.

(342) Then, in the center of this heart-mind [space], from the liveliness of the light and awakened awareness, the wind of the space element arises. From that, the door of the heart-mind opens to the channels. [This is the great golden channel that goes from the heart to the central channel]. From that, by means of the upwardly moving winds, the interior of the central channel opens upwards. This [wind] courses up the central channel and extends through the throat chakra, and emerges from the center of the [throat chakra]. It penetrates the chakra of great bliss at the top of the crown. At the crown protuberance is a gateway that is a completely open hole. This is the pathway to pass beyond [all] suffering [i.e., the path of *nirvāṇa*]. [It is also called the channel of threads of white silk].

Now, the downward-moving wind [also] opens [at the heart-mind sphere] and a passage opens into the central channel downwards. This wind then departs into the central channel and moves down the interior tube of the central channel, extends through the navel chakra of emanation, then penetrates the great mouth that is the juncture of the channels, (343) and finally extends to the gateway of the chakra of the secret place of wisdom and means [at the sex organs]. This is the path of *samsāra*. From the steps of the great mouth at the juncture of the channels, two [side] channels open—the right channel of *samsāra* and the left channel of *nirvāṇa*. These [channels] extend from the juncture through a small hole at the back of the Adam's apple [at the occiput] then meander around the outside border of the brain, where at the top they begin to turn downwards between the eyes until extending to the nostrils. On the right is the channel of *samsāra*. Herein are the [impure] wind drops [normally] associated with the five dregs, the seven subtle bodily constituents, and the wind that moves the afflictive emotions, and through which the accumulation of all the defilements arise. On the left is the channel of *nirvāna* wherein one passes beyond mental suffering. Herein are the wind drops of the brightness of mind and also the movement of the winds of primordial wisdom, through which comes the accumulation of all good qualities. Herein, the immense original purity of awakened awareness shines forth. That third channel is also the channel of the [expanse of] space of universal ground. In the central channel there is movement of neither defilements nor good qualities whatsoever. Herein, the immense original purity of awakened awareness shines forth. That third channel is also the channel of the [expanse of] space of universal ground. The heart-mind resides there like an erected tent, and the three channels go straight up like central tent poles.

Commentary A:

A.2.2.2.4.2.2.2 Explaining the Way the Three Channels and Six *Chakras* Develop

To explain the way the three channels and six *chakras* develop [the root text] says, "Then, in the center of this heart-mind [space], from the liveliness of awakened awareness and its light, the wind of the space element arises. From that, the door of the heart-mind opens to the channels. From that, by means of the upwardly moving winds, the interior of the central channel opens upwards. This [wind] courses up the central channel and extends through the throat *chakra*, and emerges from the center of the [throat *chakra*]. It penetrates the *chakra* of great bliss at the top of the crown. At the crown protuberance is a gateway to pass beyond [all] suffering." If you were to transfer consciousness[21] of awakened awareness along this path, you would attain the fruition of

---

21. '*pho ba*: "consciousness-transference."

Buddhahood. (357) [The root text] continues, "Now, the downward-moving wind [also] opens [at the heart-mind sphere], and a passage opens into the central channel downwards. This wind then departs into the central channel and moves down the interior tube of the central channel, extends through the naval *chakra* of emanation, then penetrates the great mouth that is the juncture of the channels, and finally extends to the gateway of the *chakra* of the secret place of wisdom and means. This is the path of *saṁsāra*." If you were to transfer consciousness of awakened awareness along this path, you would be born and remain in the hell-realms. [The root text] continues, "From the steps of the great mouth at the juncture of the channels, two [side] channels open—the right channel of *saṁsāra* and the left channel of *nirvāṇa*. These [channels] extend from the juncture through a small hole at the back of the Adam's apple [at the occiput], then meander around the outside border of the brain, where at the top they begin to turn downwards between the eyes until extending to the nostrils. On the right is the channel of *saṁsāra*. Herein are the [impure] wind drops [normally] associated with the five dregs, the seven subtle bodily constituents, and the wind that moves the afflictive emotions." If there is consciousness-transference of awakened awareness along this path, there will be mainly a bad rebirth, with the accumulation of many faults arising. [The root text] continues, "On the left is the channel of *nirvāṇa*, wherein one passes beyond mental suffering. Herein are the wind drops of the brightness of mind and also the movement of the winds of primordial wisdom, through which comes the accumulation of all good qualities." If there is consciousness-transference of awakened awareness along this path, there will be mainly a very positive re-birth. [The root text] continues, "In the central channel there is movement of neither defilements nor good qualities whatsoever.... Herein, the immense original purity of awakened awareness shines forth." This means that in the central channel there can be no movement of any defilements or positive qualities whatsoever, and the immense original purity of awakened awareness is said to reside there. [The root text] continues, "That third channel is also the channel of [the expanse of] the space of groundless-ground." The three refers to the right, left, and central channel. If we were to give it a name, groundless-ground could be called the "channel of space." The basic structure of the three includes the white right channel, the left red channel, and the blue central channel. (358) These are called the [right] *rom ma*, [left] *rkyan ma*, and [central] *kun 'dar ma* [ever-pulsing] channels. [The root text] continues, "The heart-mind resides there like an erected tent, and three channels go straight up like the central tent poles." The heart-mind resides like an erected tent, and the three channels go straight up like central tent poles. The specific [side channels] do not have contact with the central channel.

A.2.2.2.4.2.2.3 Explaining the Way Ultimate Truth Develops in the Vessel Via the Arising of Branch Channels, and Further Branch Channels to the Sense-organs

Explaining the way ultimate truth develops in the vessel via the arising of branch channels, and further branch channels to the sense-organs has four parts:

(1) explaining how ultimate truth arises in the heart-mind,

(2) explaining how it arises in the branches,

(3) explaining how it arises in the sense-organs, and

(4) explaining how liberation arises inside the vessel.

Commentary B:

B.2.3.2.2.2.1 The Way the Main Channel and the Branch Channels Develop

First, the root text says, "At the onset [of seeming existence], the white and red [vital] essences become mixed inside the physical heart-mind space." This refers to development from that [space] at the very onset, inside the heart. The root text says, "The space element is the support." This refers to the support of the domain of space. The root text says, "Then, in the center of this heart-mind [space], from the liveliness of the light and awakened awareness, the channel winds arise in the space element. From that, the door of the heart-mind opens to the channels." [These winds] come from the liveliness of primordial wisdom and whatever color of light [manifests] in the center of the heart. This wind arises from space and opens up inside the central channel. This means that winds from space become the five primordial winds in the heart-mind, and each type of wind develops from the earlier central channel [development]. The root text says, "From that comes a passage wherein the upward-moving wind opens into and moves up the interior tube of the [upper] central channel. From these [five winds of the channel] comes a passage wherein the upward-moving wind opens into and moves up the interior tube of the [upper] central channel. This [wind] courses up the central channel and extends through the [throat] *chakra*, and emerges from the center of the [throat *chakra*]." It emerges from this. The root text says, "It penetrates the *chakra* of great bliss at the top of the crown." It penetrates this *chakra* of bliss at the crown in which there is a continuous descending of wind drops, which is why the root text says, "It penetrates the *chakra* of great bliss at the top of the crown." Then the root text says, "At the crown protuberance is a gateway that is a completely open hole. This is the pathway beyond all suffering." (422) From awakened awareness in the central channel to where it emerges as a completely open hole is all the potential pure and impure *karma*, [and from this] comes *Buddhahood*. It is here you meet with all the essential points of the profound consciousness-transference. The root text continues, "Now, the downward-moving wind [also] opens [at the heart-mind sphere], and a passage opens into the central channel downwards." By that wind there is an opening downward inside the central channel. The text then says, "This wind then departs into the central channel and moves down the interior tube of the central channel, and extends through the navel *chakra* of emanation." It increases everywhere in the body and then departs from the navel *chakra* of emanation. The text says, "…then penetrates the great mouth that is the juncture of the channels." It penetrates at the root [of the channels]. The text continues, "…and finally extends to the gateway of the *chakra* of the secret place of wisdom and means [at the sex organs]." The white and red [side] channels of wisdom and means support the wind drops and extend [from the root] to the gateway of the *chakra* of bliss [at the crown]. The text continues, "This is the path of *saṁsāra*."

From the steps of the great mouth at the juncture of the channels, two [side] channels open—the right channel of *saṁsāra* and the left channel of *nirvāṇa*." These two side channels extend from the lowest point of the central channel, opening into a white channel on the right and a red channel on the left, each shaped like legs. The root text continues, "These [channels] extend from the juncture through a small hole at the back of the Adam's apple." Both the right and left side channels are supported by the central channel. Both channels continue upwards from only one channel and extend from an opening just above the back of the Adam's apple. The text says, "They then meander around the outside border of the brain, where at the top they begin to turn downwards between the eyes until extending to the nostrils." They penetrate the gateway of the nostrils and come together, uniting the soft and rough channels wherein the wind is devoid of any essence. (423) The heat from the wind in the central channel will cause many positive qualities to arise in the mind as the clear-light of the realization of sameness. The text continues, "On the right is the channel of *saṁsāra*." On the right is the white channel, and opening from that are all the right [branch] channels. The liveliness of awakened awareness becomes the defilements, and its winds become activated and move from that. The text says, "Herein are the [impure] wind drops [normally] associated with the five dregs, the seven subtle bodily constituents, and the winds that move the afflictive emotions." This refers to the wind drops of the ordinary body and the movement of the coarse winds of the afflictive emotions. The text says, "...and through which the accumulation of all the defilements arise." Through this movement [of the winds], the greater part of the defilements arises. The root text continues, "On the left is the channel of *nirvāṇa* wherein one passes beyond mental suffering." The left channel is red, and opening from that are all the left [branch] channels. The liveliness of awakened awareness becomes the positive qualities, and its winds become activated and move out from that. The root text continues, "Herein are the wind drops of the brightness of mind, and also the movement of the winds of primordial wisdom, through which comes the accumulation of all good qualities." Through the activation of this wind, primordial wisdom and the bliss of primordial wisdom comes forth. The greater part of the positive qualities arises. The root text says, "In the central channel there is movement of neither defilements nor good qualities whatsoever. Herein, the immense original purity of awakened awareness shines forth." In the central channel there is no movement of either the stains of defilement or the positive qualities. The text says, "Herein, the immense original purity of awakened awareness shines forth. That third channel is also the channel of the [expanse of] space of groundless-ground." Of the three—the right, left, and central channels—the central channel is the principle channel. It is the channel of space-like groundless-ground. The root text continues, "The heart-mind resides there like an erected tent, and the three channels go straight up like central tent poles." It resides with the channels and the heart in the shape [of an offering tent].

(343) Then, from the center of the heart-mind, from the liveliness of the light of awakened awareness, the four elemental winds arise. These elemental winds open in the interior tube of the channels, as if pulling tent flaps to four sides. The four vital organs develop with the support of the four elements [the lungs by air, the liver by fire, the kidneys by water, and the spleen by earth].

Commentary A:

A.2.2.2.4.2.2.3.1 Explaining How Ultimate Truth Arises in the Heart-mind

[The root text] says, "Then, from the center of the heart-mind, from the liveliness of the light and awakened awareness, the four elemental winds arise." This refers to the four winds that are active inside the channels—the winds of the wind element, the fire element, the water element, and the earth element. [The root text] continues, "These [elemental] winds open in the interior tube of the wind channels, as if pulling tent flaps to four sides. The four vital organs develop…" As explained earlier there are the four truths, namely what happens in the heart-mind, and the five [primordial wisdoms], the ultimate truth of the heart-mind. [The root text] continues, "…with the support of the four elements." This refers to [how the vital organs develop] with the support of the elements. From the support of space, the heart develops; from the support of wind, the lungs develop; from the support of fire the liver develops; from the support of water, the kidneys develop; and from the support of earth, the spleen develops.

(343) From the five vital organs, the five elemental branch winds arise. Through the division of the interior of the channels, the five elemental branch winds arise.

Commentary B:

B.2.3.2.2.2.2 How the *Chakras* and Branch Channels Develop

Second, how the *chakras* and branch channels develop. The root text says, "Then from the center of the heart-mind, (424) from the liveliness of the light of awakened awareness…" This means that all the branch channels and winds that arise in the vessel arise from the liveliness of whatever is the respective color of primordial wisdom and its light. The text continues, "…the four winds of the elements arise." The four winds that arise are the wind of wind, the wind of fire, the wind of water, and the wind of earth. The text says, "These [four] elemental winds open in the interior tube of the channels, as if pulling tent flaps to four sides." The four winds open in the interior of the channel like a four-sided open tent. Then, the four branch channels develop. The text says, "The four vital organs develop with the support of the four elements [the lungs by air, the liver by fire, the kidneys by water, and the spleen by earth]." This refers to the lungs from the support of wind, the liver from the support of fire, the kidneys from the support of water, and the spleen from the support of earth. The text says, "From the elements and the five vital organs the five ancillary winds arise. The five ancillary channels associated with the elements project from an opening inside the channels." The branch winds of space arise from the heart, and from an opening in the interior of the channel these branches of space project to the head. The branch winds of wind arise from the lungs, and project into the right leg. The branch winds of fire arise from the liver and project into the right arm. The branch winds of water arise from the kidneys and project to the left leg. The branch winds of earth arise from the spleen and project to the left arm.

(343) From these, the elements differentiate into the five winds of the secondary limbs, differentiating into the five sense-organs in the head, and differentiating into each of the five fingers and toes of the

four limbs.

Commentary A:

A.2.2.2.4.2.2.3.2 **Explaining How it Arises in the Ancillary Channels**

Explaining how it arises in the ancillary channels is as follows. [The root text] says, "From the elements and the five vital organs the five ancillary winds arise. The five ancillary channels associated with the elements project from an opening inside the channels." In the heart-mind, the wind in the ancillary channel associated with space arises. (359) It opens from the interior of the channel and projects as an ancillary channel associated with space to the head. In the lungs, the wind of the ancillary channel associated with wind arises. It opens from the interior of the channel and projects as an ancillary channel associated with the right leg. In the liver, the wind in the ancillary channel associated with fire arises. It opens from the interior of the channel and projects as an ancillary channel associated with fire to the right arm. In the kidneys, the wind in the ancillary channel associated with water arises. It opens from the interior of the channel and projects as an ancillary channel associated with water to the left leg. In the spleen, the wind in the ancillary channel associated with wind arises. It opens from the interior of the channel and projects as an ancillary channel associated with earth to the left arm. [The root text] continues, "From these, the elements differentiate into the five winds of the secondary limbs, differentiating into the five sense-organs in the head, and differentiating into each of the five fingers and toes of the four limbs." For example, with respect to the head, the space element becomes the wind of space and differentiates into the five winds of space—the wind of space, the fire of space, the water of space, the earth of space , and the space of space. These become the supports for the sense-organs in the head. With respect to the right leg, it differentiates into each of the five winds—the wind of wind, the wind of fire, the wind of water, the wind of earth, and the wind of space. With respect to the right arm, it differentiates into each of the five fire winds—the fire of wind, the fire of fire, the fire of water, the fire of earth, and the fire of space. With respect to the left leg, it differentiates into each of the five water winds—the water wind of wind, the water wind of fire, the water wind of water, the water wind of earth, and the water wind of space. (360) With respect to the left arm, it differentiates into each of the five earth energies—the earth wind of wind, the earth wind of fire, the earth wind of water, the earth wind of earth, and the earth wind of space.

Commentary B:

B.2.3.2.2.2.3 How the Minor Branches Develop From the Elements

Third, how the minor branches develop from the elements. The root text says, "From these, the elements differentiate into the five winds of the secondary limbs, differentiating into the five sense-organs in the head and differentiating into each of the five fingers and toes of the four limbs." With respect to the head, through the differentiation of the space element into the five elemental winds—the space wind into the fire wind, (425) the space wind into the water wind, the space wind into the earth wind, the space wind into the wind wind, and the space wind into the space wind. In the head these further differentiate into the five supports for the sense-systems. With respect to the right leg, there is differentiation of the space element into each of the five elemental winds—the wind wind into wind wind, the wind wind into fire wind, the wind wind into water wind, the wind wind into earth wind, and the wind wind into space wind. With respect to the right arm, there is differentiation of space element into each of the five elemental winds—the fire wind into wind wind, the fire wind into fire wind, the fire wind into water wind, the fire wind into earth wind, and the fire wind into space wind. With respect to the left leg, there is differentiation of the space element into each of the five elemental energies—the water wind into wind wind, the water element into fire wind, the water element into water wind, the water element into earth wind, and the water element into space wind. With respect to the left arm, there is differentiation of the space element into each of the five earth elemental energies—the earth wind into earth wind, the earth wind into wind wind, the earth wind into fire wind, the earth wind into water wind, and the earth wind into space wind.

(343) From that, the respective pure subtle essences of each element [originating] in each of the five vital organs arises from the el-

emental wind of the five lights, and flows up the interior of the channel. Each of the respective elemental winds of the five elements arises. From that, by generating the liveliness that distinguishes the five sense-objects and five sense-consciousnesses, the so-called "five sense faculties" arise.

Commentary A:

A.2.2.2.4.2.2.3.3 **Explaining How It Arises in the Five Sense-organs**

Explaining how it arises in the sense-organs is as follows. [The root text] says, "From the pure essence of each element [originating] in each of the five vital organs, manifesting as wind, then flowing up the interior of the channel, then at the gateway associated with each of the elements projecting through these gates as supports for the sense-organs, and then at each gateway associated with the respective element arising as one of the five sense-objects…" For example, the pure essence of space originates in the heart and manifests as wind that flows up the interior of the channel and projects through the gateway where it serves as a support for the eye sense-organ, from which form appears at the gateway associated with space. The pure essence of wind originates in the lungs and manifests as wind that flows up the interior of the channel and projects through the gateway where it serves as a support for the nose sense-organ, from which smell occurs at the gateway associated with wind. The pure essence of fire originates in the liver and manifests as wind that flows up the interior of the channel and projects through the gateway where it serves as a support for the tongue sense-organ, from which taste occurs at the gateway associated with fire. The pure essence of water originates in the kidneys and manifests as wind that flows in the interior of the channel and projects through the gateway where it serves as a support for the ear sense-organs, from which sound occurs at the gateway associated with water. The pure essence of earth originates in the spleen and manifests as wind that flows in the interior of the channel and projects through the gateway where it serves as a support for body sense-organs, from which touch sensations occur at the gateway associated with the earth element. [The root text] continues, "Within the interior passage of [each of] these five channels the pure essence of each of these [respective] elements shines forth as the brightness of the five respective [wisdom] lights. By knowing these as being generated from the liveliness [of primordial wisdom] in a way that cuts through the five sense-objects known by the so-called 'five sense-organs'..." Thus, inside the interior of the eye channel is the bright white light arising from the pure essence of the space element. (361) Knowing this as being generated from liveliness cuts through the forms seen by the eye by the so-called "eye sense-organ." Inside the interior of the nose channel is a green light arising from the pure essence of the wind element. Knowing this as being generated from liveliness cuts through the smells smelled by the so-called "nose sense-organ." Inside the interior of the tongue channel is a bright red light arising from the pure essence of the fire element. Knowing this as being generated from liveliness cuts through the tastes tasted by the so-called "tongue sense-organ." Inside the interior of the ear channel is a bright blue light arising from the pure essence of the water element. Knowing this as being generated from liveliness cuts through the sounds generated by the so-called "ear sense-organ." Inside the interior of the body channel is a bright yellow light arising from the pure essence of the earth element. Knowing this as being generated from liveliness cuts through the touch sensations generated by the so-called "body sense-organ."

Commentary B:

B.2.3.2.2.2.4 How the Support of the Senses Develops From the Pure Essence of the Wind in the Channels

Fourth, how the support of the senses develops from the pure essence of the winds in the channels. The root text says, "From the pure essence of [each] element [originating] in each of the five vital organs manifesting as elemental wind, then flowing up the interior of the channel, then at the gateway associated with each of the elements projecting through these gates as supports for the sense-organs, and then at each gateway associated with the respective element arising as one of the five sense-objects." With respect to the heart, the wind of the pure essence of the space element opens upward inside the channel and projects to the gateway that supports the eye sense-organ. This gateway of space arises as form. With respect to the lungs, the wind of the pure essence of the wind element opens upward inside the channel and projects to the gateway that supports the nose sense-organ. This gateway of wind arises as smell. With respect to the liver, the wind of the pure essence of the fire element (426) opens upward inside the channel and projects to the gateway of the tongue sense-organ. This gateway of fire arises as taste. With respect to the kidneys, the wind of the pure essence of the water element opens upward inside the channel and projects to the gateway of the ear sense-organ. This gateway of water arises as sound. With respect to the spleen, the wind of the pure essence of the earth element opens upward inside the channel and projects to the gateway of the body touch sense-organ. This gateway of earth arises as touch sensation. The root text continues, "Within the interior passage of [each of] these five channels, the pure essence of each of the respective five elements arises as the pure essence of the five respective [wisdom] lights. Know these as being generated from liveliness [in a way that] cuts through the five sense-objects. This is what is known as the 'five senses.'" Within the interior passage of the eye channel is an opening of white light that arises from the pure essence of space. This eye consciousness is generated from the liveliness that cuts through form. This is what is known as the "eye-consciousness." Within the interior passage of the nose channel is an opening of green light that arises from the pure essence of wind. This nose consciousness is generated from the liveliness that cuts through smell. This is what is known as "smell-consciousness." Within the interior passage of the tongue channel is an opening of red light from the pure essence of fire. This taste consciousness is generated from the liveliness that cuts through taste. This is what is known as "taste-consciousness." Within the interior passage of the ear is an opening of blue light that arises from the pure essence of water. This ear consciousness is generated from the liveliness that cuts through sound. This is what is known as "ear-consciousness." Within the interior passage of the body channels is an opening of yellow light that arises from the pure essence of earth. This body sensation consciousness is generated from the liveliness that cuts through sensation. This is what is known as "body sensation-consciousness."

(344) Also, from the five vital organs, the five winds of the residual [impure] substances arise through the interior tube of the channel and divide downward. These five elements become the five means to liberation inside the vessel. Inside of this [vessel] the contents of these five elements stir as the five types of sacred substances.

Commentary A:

A.2.2.2.4.2.2.3.4 **Explaining How Liberation Arises Inside the Vessel**

Explaining how liberation arises inside the vessel is as follows. [The root text] says, "Also, from the elements associated with the five vital organs, the five impure substances[22] arise and flow downwards in the interior of the wind channels. These five elements become the five means to liberation inside the vessel. Inside the vessel the contents of these five elements stir as the five types of sacred substances." The impure substance associated with space originates in the heart and manifests as a wind that flows down inside the channel and once inside the seminal vesicles, the movement of the sperm can become liberated inside this vessel as the vital essence of the mind associated with the space element. The impure substance associated with wind originates in the lungs and manifests as a wind that flows down inside the channel and once inside the bowels, the movement of the feces can become liberated inside this vessel as the vital essence of the wind element. (362) The impure substance associated with the fire element originates in the liver and manifests as a wind that flows down inside the channel and once inside the gall bladder, the movement of the blood can become liberated inside this vessel as the vital essence of the fire element. The impure substance associated with the water element originates in the kidneys and manifests as a wind that flows down inside the channel and once inside the urinary bladder, the movement of the urine can become liberated inside this vessel as the vital essence of the water element. The impure substance associated with the earth element originates in the spleen and manifests as a wind that flows down inside the channel and once inside the stomach, the movement of flesh can become liberated inside this vessel as the vital essence

---

22. *snyings ma*: "degraded or impure substances."

of the earth element.

Commentary B:

B.2.3.2.2.2.5 The Meaning of the Impure Wind in the Channels and How It Develops Into the Sacred Substances of the [Suitable] Vessel

Fifth, the meaning of the impure wind in the channels and how it develops into the sacred substances of the [suitable] vessel. (427) The root text says, "Also, from the elements associated with the five vital organs, the winds of the five impure substances arise, and open downward in the interior of the channels. These five elements become the five means to liberation inside the vessel [of the five vessels of the body]. Inside of this [vessel] the contents of these five elements stir as the five types of sacred substances." With respect to the heart, the wind of the impurity of space opens downward inside the channel into the vessel of space in the seminal vesicle. Within this vessel, the contents of space-like mind stir as nectar, the wind [manifesting as] drops of *bodhicitta*. With respect to the lungs, the wind of the impurity of wind opens downward inside the channel into the vessel of wind in the small and large intestines. Within this vessel, the contents of wind stir as the nectar of feces. With respect to the liver, the wind of the impurity of fire opens downward inside the channel into the vessel of fire in the gall bladder. Within this vessel, the contents of fire stir as the nectar of bile. With respect to the kidneys, the wind of the impurity of water opens downward inside the channel into the vessel of water inside the urinary bladder. Within this vessel, the contents of water stir as the nectar of urine. With respect to the spleen, the wind of the impurity of earth opens downward inside the channel into the vessel of the stomach. Within this vessel, the contents of earth stir as the nectar of flesh.

(344) These three channels are the trunk. The [five ancillary] channels associated with the elements are the main branches. From there they differentiate into three hundred and sixty branch channels, and from there they differentiate further into twenty-one thousand branch channels, and then eighty-four thousand branch channels, like diverse leaves, the diversity of which shines forth from

knowing them as liveliness.

Commentary A:

A.2.2.2.4.2.2.4 **Explaining How the Branch Channels and Further Branch Channels Become Differentiated**

Explaining how the branch channels and further branch channels become differentiated is as follows. [The root text] says, "These three channels are the trunk. The [five ancillary] channels associated with the elements are the main branches. From there they differentiate into three hundred and sixty branch wind channels, and from there differentiate further into twenty-one thousand branch channels, and then eighty-four thousand branch channels, like diverse leaves, the diversity of which shines forth from knowing them as liveliness." Because many channels become differentiated from the trunk of the three main channels, it would be inappropriate to know these many various channels as anything other than liveliness.

(344) Even though so many channels arise, "the lamp of the channels" pertains to the [the upper] central channel.

Commentary A:

A.2.2.2.4.2.2.5 **Explaining How Primordial Wisdom Arises in the Path of the [Upper] Central Channel**

Explaining how primordial wisdom arises in the path of the central channel has two parts: (1) recognizing the lamp of the channels, and (2) explaining the way primordial wisdom arises.

A.2.2.2.4.2.2.5.1 **Recognizing the Lamp of the Channels**

[The root text] says, "Even though so many channels arise, the lamp of the channels pertains to the [upper] central channel." This is the channel of *avadhuti*, the central channel, the channel of *bodhicitta*, free of any stains whatsoever of *saṃsāra* or *nirvāṇa*. This is the path of *bodhicitta*.

Commentary B:

B.2.3.2.2.3 **Based on the Support the Division of the Channels**

Third, based on the support the division of the channels. The root text says, "These three channels are the trunk. The [five ancillary] channels associated with the elements are the main branches. From there they differentiate into three hundred and sixty branch wind channels, and from there differentiate further into twenty-one thousand branch channels, and then eighty-four thousand branch channels, like diverse leaves, the diversity of which shines forth from knowing them as liveliness. Even though so many channels arise, the lamp of the channels pertains to the central channel." In these other [ancillary] channels, primordial wisdom's awakened awareness is not clear because it is obscured by the clouds of deluded thought. [However,] in the path of the central channel [primordial wisdom] arises as clear, like a lamp, and is not obscured by anything whatsoever.

(344) Universal ground saturates everything in all the channels like pouring everything into space. Here is the clarity without obscuration by clouds of delusion. This central channel is like a cloudless sky, wherein primordial wisdom shines forth with complete transparency. Awakened awareness is like the sun inside the channels that stays there, pervades everything, and spreads everywhere. Being obscured by the darkness of conceptual thought, it is without clarity. The path of the central channel is like the sun freed of clouds, wherein self-awakened awareness arises as the great original purity. Like the sun that arises in a cloudless sky, this so-called "pathway of the central channel" is the way the infant [of individual consciousness] and the mother [consciousness of *dharmakāya*] become inseparable.

Commentary A:

A.2.2.2.4.2.2.5.2 **Explaining the Way Primordial Wisdom Arises**

Explaining the way primordial wisdom arises is as follows. [The root text] says, "Universal ground saturates everything in the channels like pouring everything into space. Here is the clarity without obscuration by the clouds of delusion. (363) This central channel is like a cloudless sky, wherein primordial wisdom shines forth with complete transparency. Awakened awareness is like the sun inside the channels that stays there, pervades everything, and spreads everywhere. Here is the clarity without ever being obscured by the darkness of conceptual thought." The text says that universal ground and awakened awareness are the sun in [vast] space that pervades the body and all the wind channels without outside or inside. Even though it pervades everything as space, it can become covered by clouds, as the sun can be covered by darkness, yet they remain [the way they are even if not seen]. [The root text] continues, "The path of the central channel is like the sun free of clouds, wherein self-awakened awareness arises as the great original purity." This means that in the pathway of the central channel, groundless-ground and awakened awareness arise like the sky free of clouds and the sun free of darkness. [The root text] continues, "Like the sun that arises in a cloudless sky, this so-called 'pathway of the central channel' is the way the infant [of individual consciousness] and the mother [consciousness of *dharmakāya*] become inseparable." Because groundless-ground and awakened awareness are a non-dual pair, they arise like the sun in a cloudless sky within the pathway of the central channel. This is where primordial wisdom shines forth with complete transparency.

This completes the Lamp of the Soft White Channels. *Samaya!*

Commentary B:

B.2.3.2.3 The Way it Arises Just As It Is

Third, the way it arises. Groundless-ground generally fills all the channels like space, but when obscured by the clouds of delusion there is no clarity. The root text says, "Universal ground saturates everything in the channels like pouring everything into space. Here is the clarity without obscuration by clouds of delusion. This central channel is like a cloudless sky, wherein primordial wisdom shines forth with complete transparency. Awakened awareness is like the sun inside the channels that stays there, pervades everything, and spreads everywhere. Being obscured by the darkness of conceptual thought, it is without clarity." That which remains unclear due to being obscured by the activity of conceptual thought in all the channels is awakened awareness. The root text says, "The path of the central channel is like the sun free of clouds, wherein self-awakened awareness arises as the great original purity." In the path of the central channel, awakened awareness arises nakedly free of being covered by conceptual thought. The root text says, "Like the sun that arises in a cloudless sky." The way groundless-ground and awakened awareness as non-dual lucidity/emptiness arises is as self-occurring in the path of the central channel.

Commentary A:

A.2.2.2.4.3 **A Brief Summary**

The extensive explanation is clear. [The root text closes], "*Samaya!*" This completes the commentary on the third lamp.

Commentary B:

B.2.3.3 **The Conclusion**

Third, the conclusion. The root text says, "This completes the Lamp of the Soft White Channels. *Samaya!*" This has been explained previously.

(4) The Fluid Lamp of the Extensive Lasso

(344) Homage to Kun tu bZang po, who is the enlightened embodiment of self-arisen primordial wisdom.

Commentary A:

A.2.2.2.5 **The Fluid Lamp of the Extensive Lasso**

The lamp of the fluid extensive lasso has three parts.

A.2.2.2.5.1 **Homage**

[The root text begins], "Homage to Kun tu bZang po, who is the enlightened embodiment of self-arisen primordial wisdom." The explanation of the homage is the same as before, as is the explanation of Kun tu bZang po. The enlightened body of self-arisen primordial wisdom refers to the fact that primordial wisdom is known by-itself and comes to the victorious endpoint by-itself in a way that becomes self-evident without being covered by any obscurations. (364)

Commentary B:

B.2.4 **The Fluid Lamp of the Extensive Lasso**

Fourth, the fluid lamp of the extensive lasso has three parts:

(1) the explanation,

(2) the extensive explanation, and

(3) the conclusion.

(344) Oh, Children of the lineage! Here is what is called "the essential point on the Fluid Lamp of the Extensive Lasso, to see awakened awareness nakedly in whatever has arisen from the [sense] gateway [of the eyes]."

B.2.4.1 The Explanation

First, as before, there is Kun tu bZang po. With respect to self-arising primordial wisdom, groundless-ground (429) and awakened awareness are the ultimate truths of *Buddha*-nature. In the gateway of the [eye] lamp whatever arises arises in-and-by-itself, not made by anyone. The object of the homage is the existing enlightened body of Kun tu bZang po. The root text says, "Here is the essential point of the fluid lamp of the extensive lasso, to see awakened awareness nakedly in whatever has arisen from the [sense] gateway [of the eyes]." This means that from the gateway of the fluid eye lamp, all the enlightened *Buddha*-bodies and the *Buddha*-fields arise [as right here] without being obscured by anything whatsoever. Viewed like this it is direct seeing, so it is called "the essential point of seeing nakedly."

B.2.4.2 The Extensive Explanation

Second, the extensive explanation has three parts:

(1) whatever arises as the essence of groundless-ground,

(2) the gateway of the lamp by which it arises, and

(3) the ultimate truth of the natural state of its arising just as it is.

(344) In that way universal ground stays primordially as it is and awakened awareness stays in the heart.

Commentary B:

B.2.4.2.1 Whatever Arises as the Essence of Groundless-Ground

First, [whatever arises as the essence of groundless-ground]. The root text says, "In that way universal ground stays primordially as it is and awakened awareness stays in the heart." This means that [groundless-ground] stays in the heart unborn. Its real nature is originally pure, spontaneously present clear-light, uncompounded.

(345) The basis stays in the center of the heart. [Primordial wisdom] is drawn forth on the pathway of the [upper central] channel, and then arises in the lamp of the fluid gateway [of the eyes].

Commentary A:

A.2.2.2.5.2 **The Extensive Explanation**

The extensive explanation has two parts. [The root text] says, "Oh! Children of the lineage! Here is the essential point of the fluid lamp of the extensive lasso, to see awakened awareness nakedly in whatever has arisen from the [sense] door [of the eyes]." This is about how primordial wisdom's self-awakened awareness arises in-and-by-itself. Externally, it becomes evident nakedly at the gateway of the eyes; internally, in the interior tube manifesting as the five wisdom lights; and secretly, arising in the space of groundless-ground. [The root text] continues, "Universal ground stays primordially as it is and awakened awareness stays in the heart." Of the three main wind channels, the heart essence "stays in the central channel." Groundless-ground also stays in the central channel. [The root text] continues, "[Primordial wisdom] is drawn forth on the pathway of the [upper central] channel, and then arises in the lamp of the fluid gateway [of the eyes]." There is a brief and extensive explanation of this.

(345) Emerging from the central channel at its top, like the spout of a conch shell, comes a channel known as the so-called "*tsang ri pu* [the eye] channel," that arises like a bolt-like mountain. This single channel divides into two at its very tip and penetrates both eye lamps. The door of the channel gateway opens like a blossoming flax flower. The gateway for seeing awakened awareness projects out [just below the eyebrow fence].

Commentary A:

A.2.2.2.5.2.1 The Brief Explanation

[The root text] says, "Emerging from the central channel at its top, like the spout of a conch shell, comes a channel known as the '*tsang ri pu* [the eye] channel' that rises like a bolt-like mountain." These channels emerge from the central channel. As the text says, "This single channel divides into two at the very tip and penetrates both eye lamps. The door of the channel gateway opens like a blossoming flax flower. The gateway for seeing awakened awareness projects out [just below the eyebrow fence]." This means that awakened awareness [and its liveliness] becomes evident at the gateways of the eye lamps. Because the real nature [of everything seen] occurs in the fluid eye lamps, it is called "the lamp of the extensive lasso."

(345) From the interior of this channel the five [wisdom] lights arise like [the eye of a] peacock feather.

Commentary B:

B.2.4.2.2 The Gateway of the Lamp by Which it Arises

Second [the gateway of the lamp by which it arises]. The gateway is described in the root text where it says, "The basis stays in the center of the heart. Primordial wisdom is [drawn forth] along the pathway [of the upper central] channel, and then arises in the lamp of the fluid gateway [of the eyes]." Awakened awareness stays at the level of the heart-mind. The path refers to the channel. Whatever arises is in the gateway of the eye [lamp]. The root text says, "Emerging from the central channel at its top, like the spout of a conch shell, comes a channel known as [the eye channel] that arises like a bolt-like mountain." [Two] eye channels emerge, separating from the top of the central channel. The root text says, "This single channel divides into two at the very tip and penetrates both eye lamps." After becoming separated into two like this, [each channel] penetrates the two eyes. The root text says, "The door of the channel gateway opens like a blossoming flax flower." This refers to the gateway of the channel at the eye sense-organ. The shape of this abides like the open mouth of a flax flower. The root text says, (430) "And from this gateway awakened awareness projects out." Knowing projects from the gateway wherein forms are seen. The root text says, "From the interior of the channels the five [wisdom] lights arise like [the eye of a] peacock feather." This means that from the interior of the channels the five lights of awakened awareness arise in-and-by-themselves, like the eye of a peacock feather. Depending on that [channel] is what distinguishes the gateway for awakened awareness's seeing.

(345) With respect to the gateway of seeing these lights, the mother [consciousness], universal ground, is like [vast] space, without outside or inside, wherein primordial wisdom arises and completely saturates everything. Awakened awareness shines forth in this gateway of seeing like the heart of the sun without any conceptual thought. Herein, ordinary conceptual thought and the activity of ordinary mindfulness and various activities toward sense-objects are like the rays of the sun. Light is the self-light of awakened awareness, like a rainbow in the sky. The light-rays are the self-emitting rays of awakened awareness seen like rays of a matrix of sunlight.

Commentary A:

A.2.2.2.5.2.1.1 **The Extensive Explanation**

The manner in which primordial wisdom arises has two parts:

(1) explaining how it stays as complete, and

(2) explaining how it is seen nakedly.

A.2.2.2.5.2.1.1.1 **Explaining How it Stays as Complete in Itself**

With respect to the lamp of the eye-consciousness, the natural state of groundless-ground and awakened awareness (365) stays in its primordial condition as the three—ultimate sound, light, and light-rays. This natural state is thoroughly complete in itself with nothing left out. It arises just as it is. [The root text] continues, "From the interior of the channels the five wisdom lights arise like the [eye of a] peacock feather. With respect to the gateway of seeing[23] these lights, the mother consciousness,

---

23. *mthong sgo*: "gateway of seeing."

groundless-ground, is like [vast] space, without outside or inside, wherein primordial wisdom arises and completely saturates everything. Awakened awareness shines forth in this gateway of seeing like the heart of the sun, without any conceptual thought. Herein, ordinary conceptual thought[24] and the activity of ordinary mindfulness and various thoughts toward sense-objects are like the rays of the sun. Light is the light-itself of awakened awareness, like a rainbow in the sky, as if showing the way home. The light-rays are the rays-themselves of awakened awareness. Having seen [ordinary thought as light-rays of awakened awareness, thought] arises like rays of the matrix of sun rays."

(345) In that way, the heart-essence always stays primordially. In the gateways of the [fluid eye] lamps these can never diminish, and there, there can be no activity of ordinary thought. Because these arise nakedly as three kinds of direct perception associated with the eye sense-organ, this is called, "the essential point of seeing awakened awareness nakedly."

Commentary A:

A.2.2.2.5.2.1.2 **Explaining How it is Seen Nakedly**

To explain how it is seen nakedly [the root text] continues, "In this way, [seeing is seeing] the heart-essence that always stays primordially." The text explains how the natural state of groundless-ground and awakened awareness arises. [The root text] continues, "In the gateways of the [fluid eye] lamps these can never diminish, and there, there can be no activity of ordinary thought. Because these arise nakedly as three kinds of direct perception[25] associated with the eye sense-organs, this is called 'the essential point of seeing awakened awareness nakedly.'" This explains that in the eye lamps, the natural state [leading to] the fruition of the enlightened *Buddha*-bodies never diminishes. Because there is no activity of ordinary thought here, seeing arises nakedly manifesting as the three kinds of direct [non-conceptual] seeing, and such direct seeing is called "the essential point of seeing nakedly."

---

24. *blo*: "ordinary conceptual thought."

25. *mngon gsum* = *mngon sum gsum*: "three kinds of direct perception."

Commentary B:

B.2.4.2.3 The Ultimate Truth of the Natural State of its Arising Just As It Is

Third, the ultimate truth of the natural state of its arising just as it is. The root text says, "With respect to the gateway of seeing these lights...groundless-ground is like [vast] space, without outside or inside, wherein primordial wisdom arises and completely saturates everything." Emptiness/lucidity arises entirely pervading [everything] whose fundamental nature is like space. The root text continues, "Awakened awareness shines forth in this gateway of seeing like the heart of the sun without any conceptual thought." In this gateway, primordial wisdom's awakened awareness arises nakedly free of conceptual thought like the heart of the sun. The root text says, "Herein, ordinary conceptual thought and the activity of ordinary mindfulness and various activities toward sense-objects are like the rays of the sun." In primordial wisdom's awakened awareness, so much liveliness of ordinary mindfulness and conceptual thought arises and reaches toward sense-objects. The root text says, "Light is the light-itself of awakened awareness, like a rainbow in the sky." This means that from the gateway of the lamp, the self-emitting light of awakened awareness arises lucidly and splendidly like rainbow light. The text says, "The light-rays are the self-emitting rays of awakened awareness seen like rays of a matrix of sunlight." These light-rays are the self-emitting light-rays of awakened awareness that arise as self-radiance in the gateway of the eye sense-organs, seen for example, like light-rays from the sun. The root text says, "In that way, the heart-essence always stays primordially." The heart-essence refers to the quintessence of the path, the liveliness of awakened awareness as the three—sound, light, and light-rays—the path of the radiant magical display. The root text says, "In the gateways of the [fluid eye] lamps (431) these can never diminish, and there, there can be no activity of ordinary thought. Because these arise nakedly as three kinds of direct perception associated with the eye sense-organ..." In the gateway of the [eye] lamp is the self-emitting radiance that increases without obscuration just as it is, without any deliberate effort associated with the causes and conditions of conceptual thought. The [eye] sense-organ refers to naked direct [seeing]. The root text continues, "This is called, 'the essential point of seeing awakened awareness nakedly.'" By relying on whatever arises, you take up the meditation experiences, you train liveliness, and walk the path through which the natural state is seen just as it is. This is called "staying that sees nakedly."

This completes the Fluid Lamp of the Extensive Lasso. Samaya!

Commentary A:
A.2.2.2.5.3 A Brief Summary

The extensive explanation makes this clear. [The root text ends], "*Samaya!*" This completes the commentary on the fourth lamp.

Commentary B:
B.2.4.3 The Conclusion

Third, the conclusion is clearly condensed when the root text says, "This completes the Fluid Lamp of the Extensive Lasso." "*Samaya!*" has been explained previously.

(5) The Lamp of the *Buddha*-fields

(345) Homage to Kun tu bZang po, who directly manifests as self-awakened awareness.

Commentary A:
A.2.2.2.6 The Lamp of the *Buddha*-fields

Explaining the lamp that points out the *Buddha*-fields has three parts: (366)

A.2.2.2.6.1 Homage

[The root text] says, "Homage to Kun tu bZang po, who directly manifests as self- awakened awareness." The explanation of the homage to Kun tu bZang po has been given previously. Actualizing awakened awareness in-and-by-itself refers to directly drawing forth the enlightened *Buddha*-bodies nakedly on the path, based on the compassion of Kun tu bZang po.

A.2.2.2.6.2 The Extensive Explanation

The extensive explanation has two parts—a brief and a more extended explanation.

Commentary B:

B.2.5 The Lamp of the *Buddha*-fields

The lamp of the *Buddha*-fields has three parts:

(1) the explanation,

(2) the extended explanation, and

(3) the conclusion.

(345) Oh! Children of the Lineage! Here is the lamp on pointing out the *Buddha*-fields, and once having some meditative experience like that along this path, here are the so-called "close-to-the-heart" essential points [that establish certainty] about the three-fold embodiment of enlightenment directly manifesting.

Commentary A:

A.2.2.2.6.2.1 A Briefer Explanation

[The root text] says, "Oh! Children of the Lineage! Here is the lamp for pointing out the *Buddha*-fields, and once having some meditative experience like that along this path, here are the so-called 'close-to-the-heart' essential points [that establish certainty] about the three-fold embodiment of enlightenment." With respect to *bodhicitta*, those Victorious Ones who know self-awakened awareness explain this teaching as the three-fold embodiment of enlightenment being spontaneously present, self-arising, and staying.

Commentary B:

B.2.5.1 The Brief Explanation

First, "*Kun tu*" refers to all the ways, good, bad, etc., that thought arises from the ground. "*bZang po*" refers to all of these arising from the state of mind-itself as self-arising, self-liberating. Having arisen from the liveliness of primordial wisdom, they are [not mentally engaged], neither accepted nor rejected. "Self-awakened awareness" refers to primordial wisdom, which is the essence of awakened mind-itself. "Directly manifesting" refers to the fact that self-awakened awareness directly manifesting brings the direct realization of *Buddhahood*. "Homage" refers to being mindful of the homage to its self-lucidity. The root text continues, "Oh! Children of the Lineage! Here is the lamp on pointing out the *Buddha*-fields." This means that the enlightened *Buddha*-bodies and the *Buddha*-fields are innate. Having relied upon the six essential points and their skillful means these become directly evident, so this is the lamp that directly and nakedly points these out. (432) The root text says, "And once having some meditative experience like that along this path, here are the so-called 'close-to-the-heart' essential points [that establish certainty] about the three-fold embodiment of enlightenment." These are the teachings through which you make a firm determination that the three enlightened *Buddha*-bodies of the universal basis become directly manifest, and having arisen, everything ends up in its own way as awakened mind-itself.

(345) There are two [sets of instructions]:

(1) pointing out, and

(2) close-to-the-heart [instructions for establishing certainty].

Commentary A:

A.2.2.2.6.2.2 **A More Extended Explanation**

The extended explanation has two parts: (1) pointing out the three enlightened *Buddha*-bodies, and (2) the close-to-the-heart instructions.

Commentary B:

B.2.5.2 **The Extended Explanation**

Second, the extended explanation has two parts:

(1) pointing out the three enlightened *Buddha*-bodies, and

(2) the close-to-the-heart instructions.

(345) Here are the first, the pointing out instructions. Oh! Children

of the Lineage! The natural state, universal ground, stays as [ultimate] *bodhicitta*, that which entirely pervades everything and is without boundaries or divisions. This is the expanse of the *dharmadhātu*. When this stays, only this stays and nothing else, as the immense original purity of self-awakened awareness. (346) This is the self-arising *dharmakāya*, wherein the *Buddha*-fields of the *dharmadhātu* abide in their own way. Even though it accompanies you perpetually across the three times, it remains unrecognized.

Commentary A:

A.2.2.2.6.2.2.1 **Pointing out the Three Enlightened *Buddha*-bodies**

What is pointed out with respect to the three enlightened *Buddha*-bodies is that the enlightened *Buddha*-bodies stay in the expanse of *dharmakāya* and remain there. The *dharmakāya* arises in-and-by-itself. It always remains just as it is. [The root text] says, "Oh! Children of the Lineage! The natural state, universal ground, stays as [ultimate] *bodhicitta*, that which entirely pervades everything and is without boundaries or divisions. This is the expanse of *dharmadhātu*. When this stays, only this stays and nothing else, as immense original purity of self-awakened awareness. This is the self-arising *dharmakāya*, wherein the *Buddha*-fields of the *dharmadhātu* abide in their own way. Even though it accompanies you perpetually across the three times, it remains unrecognized." [The *dharmadhātu*] is pointed out. It and the unsurpassable *Buddha*-fields stay [just the way they are].

Commentary B:

B.2.5.2.1 **Pointing out the Three Enlightened *Buddha*-bodies**

B.2.5.2.1.1 **Pointing out the Enlightened *Dharmakāya***

First, [pointing out the three enlightened *Buddha*-bodies]. The first of three parts is pointing out the enlightened *dharmakāya*. The root text says, "Oh! Children of the Lineage! The natural state, universal ground, stays as [ultimate] *bodhictta*, that which entirely pervades everything and is without boundaries or divisions. This is the expanse of *dharmadhātu*." This is the great mind-itself emptiness/lucidity entirely pervading everything. It is the expanse of *dharmadhātu*. The root text says, "When this stays, only this stays and nothing else, as immense original purity." From within the state of the lucid space of groundless-ground, primordial wisdom's awakened awareness is like the sun that is never covered by faults. It arises stainless and bare. The root text says,

> This is the self-arising *dharmakāya*, wherein the *Buddha*-fields of the *dharmadhātu* abide in their own way. Even though it accompanies you perpetually across the three times, it remains unrecognized. These *Buddha*-fields and the *dharmakāya* exist primordially in oneself, but when failing to recognize them, you wander in *saṁsāra*. For example, it is like being acquainted with an individual but not recognizing their face, or like a lowly, poor person who remains hungry by not recognizing that he has wealth.

(346) Oh! Children of the Lineage! It stays in that inner place, the dark crystal in the offering tent [in the sphere of the heart-mind], where its appearance has the clarity of immeasurable light. Herein are the unsurpassable highest *Buddha*-fields of 'Og Min. Here primordial wisdom's self-awakened-awareness stays. Here the three [visions]—ultimate sound, light, and light-rays—are spontaneously present. Here, everything in *samsāra* and *nirvāna* is spontaneously present and complete. Here the *sambhogakāya* shines forth in-and-by-itself, and the *Buddha*-fields of the *sambhogakāya* also remain in-and-by-themselves. If there is no direct realization, only the deluded realms come forth.

Next, the completion *Buddha*-body also remains and arises in-and-by-itself, [as described in the root text], "Oh! Children of the Lineage! It stays in that inner place, the dark crystal in the offering tent [in the sphere of the heart-mind], where its appearance (367) has the clarity of immeasurable light. Herein are the unsurpassable highest *Buddha*-fields of 'Og Min. Here primordial wisdom's self-awakened awareness stays. Here the three [visions]—ultimate sound, light, and light-rays—are spontaneously present. Here, everything in *saṁsāra* and *nirvana* is spontaneously present and complete. Here, the *sambhogakāya* shines forth in-and-by-itself, and the *Buddha*-fields of the *sambhogakāya* also remain in-and-by-themselves. If there is no direct realization, only the deluded realms come forth." The root text passage points out the *sambhogakāya* [the completion *Buddha*-body].

Commentary B:
B.2.5.2.1.2 Recognizing the *Buddha*-fields of the Enlightened Completion Body

Second, recognizing the *Buddha*-fields of the *sambhogakāya* [enlightened completion body]. The root text says, "Oh! Children of the Lineage! (433) It stays in that inner place, the dark crystal in the offering tent [in the sphere of the heart-mind], where its appearance has the clarity of immeasurable light. Herein are the unsurpassable highest *Buddha*-fields of 'Og Min." Externally, in the heart it appears in the shape of an eight-sided jewel. Internally, it appears within the center of a very lucid eight-petalled lotus. It is like a pavilion of five [rainbow] lights. This is the ultimate truth of the subject matter [of these teachings] with nothing higher. The root text continues, "Here primordial wisdom's self-awakened-awareness stays." This refers to the stainlessness of awakened awareness, staying as the identitylessness of everything good. The text says, "Here the three—ultimate sound, light, and light-rays—are spontaneously present." Here the three great visions of the liveliness of awakened awareness arise in-and-by-themselves without obstruction. The text says, "Here, everything in *saṁsāra* and *nirvāṇa* is spontaneously present and complete."

With respect to primordial wisdom's awakened awareness, these innate five livelinesses of the visions and the five [rainbow] lights are complete [in themselves]. Being complete, [all] the appearances of *saṁsāra* and *nirvāṇa* are completed without exception. All the sacred visions are complete and spontaneously present without effort—the immeasurable visions of the *Buddha*-fields of *nirvāṇa*, the five enlightened bodies and deity forms of the five *Buddha* families and principal deities of the *mandala*, such as the their facial expressions, their forms taken, their hand instruments, the color of their bodies, and their ornaments. [Likewise], all the mundane appearances of *saṁsāra* are complete and spontaneously present without effort—the external vessel [external reality], the internal contents [of mind], the times in history, lives, and residences of the six classes of beings, the *mandala* of the three realms, the five elements, the aggregates, the five poisons, the five vessels, the five limbs, the five sense-organs, the five sense supports, and the five sense-objects, etc. (434)

With respect to primordial wisdom's awakened awareness, the illustrious root of innate sound is complete in-itself. Externally, it is the sound of the elements. Internally, it is the sound of awakened awareness. Secretly, it is the emanation of *Buddhahood* with all the possibilities of the speech and sign language of sentient beings. All the particulars of renowned speech are complete and spontaneously present without effort.

With respect to primordial wisdom's awakened awareness, the root of conceptual thought as [immeasurable] innate light-rays is complete in itself. Being complete like this, all possible eighty-four thousand specific conceptual thoughts of sentient beings, and ten thousand and one hundred thousand omniscient primordial wisdoms of *Buddhas*, are all specifically known by beings as complete and spontaneously present without effort. The root text says, "Here, the *sambhogakāya* shines forth in-and-by-itself, and the *Buddha*-fields of the *sambhogakāya* also remain in-and-by-themselves." Thus, with respect to primordial wisdom's awakened awareness, all phenomena of *saṃsāra* and *nirvāṇa* are completed as spontaneously present without effort, and so, the enlightened completion *Buddha*-body and the *Buddha*-fields stay in their own way. Thus, all the appearances of *saṃsāra*—the aggregates and sense-fields of dependent origination, the five enlightened *Buddha*-bodies, the five *Buddha* families, etc., stay as the completion *Buddha*-fields. The essence of primordial wisdom's awakened awareness stays as empty. From the radiance of primordial wisdom's emptiness comes a clear white light. In the clarity of awakened awareness, primordial wisdom is like a mirror without inherent nature. From the radiance comes a yellow light. From the heart of this [yellow light] in the east comes a yellow-colored *Sugata* of the *gYung Drung* family. Here awakened awareness stays the same, never divided, (435) as the primordial wisdom of equanimity. From the radiance of this comes a green light. From the heart of this [green light] in the north comes a green-colored *Sugata* of the *mandala* family, the holder of the *mandala*. Here awakened awareness stays unadulterated, thoroughly completed as discriminating primordial wisdom. From the radiance of this comes a red light. From the heart of this [red light] in the west comes a red-colored *Sugata* of the lotus family, the holder of the lotus. Here awakened awareness is spontaneously present, without [needing to] search for it, as all-accomplishing primordial wisdom. From the radiance of this comes a blue light. From the heart of this [blue light] in the south comes a blue-colored *Sugata* of the jewel family, the holder of the jewel. Here is awakened awareness. Thus, from the radiance of the five [*Buddha*] families, the *dharmakāya* stays as these [five] deity bodies. The root text says, "If there is no direct realization, only the deluded realms come forth." Primordially, the completion *Buddha*-fields stay in their own way. When these are not realized, they become the five *Maras*, five poisons, five elements, and five aggregates, etc. These then arise as various impure appearances, the subject of deluded appearance.

(346) Oh! Children of the Lineage! Here, the completion of the three main channels, the six chakras, the trunk, the main ancillary branch channels, and the smaller branch channels are to be found in the *Buddha*-fields that complete the *mandala* of the seed syllables. Remaining in this way is primordial wisdom's self-awakened awareness; then the six sense-systems and six sense-objects arise as the liveliness [of awakened awareness]. The seemingly ordinary various activities of the three [doors]—body, speech, and mind—are the *nirmānakāyas* arising in-and-by-themselves, yet staying in-and-by-themselves as the *Buddha*-fields of the *nirmānakāyas*. If there is no direct realization, only the six classes of ordinary beings seem to arise.

Commentary A:

The *Buddha*-fields that complete the *mandala* of the seed syllables, and the *nirmānakāyas* [emanation *Buddha*-bodies] also remain and arise in-and-by-themselves [as described in the root text]. "Oh! Children of the Lineage! Here, the completion of the three main channels, the six *chakras*, the trunk, the main ancillary branch channels, and the smaller branch channels, are to be found in the *Buddha*-fields that complete the *mandala* of the seed syllables. Remaining in this way is primordial wisdom's self-awakened awareness; then the six sense systems and six sense-objects arise as the liveliness [of awakened awareness]. The seemingly ordinary various activities of the three [doors]—body, speech, and mind—are the *nirmāṇakāyas* arising in-and-by-themselves, yet staying in-and-by-themselves as the *Buddha*-fields of the *nirmāṇakāyas*. If there is no direct realization, only the six classes of ordinary beings seem to arise." The passage points out the *nirmāṇakāyas* [emanation *Buddha*-bodies]. If the three-fold embodiment of enlightenment stays [stable] in this way, then they remain [permanently] *nirmāṇakāyas* as spontaneously present. There is nothing existing other than this. They stay so as to shine forth in-and-by-themselves.

Commentary B:

B.2.5.2.1.3 Pointing out the *Nirmāṇakāyas* [Enlightened Emanation Bodies]

Third, pointing out the *nirmāṇakāyas* [enlightened emanation bodies]. The root text says, "Oh! Children of the Lineage! Here, the completion of the three main channels, the six *chakras*, the trunk, the main ancillary branch channels, and the smaller branch channels, are to be found in the *Buddha*-fields and realms that complete the *mandala* of the seed syllables." There are three main channels—right, left, and central channel—and six *chakras*—the crown *chakra* of bliss, the throat *chakra* of enjoyment, the heart *chakra* of the *dharmadhātu*, the navel *chakra* of emanation, the secret *chakra* of wisdom and means, and the floor *chakra* of wind. (436) From the *Buddha*-fields of the *nirmāṇakāyas* come the channel of the trunk of life, the branch channels of the true vessel and the sense-organs, the branch channels of the head, body, legs, and arms. These differentiate into the three primary external, internal, and in-between channels, and then into twenty-one thousand and eighty-four thousand channels. These channels serve as the basic support for the light and seeds of the deities, namely the five seed syllables, winds, drops, etc. The root text says, "Remaining in this way is primordial wisdom's self-awakened awareness; then the six sense-systems and six sense-objects arise as the liveliness [of awakened awareness]." This means that from the liveliness of awakened awareness, the six sense-consciousnessness and six sense-objects arise. The liveliness of these consciousnesses is impartial. The activities of the various characteristics of effortful activities of the three—body, speech, and mind—arise as impartial. They arise as [various] *nirmāṇakāyas*.

The root text says, "The seemingly ordinary various activities of the three [doors]—body, speech, and mind—are the *nirmāṇakāyas* [emanation *Buddha*-bodies] arising in-and-by-themselves, yet staying in-and-by-themselves as the *Buddha*-fields of the *nirmāṇakāyas*." This refers to whatever emanations arise from all the *Buddha*-fields belonging to the channels of the *mandala*. In the middle of the crown *chakra* of great bliss, the subduer of gods, gShen ye gShen gTsyg Pyhug, resides. In the throat *chakra*, the subduer of the demi-gods, gShen lCe rGyal, resides. In the heart *chakra*, the subduer of humans, gShen gSang 'Dus, resides. In the navel *chakra*, the subduer of animals, gShen ti Sangs, resides. In the secret *chakra*, the subduer of the hungry ghosts, gShen Mu Cho Ldem Drug, resides. In the base *chakra*, the subduer of hell beings, gShen gSang Ba Ngang Ring, resides. Furthermore, there are seventy-five consorts of the five *Buddha* families. From the liveliness of the eight assemblies, there are eight primordial gShen *Buddhas* and 8 primordial pillars. (437) There are the four flowers of the head, legs, eyes, and tongue. There are the three deities that remove the three poisons of body, speech, and mind. In the branch channels are the Victorious Ones of the four times. There are forty-five peaceful deities, and from their transformation, the thirty-four wrathful deities, and the one hundred twenty-eight assembly deities as the victors of time. In addition to that, all the assemblies of deities of the three-outer, inner, and secret—occur in the middle of the *mudra* of the *chakras* of one's own body by having connected the aggregates of body and mind. In fact, everything stays in the channels where there is nothing not pervaded by the enlightened emanation bodies of the *Buddhas*.

The root text says, "If there is no direct realization, only the six classes of ordinary beings seem to arise." Even when these stay, if there is no realization, the mind and the winds stay as seed syllables in the channels of the six *chakras*. There, the appearance of the six classes of beings arises, or through the coming together of the mind and the winds in the heart *chakra*, as the greater part of what is especially present, the appearances of human preoccupations and afflictions arise. The five poisons are combined in the five visceral organs and combined into the eighty-four thousand small wind channels, through which they arise as the liveliness of the mass of eighty-four thousand conceptual thoughts.

(346) Now come the close-to-the-heart instructions [for establishing certainty] regarding the three-fold embodiment of enlightenment. First, with respect to pointing out the essence-itself of awakened awareness, there are the close-to-the-heart instructions on the enlightened *dharmakāya*. Second, with respect to pointing out the special insight [seeing beyond] awakened awareness, there are the close-to-the-heart instructions on the Enlightened Form-bodies.

Commentary A:

A.2.2.2.6.2.2.2 **The Close-to-the-Heart Instructions**

The close-to-the-heart instructions regarding the three-fold embodiment of enlightenment has two parts: [As the root text] says, "(1) with respect to pointing out the essence-itself of awakened awareness, the close-to-the-heart instructions on the *dharmakāya*[26]; and (2) with respect to pointing out that gives insight into awakened awareness, the close-to-the-heart instructions of the Enlightened Form-bodies."[27] The first has two parts—pointing out and close-to-the-heart instructions.

Commentary B:

B.2.5.2.2 **The Close-to-the-Heart Instructions**

Second, the close-to-the-heart instructions have two parts.

(1) The root text says, "First, with respect to pointing out the essence-itself of awakened awareness, there are the close-to-the-heart instructions on the *dharmakāya*.

(2) Second, with respect to pointing out the special insight into awakened awareness, there are the close-to-the-heart instructions on the Enlightened Form-bodies [*gzhugs sku*]."

B.2.5.2.2.1 **Pointing out the Enlightened Dharmakāya**

The first has two parts:

(1) pointing out, and

---

26 *bod sku* = *chos sku*: literally, "Body of Bon," i.e., *dharmakāya*.

27 *gzugs sku*: "Enlightened Form-bodies."

(2) close-to-the-heart instructions.

(346) Recognizing the essence-itself of awakened awareness is pointed out by means of the three lamps. First, recognizing the basis, [universal ground], through the Lamp of the Basis that stays. Second, the Lamp of Illustrative Examples is used to illustrate the truth by examples. Third, pointing out the extent of signs that occur through the Lamp of the Signs of primordial wisdom.

Oh! Children of the Lineage! Recognizing the basis.

Commentary A:

A.2.2.2.6.2.2.2.1 **With Respect to Pointing out the Essence-itself of Awakened Awareness, the Close-to-the-Heart Instructions on the Body of Bon [*Dharmakāya*]**

A.2.2.2.6.2.2.2.1.1 **Pointing out Instructions**

The pointing out instructions have three parts, according to the root text:

"(1) through the lamp of groundless-ground that stays, recognizing the basis;

(2) through the lamp of illustrative examples, illustrating ultimate truth by example; and

(3) through the lamp of the signs of primordial wisdom, in addition recognizing the signs.

The first is: Oh! Children of the Lineage! Recognizing the basis."

Right now, establish the lamp [of the basis] in its own way until [direct] knowing of sense-objects is established in its own right, without any conceptual analysis. Without examining sense-objects, (347) this knowing of objects remains uncovered. At that time, the emptiness/clarity of the universal ground is never covered by obscurations and distinctly becomes clear. [Within universal ground]

the many seeming appearances of sense-objects distinctly become clear, like reflections in a mirror.

Commentary B:

B.2.5.2.2.1.1 Pointing Out

The first [pointing out] has three parts. As the root text says, "Recognizing the essence-itself of awakened awareness is pointed out by means of the three lamps."

(1) "Recognizing the basis, [universal ground] through the Lamp of the Basis that stays," (438)

(2) "...the lamp of illustrative examples is used to illustrate the truth by examples," and

(3) "...pointing out the extent of signs that occur through the Lamp of the Signs of primordial wisdom."

B.2.5.2.2.1.1.1 Recognizing the Basis, [Groundless-ground], Through the Lamp of the Basis that stays

First, recognizing the basis, the son, [namely recognizing] awakened awareness, has three parts—pointing out the three—the mother, the son, and the liveliness.

B.2.5.2.2.1.1.1.1 Pointing out the Mother Consciousness

First, [pointing out the mother], the essential point of bringing out the brightness of awakened awareness is that through the body points and gaze the mind develops concentrated evenness, and after that, awakened awareness arises nakedly, free of conceptual thought. The root text says, "Establish the lamp [of the basis] in its own way." It refers to the view being distinguished by the gaze. Awakened awareness is seen through the gateway of the eyes when the eyes do not waver, the eyelids do not close, and they are established in their own way. The root text says, "...until [directly] knowing sense-objects is established in its own right, without any conceptual analysis." This refers to the skillful means to set up the mind without chasing after past [moments of] consciousness, without analyzing sense-objects externally, and without making any analytic thought internally toward awakened awareness, but setting up the mind one-pointedly. The root text says, "Without examining sense-objects, this knowing of objects remains uncovered." At that time, the subject, awakened awareness, stays free from grasped and grasping [duality], unspoiled, never changing color, lucidly knowing the object without being obscured. The root text says, "At that time, the emptiness/clarity is never covered by obscurations, and distinctly becomes clear." Through viewing through the gateway of the lamp, groundless-ground arises with its pervading, insubstantial, purified emptiness. This points out the practice. The root text continues, "[Within universal ground] the many seeming appearances of sense-objects distinctly become clear like reflections in the mirror." These are known at that time directly in groundless-ground. Such appearing objects arise without any inherent nature. (439)

(347) At that time, [this pure] awakened awareness has no activity of ordinary awareness, [but is] an openness, cleaned up of focus. Once staying in bare [awareness] without grasping, open, and free of conceptual thought, then all seeming appearances of sense-objects become like reflections in a crystal ball, and shine forth with vivid wakefulness.

Commentary B:
B.2.5.2.2.1.1.1.2 **Pointing out the Son Consciousness**

Second, pointing out the son. The root text says, "At that time, [this pure] awakened awareness has no activity of ordinary awareness, [but is] an openness, cleaned up of focus." This refers to being free from ordinary mindfulness [wherein thoughts come] before or after, and in being without mindfulness, there are no words [that get in the way]. The text continues, "…cleaned up of focus." Being free of focus is a pervasive bliss without any representation. This means that it is free of any fluctuating focus. When the text says, "…an openness…without grasping," it means that there is no reflecting on anything external or internal whatsoever. The text continues, "Once staying in bare [awareness] without grasping…" This means that by not being obscured by anything whatsoever, whatever arises comes forth nakedly, not covered by conceptual thought. The text continues, "Then all seeming appearances of sense-objects become like reflections in a crystal ball, and shine forth with vivid wakefulness." What is pointed out is that whenever whatever [seeming appearances] arise like this, all the seeming external appearing objects are appearance/emptiness, insubstantial, lucid in-and-by-themselves, bare, and ungrasped. They arise in-and-by-themselves as the very first adornments of the profound crystal, or they arise without inherent nature appearing like reflections in a mirror.

(347) As for conceptual thought, [seemingly ordinary] reflective thought and ordinary awareness act to distinguish each and every one of the various objects.

Commentary A:

A.2.2.2.6.2.2.2.1.1.1 Through the Lamp of Groundless-ground that Stays, Recognizing the Basis

To recognize the basis is to recognize it just as it is. [The root text] continues, "Right now, establish the lamp [of the basis] in its own way." The body is established in the gesture[28] of concentrated evenness; the eyes remain wide open, never shut. [The root text] continues, "Until [direct] knowing of sense-objects is established in its own right,[29] without any conceptual analysis." This explains the skillful way to establish the mind. [The root text] then says, "Without examining sense-objects, this knowing of objects remains uncovered." Then, once established in this way, the natural state stays without duality. In this case, groundless-ground is clear just the way it is. [The root text] continues, "The emptiness/clarity of the universal ground is never covered by any obscurations and distinctly becomes clear. [Within groundless-ground] the many seeming appearances of sense-objects distinctly become clear, like reflections in a mirror." Seeing through the door of the eyes from groundless-ground is seeing wherein [seeming appearances] are unobstructed and completely transparent, and so [this kind of seeing] is called "primordial wisdom in the expanse of *dharmakāya.*" All seemingly external appearances of sense-objects remain clear, without obscuration, as illustrated by the ex-

---

28. *phyag rgya* = *mudra*: "gesture."

29. *rang sor*: "in its own right."

ample of reflections in a mirror. In this case, awakened awareness stays just as it is. [The root text] continues, "At that time, [this pure] awakened awareness has no activity of ordinary awareness, [but is] an openness cleaned up of focus. Once staying in bare [awareness] without grasping, open, and free of conceptual thought, then all seeming appearances of sense-objects become like reflections in a crystal ball (369), and shine forth with vivid wakefulness."[30] In this case, [appearances] arise just as they are. [The root text] continues, "As for conceptual thought, [seemingly ordinary] reflective thought and ordinary awareness act to distinguish each and every one of the various objects." In other words, these various objects [ultimately appear] from the liveliness of the inseparable pair of groundless-ground and awakened awareness, so that seemingly ordinary conceptual thought and ordinary awareness are able to distinguish each and every one of the various appearances that arise as the five sense-objects. With respect to this directly knowing [appearances] as emptiness/clarity, without obscuration, the seeming external appearances of sense-objects shine forth, lucidly and flashing. Because the victory of knowing-awareness[31] is [the realization of] groundless-ground, this is what is pointed out. To make this clear, if there is any doubt about this, the five seemingly external sense-objects shine forth lucidly and flashing from groundless-ground. Not even the smallest ordinary conceptual thought ever arises from groundless-ground. The eyes are [like fluid] bubbles, wherein [all seeming sense-objects] seem to be the same [vision]. The same is true for all five supporting sense-organs. The five sense-organs or the bubble-like eyes are just the gateways through which the five sense-objects arise from groundless-ground. To illustrate how the five sense-objects arise from groundless-ground without obscuration, the metaphor of water and a water-moon [reflection] is used, or the metaphor of a dream. This should make it more clear, if there is any doubt, how these three [groundless-ground, awakened awareness, and ordinary conceptual thought] come to exist.

---

30. *hrig ge*: "vivid wakefulness."

31. *shes rig*: "knowing-awareness," awakened awareness in its capacity to know directly, free of conceptualization.

Commentary B:

B.2.5.2.2.1.1.1.3 **Pointing out Liveliness**

Third, [pointing out liveliness]. The root text says, "As for conceptual] thought, [seemingly ordinary] reflective thought and ordinary awareness act to distinguish each and every one of the various objects." Whenever there is conceptual thought that grasps, through reflecting on this, or tries to stop everything, it is pointed out that this is empty movement, much like a gentle breeze that appears, or like waves on the ocean that appear in-and-by-themselves and become liberated in-and-by-themselves, and it is pointed out that these arise as the liveliness of primordial wisdom.

(347) Oh! Children of the Lineage! Here is the *Lamp of Illustrative Examples*. The example and meaning of the self-clarity of awakened awareness is illustrated through the example of a butter lamp [that stays lit by itself]. The sign of being stainless and originally pure is illustrated by a lotus. The sign of being spontaneously arisen clear-light is illustrated by the heart of the sun. The sign of being naturally clear without obscuration is illustrated by a spotless mirror. The sign of being naked and transparent is illustrated by a clear crystal ball. The sign of primordial wisdom is illustrated by pouring empty space into empty space.

Commentary B:

B.2.5.2.2.1.1.2 **The Lamp of Illustrative Examples**

Second, the lamp of illustrative examples. There are metaphors to illustrate the meaning. These are used for insiders who believe. They serve as miraculous signs regarding attaining confidence and having definitive knowledge arise. (440) Through acting to bring about the realization of ultimate truth, they make any untruths clear.

(347) Oh! Children of the Lineage! Here is pointing out the *Lamp of the Extent of the Signs*. First, the truth of the universal ground and awakened awareness is pointed out. With respect to pointing out the truth of the universal ground, it is like lighting a butter lamp that

separates the brightness from the darkness and shadows that had obscured it. It is like discovering a sudden, intensely awake clarity as natural clarity. In the gateway of the lamp, universal ground is free from any darkness and obscuration whatsoever, wherein primordial wisdom stays as a sudden, intensely awake natural clarity. Although a lotus lives in the mud, it is never covered by the stench of the mud. It remains stainless and naked. In the gateway of the lamp, the universal ground is never covered by the stench of anything whatsoever.

It stays originally pure and naked. It is also like the sun whose immense primordial clear-light shines forth self-evidently, without doing anything whatsoever. In the gateway of the lamp, universal ground is without any activity whatsoever. Primordially, it spontaneously arises as immense clear-light, (348) wherein the greatness of self-originating primordial wisdom shines forth self-evidently, with a clarity free of all obscurations, like all the reflections shining forth in a spotless mirror. In the gateway of the lamp, the universal ground shines forth as self-arising primordial wisdom without anything whatsoever obscuring it, so that the appearance of all seeming external sense-objects shine forth without obscuration, and the pure, naked transparency stays, like a crystal ball that separates the lucid from what seemed covered by whatever obscurations [occur]. In the gateway of the lamp, groundless-ground stays, free from what seemed covered by obscurations, wherein primordial wisdom stays stark naked and transparent. In the doorway of the lamp, groundless-ground saturates everything, like space without an inside or outside, wherein the remarkable transparency of primordial wisdom saturates everything without inside or outside.

Commentary A:

A.2.2.2.6.2.2.2.1.1.2 **Through the Lamp of Illustrative Examples, Illustrating Ultimate Truth by Example**

Next is the lamp of illustrative examples. The root text uses six metaphors to bring victory about knowing awakened awareness. Each of these illustrates the same thing. The lengthy discussion in the root text makes it clear [so they are not discussed further here].

(348) Oh! Children of the Lineage! Pointing out the truth of awakened awareness. Just as the universal ground stays, so awakened awareness also stays.

Commentary A:

A.2.2.2.6.2.2.2.1.1.3 **Through the Lamp of the Signs of Primordial Wisdom, in Addition Recognizing the Signs**

Pointing out the additional signs. For example, after leaving the house, it is like the light of the [house's] fire coming through an open window. In everyone's mind-stream, groundless-ground arises free of conceptual thought as a lucid knowing in the window of the eye [lamps], as a sign of its having arisen in-and-by-itself. (370) This is illustrated like the red light of a fire that guides the way again and again by shining from a window. This is the sign of fire existing inside a house. Similarly, in the window of the eye [lamps], this arises as direct knowing, free of conceptual thought. This is the sign of groundless-ground having arisen through its own self-clarity. What has been pointed out, in addition to the natural state of groundless-ground and awakened awareness itself, are the signs that illustrate a lucid, non-conceptual knowing arising in the window of the eye lamps.

Pointing out the natural state to be like a butter lamp and its flame. The lamp of primordial wisdom, clear-in-itself, is free of the darkness and obscurations of ordinary appearing sense-objects; free of the darkness and obscurations of ordinary conceptual thought; and free of the darkness and obscurations of the illusory body.

[Pointing out] like a lotus. [Just as a lotus emerges from the mud,] you escape from dwelling within the three [kinds of] impure [states, and realize] the raw original purity [of the mind].

[Pointing out] like the sun. What becomes evident is the immense lucid light.

[Pointing out] like a mirror. It is free from the three types of obscurations, like refined gold free of impurities.

[Pointing out] like a crystal ball. Primordial wisdom is transparent and bare.

[Pointing out] like space. Primordial wisdom arises in a manner that is without outside or inside.

Pointing out the ultimate truth of awakened awareness is as follows: [The root text] says, "Just as universal ground stays, so awakened awareness also stays." With respect to the pair, groundless-ground and awakened awareness, it is customary to refer to groundless-ground as associated with emptiness, and awakened awareness as associated with clarity, but there is no difference. In the single interconnected thread [of ultimate reality] both remain as the same.

A.2.2.2.6.2.2.2.1.2 Close-to-the-Heart Instructions

The close-to-the-heart instructions have two parts:

(1) explaining the actuality of the close-to-the-heart instructions, and

(2) showing the fruition of the close-to-the-heart instructions. (371)

Commentary B:

B.2.5.2.2.1.1.3 The Lamp of the Extent of the Signs

Third, the lamp of the extent of the signs has two parts.

B.2.5.2.2.1.1.3.1 Pointing out the Truth of Groundless-ground

First, the root text says, "Oh! Children of the Lineage! Here is pointing out the Lamp of the Extent of the Signs." This refers to pointing out the truth of groundless-ground and awakened awareness. The root text says, "With respect to pointing out the truth of the universal ground, it is like lighting a butter lamp that separates the brightness from the darkness and shadows that had obscured it. It is like discovering a sudden, intensely awake clarity as natural clarity." With respect to what is made known with the metaphor, the meaning is that "in the gateway of the lamp, universal ground is free from any darkness or obscurations whatsoever, wherein primordial wisdom stays as a sudden, intensely awake natural clarity." To know the illusory body, the appearing objects, the conceptual thoughts, and the afflictive emotions, is to know them clearly and nakedly without any obscuration whatsoever. Putting together the meaning of these, in the gateway of the lamp, groundless-ground is like a lotus wherein to know the afflictive emotions of *saṁsāra* and *nirvāṇa* is to know them arising "originally pure and naked...never covered by the stench of the mud." In the gateway of the lamp, groundless-ground is "like the sun," in that there is no karmic activity of causes or conditions or effort whatsoever. "Primordially, it spontaneously arises as immense clear-light." In the gateway of the lamp, groundless-ground is "like a [spotless] mirror...without anything whatsoever obscuring it." No karmic activity whatsoever of causes and conditions occurs. "Self-originating primordial wisdom" shines forth self-evidently, "so that the appearance of every seeming external sense-object shines forth without obscuration." In the gateway of the lamp, groundless-ground is "like a crystal ball" and "primordial wisdom stays stark naked and transparent," free of being covered by the duality of afflictive emotions or conceptual thought. (441) In the gateway of the lamp, groundless-ground is "like space," wherein "primordial wisdom saturates everything, like space without inside and outside."

B.2.5.2.2.1.1.3.2 Pointing out the Truth of Awakened Awareness

Second, the root text says, "Pointing out the truth of awakened awareness. Just as the groundless-ground stays, so awakened awareness also stays." This points out the meaning, namely that groundless-ground and awakened awareness have always been inseparable.

(348) As for the close-to-the-heart instructions on ultimate truth, establish primordial wisdom nakedly, not dressed in the outer garments of discursive thought. Establish raw awakened awareness untainted by hatred and desire or by ordinary conceptual thought. Establish the mind in its own way, free from the dualism of activity/no activity or constructing/not constructing. Establish the mind without chasing after ordinary awareness or thought, and without grasping [sense-objects] with the ordinary sense-mind. Establish the mind in great equanimity, free from its many intrigues. Extend the duration of this natural state until the stream of awakened awareness is [automatic and] without interruption.

Commentary A:

A.2.2.2.6.2.2.2.1.2.1 Explaining the Actuality of the Close-to-the-Heart instructions

The first has two parts:

(1) close-to-the-heart meditation, and

(2) close-to-the-heart view.

A.2.2.2.6.2.2.2.1.2.1.1 Close-to-the-Heart Meditation

[The root text] says, "As for the close-to-the-heart instructions on ultimate truth, establish primordial wisdom nakedly, not dressed in the outer garment of discursive thought. Establish raw awakened awareness untainted by hatred and desire or by ordinary conceptual thought. Establish the mind in its own way, free from the dualism of activity/no activity or constructing/not constructing. Establish the mind without chasing after ordinary awareness or thought, and without grasping [sense-objects] with the ordinary sense-mind. Establish the mind in great equanimity, free from its many intrigues. Extend the duration of this natural state until the stream of awakened awareness is [automatic and] without interruption." This refers to establishing great equanimity in the mind, wherein nothing changes in the sphere of ultimate *bodhicitta*. You take up the meditative experience in such a way that the state is established in-and-by-itself without interruption.

Commentary B:

B.2.5.2.2.1.2 The Close-to-the-Heart Instructions

Second, the close-to-the-heart instructions have three parts:

(1) explaining what kind of close-to-the-heart instructions,

(2) close-to-the-heart instructions about whatever, and

(3) the positive benefit of the close-to-the-heart instructions.

B.2.5.2.2.1.2.1 Explaining What Kind of Close-to-the-Heart Instructions

First, the root text says, "Establish primordial wisdom nakedly, not dressed in the outer garments of discursive thought." Primordial wisdom's awakened awareness is established as naked and bare, free from the covering of conceptual thought. The root text continues, "Establish raw awakened awareness untainted by hatred and desire or by ordinary conceptual thought." Primordial wisdom's awakened awareness is never covered by conceptual thought. It is completely naked, fresh, clean awakened awareness. The root text says, "Establish the mind in its own way, free from the dualism of activity/no activity or constructing/not constructing." This refers to establishing the mind in its own way without construction of emptiness/appearance, permanent/nihilistic, etc. This is to establish it without construction, softly. The root text says, "Establish the mind without chasing after ordinary awareness or thought, and without grasping [sense-objects] with the ordinary sense-mind." Even at the time that ordinary awareness or conceptual thought arises, without changing anything, set it up so that it liberates itself. The root text says, "Establish the mind in great equanimity, free from its many intrigues." This refers to not chasing after the past or future, but setting up the mind in its natural state. The root text continues, "Extend the duration of this natural state until the stream of awakened awareness is [automatic and] without interruption." (442) This means that awakened awareness is without interruption, and the condition of ordinary mindfulness is established as lucidity integrated into the mind-stream.

(348) Being in touch with this stream of awakened awareness in the mind will bury all the falsehoods, such as external/internal, container/ contents, *samsāra/nirvāna*. Get in touch with penetrating everything in the mind that is untrue. Without exception, the close-to-the-the-heart [view is to see everything] that exists as being ultimate *bodhicitta*.

Commentary A:

A.2.2.2.6.2.2.2.1.2.1.2 **Close-to-the-Heart View**

The close-to-the-heart view is as follows: [The root text] says, "Being in touch with this stream of awakened awareness will bury all falsehoods, such as external/internal, container/contents, *saṁsāra/ nirvāṇa*." All distinctions such as external/internal, container/contents, *saṁsāra/ nirvāṇa*, arise from the enlightened intention of *bodhicitta*. Staying [with this view] of the mind, all false distinctions are but the magic display of the mind. Being in touch with [the stream of awakened awareness] enables all to arise as illusions, and to bury all false distinctions. [The root text] continues, "Without exception, the close-to-the-heart [view is to see everything as] ultimate *bodhicitta*. This refers to the close-to-the-heart [view that is to see everything] that exists as being ultimate *bodhicitta*.

Commentary B:

B.2.5.2.2.1.2.2 **Close-to-the-Heart Instructions About Whatever**

Second, close-to-the-heart instructions about whatever. The root text says, "...external/internal, container/contents, *saṁsāra/ nirvāṇa*." These arise unobstructedly from primordial wisdom's liveliness, but when object/subject, external/internal, container/contents are not realized [for what they are], there is *saṁsāra*, and when realized there is only *nirvāṇa*. The root text says, "Get in touch with penetrating everything in the mind that is untrue." Thus, nothing whatsoever arises except for the essence of ultimate truth; whatever is truly so, and what is untrue or false arises as the magical display. It arises as flawless. These mental events never move from the ultimate truth of awakened awareness. The root text says, "Without exception, the close-to-the-heart [view is to see everything] that exists as being ultimate *bodhicitta*." Thus, because everything arises from *bodhicitta*, stays in that state, and is self-liberated in that state, make a decisive determination about this.

(348) Through this view, without the slightest deception by delusion, *Buddhahood* becomes evident.

Commentary A:

A.2.2.2.6.2.2.2.1.2.2 **Showing the Fruition of the Close-to-the-Heart Instructions**

Here are the close-to-the-heart instructions regarding the fruition. If you believe what has been pointed out about the natural state of *bodhicitta*, then you make a clear determination, and confidence [develops in your mind-stream]. [The root text] says, "Through this view, without the slightest deception by delusion, *Buddhahood* becomes evident." (372) No confusion exists about remaining in *saṁsāra*. The aggregates are not gone, but the enlightened intention of *Buddhahood* becomes evident. This is why it is called, "the enlightened intention of *Buddhahood* with respect to the illusory body."

Commentary B:

B.2.5.2.2.1.2.3 The Positive Benefit From the Close-to-the-Heart Instructions

Third, the positive benefit from the close-to-the-heart instructions. The root text says, "Through this view, without the slightest deception by delusion, *Buddhahood* becomes evident." The delusion of appearance is known as false, and false appearances become liberated as mind. Thus, there is no self-deception. By knowing illusory [appearance] as illusory, there is no self-deception. Even self-deception, as it is understood, leads to realization. Through coming [to this realization], whatever appears arises in the expanse. Awakened awareness remains in its own way. There is no mistake about delusion. Directly realizing [everything] as one's own mind, at this moment, *Buddhahood* becomes evident.

(348) Oh! Children of the Lineage! Pointing out that gives special insight [seeing beyond] awakened awareness, the close-to-the-heart instructions on the Enlightened Form-bodies.

Commentary A:

A.2.2.2.6.2.2.2.2 With Respect to Pointing out that Gives Special Insight into Awakened Awareness, the Close-to-the-Heart Instructions of the Enlightened Form-bodies

Pointing out that gives insight into awakened awareness. The close-to-the-heart instructions regarding the enlightened form-body have three parts:

(1) pointing out the three great appearances,

(2) close-to-the-heart instruction regarding the enlightened form-body, and

(3) explaining the secret pith instructions.

A.2.2.2.6.2.2.2.2.1 Pointing out the Three Great Appearances

Pointing out the three great appearances has two parts:

(1) explaining the essential points regarding the body, and

(2) explaining the actuality of what is being pointed out.

Commentary B:

B.2.5.2.2.2 Close-to-the-Heart Instructions on the Enlightened Form-bodies

Second, pointing out the special insight into awakened awareness, the close-to-the-heart instructions on the Enlightened Form-bodies [*gzhugs sku*], has three parts:

(1) pointing out the special insight into awakened awareness,

(2) the close-to-the-heart instructions on the Enlightened Form-bodies, (433) and

(3) the instructions with the authoritative seal.

B.2.5.2.2.2.1 Pointing out the Special Insight into Awakened Awareness

First, has two parts:

(1) the skillful means by which special insight arises, and

(2) whatever arises is pointed out as self-appearing.

The great ocean stirs and moves upwards [i.e., the eye lamps], (349) as does the focus on the domain of space at the fence of darkness [just below the eyebrow boundary].

Commentary A:

A.2.2.2.6.2.2.2.2.1.1 Explaining the Essential Points Regarding the Body

For example, the ordinary body of sentient beings seems to exist pervaded with blood, but until an illustration is made, it does not exist externally. If an illustration were to be made, it would be that what exists is beyond what seems to exist externally. Likewise, the *mandala* of the three-fold embodiment of enlightenment stays as spontaneously present in the mind-stream of each person. Yet, once the many essential points of the ordinary body are nailed, it arises beyond what seems external. The essential points regarding the body are, [as the root text] says, "The great ocean stirs and moves upwards [i.e., to the eye lamps], as does the focus on the domain of space at the fence of darkness [just below the eyebrow boundary]." The ocean refers to the eyes. The view is [looking] into space, moving [the eyes] upwards into space. The iron mountain refers to [the view] at the point just below and between the eyebrows. The view is focusing in this way. The body has the gesture of concentrated evenness, and the view is made without tilting [the head] or modifying it in any way. Until you are familiar with the eyes [gazing in this way], set it up by doing many short sessions. Once very familiar with the eyes [this way], hold the view until you no longer connect yet again with another rebirth.

Commentary B:
B.2.5.2.2.2.1.1 **The Skillful Means by which Special Insight Arises**

First, [The skillful means by which special insight arises]. The root text says, "The great ocean stirs and moves upwards [i.e., the eye lamps]." With respect to mixing together the eyes [toward] the external ocean [of space], and awakened awareness internally, move the eyes upward and turn them higher. Awakened awareness moves into the space like planting a spear. The root text adds, "…as does the focus on the domain of space at the fence of darkness [just below the eyebrow boundary]." The eyes turn upwards, so that the irises of the eyes go under the eyelids and the whites of the eyes [remain showing] turned upwards, and then focus [just below] the eyebrow fence. To show what "focus on the domain of space at the fence of darkness" means, it means to concentrate on the lamp of the seemingly outer surface [of the fluid eye lamps]; focus on the "*A*" in the internal lamp of the [eye] sense-organ, and activate the secret lamp of awakened awareness. Come to know these extensive pith instructions.

(349) Seeing appearance in the darkness as having light, until you see the miraculous display, the matrix of light-rays, like a web or fil-

igree. Light-rays [arise] right within the obscurity of darkness. Come to see the immeasurable light of these clear appearances, like a rainbow in the sky. At the hub of the coiled conch shell [i.e., the location of the central channel in the center of the cranium], ultimate sound arises in the gateway of the sphere of emptiness. From the interior tube [of the channel] comes the secret sound of the half-moon [i.e., the inner ear]. The roar of self-occurring ultimate sound-itself comes forth, the unceasing roar of "*u ru ru*" [generated by primordial wisdom].

Commentary A:

A.2.2.2.6.2.2.2.2.1.2 Explaining the Actuality of What is Being Pointed Out

Explaining the actuality of what is being pointed out is as follows: (373) [The root text] continues, "Seeing appearance in the darkness as having light,[32] until you see the miraculous display, the matrix of light-rays." This refers to seeing the [internally-generated] light-rays as if seeing them in external space. [The text] adds "…like a web or filigree." [The initial visions are also seen] like threads of white silver, or like filaments of white crystal. You see the energy drops appearing like strings of pearls, sometimes like leaves of a tree, like a bowl, like lattice work, like shrubs, etc. All [these are] seen as various reflections [in a mirror]. [The root text] continues, "Light-rays [arise] right within the obscurity of darkness. Come to see the immeasurable light of these clear appearances." This refers to seeing the light right inside the obscuration. When you are very familiar with this view over a long time, [the root text] adds that it appears "like a rainbow in the sky." This refers to the white, red, green, blue, and yellow lights. [The text] continues, "At the hub of the coiled conch shell…ultimate sound arises in the gateway of the sphere of emptiness. From the interior tube [of the channel] comes the secret sound of the half-moon [i.e., the inner ear]. The roar of self-occurring ultimate sound-itself comes forth, the unceasing sound of '*u ru ru*.'" This refers to how the experience of ultimate sound is pointed out. The coiled conch shell refers to part of the brain [the inner ear]. In this region of

---

32. '*od ldan*: "light-like."

the brain, ultimate sound arises in the gateway of emptiness, *dharmadhātu*. Although they have the same root, the two channels divide and project to the gateways of the ear sense-organs. The half-moon refers to the [inner] ear. In the hidden interior of the ear are finger-like branches as the channels differentiate in the innermost area of the ear. The region of the brain refers to where the self-occurring sound of the emptiness of the *dharmadhātu* comes forth unceasingly in the mind-stream, much like the continuous sound of thunder. That's why these three appearances are called "awakened awareness that sees beyond." With respect to the two types of bodies, both Enlightened Form-bodies shine forth.

Commentary B:

B.2.5.2.2.2.1.2 **Whatever Arises is Pointed Out as Self-appearing**

Second, whatever arises is pointed out as self-appearing. The root text says, "Seeing appearance in the darkness as having light." This refers to seeing the objects of appearance, and seeing these appearances in the expanse of space. The root text continues, "…until you see the miraculous display, the matrix of light-rays." This means that through the essential points of the body-points, the gaze, connecting the winds and the mind, etc., you come to see the various [appearances] as impartial self-emitting rays of awakened awareness. The root text says, "Like a web or filigree." Thus, seeing [the initial visions] varies like seeing columns of sun rays, or seeing the spokes of an umbrella, or seeing bright silken filaments. The root text says, "Light-rays right within the obscurity of darkness." This refers to seeing that stays without seeing external appearance or (444) [seeing] inside the veil of skin of the eyes. The root text says, "Come to see the immeasurable light of the clear appearance." This refers to seeing the various appearances as indeterminate—as the self-emitting light of awakened awareness, like a multi-colored offering tent of five lights, the energy drops of the *Buddha*-fields, or as the root text says, "like a rainbow in the sky." This is seeing it like it is. The root text says, "At the hub of the coiled conch shell [i.e., the location of the central channel in the center of the cranium], ultimate sound arises in the gateway of the sphere of emptiness." The central channel resides in the conch shell in the middle of the cranium. Inside that site [you hear] the self-occurring sound of awakened awareness, the sound of emptiness of the *dharmadhātu*; the fresh sound from groundless-ground arises as empty. The text says, "From the interior tube [of the channel] comes the secret sound of the half-moon [i.e., the inner ear]. The roar of self-occurring ultimate sound-itself comes forth." From the interior of the central channel the channel projects to the gateway of the ear sense-organ, like the cross cut of a birch tree [shaped like an ear]. Here comes the unobstructed self-occurring sound-itself of awakened awareness. What is it like? The root text says, "the unceasing roar of '*u ru ru*.'" At this time, the sound arises and becomes unceasing through the instructions on the means of the fingers [closing each ear]. Through these three ways of pointing out sound, it is pointed out as a self-occurring illusion—external sound is pointed out as self-limiting, empty sound; internal sound is pointed out as a sign [resulting from] skillful means and other conditions; and the secret sign is pointed out as the sound-itself of awakened awareness itself. Come to know this detailed explanation.

B.2.5.2.2.2.2 The Close-to-the-Heart Instructions on the Enlightened Form-bodies

Second, the close-to-the-heart instructions on the Enlightened Form-bodies have two parts:

(1) the general explanation, and

(2) the specific explanation.

B.2.5.2.2.2.2.1 The General Explanation

The first [the general explanation] has two parts:

(1) how to take up the meditative experiences like that, and

(2) the way the experience of clear-light arises.

(349) The [seeming ordinary] movement of the sense-mind is subdued by this sound. Conceptual recollection and ordinary mindfulness is held on the light. The three livelinesses of awakened awareness are skillfully trained in the light-rays, and through the purification of these light-rays.

Commentary A:

A.2.2.2.6.2.2.2.2.2 Close-to-the-Heart Instruction Regarding the Enlightened Form-body

The close-to-the-heart instruction regarding the enlightened form-body has two parts: (374)

(1) explaining the close-to-the-heart instructions in general, and

(2) explaining the close-to-the-heart instructions in particular.

A.2.2.2.6.2.2.2.2.2.1 Explaining the Close-to-the-Heart Instructions in General

The first has two parts:

(1) the way to become familiar with the three visions as mind, and

(2) explaining how the *mandala* of the three-fold embodiment of enlightenment shines forth in the mind.

A.2.2.2.6.2.2.2.2.1.1 The Way to Become Familiar with the Three Appearances as Mind

[The root text] says, "The [seeming ordinary] movement of the sense-mind is subdued by this sound. Conceptual recollection and ordinary mindfulness is held on the light. The three livelinesses of awakened awareness are skillfully trained in the light-rays." The signs occur for a person on this path from becoming familiar with the three visions, and once familiar, ultimate sound is the self-sound of the mind, light is the self-light of the mind, and light-rays are the self-rays of the mind.

Commentary B:

B.2.5.2.2.2.2.1.1 How to Take up the Meditative Experiences Like That

First, is [how to take up the meditative experiences like that]. The root text says, "The [seeming ordinary] movement of the sense-mind is subdued in this sound." With respect to the three—sound, light, and light-rays—practice liveliness at one time, (445) and take up the meditative experiences regarding this. Through being shown the essential point, namely becoming familiar with these as self-appearing, the movement of the sense-mind as conceptual thought is self-occurring, and [the realization] is expressed as integrated into the mind-stream. In this self-occurring sound, by focusing one-pointedly, the sense-mind is subdued. The root text says, "Conceptual recollection and ordinary mindfulness is held on the light." Mindful means the mind is held on the light emitted at the moment, and after that. Hold the mind focusing one-pointedly without distraction on the various visions as self-occurring light. The root text says, "The three livelinesses of awakened awareness are skillfully trained in the light-rays." The liveliness of awakened awareness without obscuration is lucid in-itself. Whatever arises as various [appearances] is light-itself and is purified as light-rays. Make the determination using the body points, the gestures, and skillful means, that whenever these three [sound, light, and light-rays] are generated they are generated as momentary clear-light. Meditate on them as self-appearing illusions.

(349) The *mandalas* of the three-fold embodiment of enlightenment self-arises. Because the awakened mind-itself is empty and selfless, they arise as the empty appearances of the miraculous display. Primordial wisdom's self-awakened awareness is formless. Special insight [seeing beyond realizes] the liveliness of awakened awareness as the Enlightened Form-bodies. These arise like a rainbow painting the sky, or like the unfolding of a rainbow-colored silk brocade, or like the reflections arising in a mirror.

Commentary A:

A.2.2.2.6.2.2.2.2.2.1.2 **Explaining how the Maṇḍala of the Three Enlightened Buddha-bodies Shines Forth in the Mind**

Explaining how the *maṇḍala* of the three-fold embodiment of enlightenment shines forth in the mind is as follows: [The root text] says, "The *maṇḍalas* of the three-fold embodiment of enlightenment self-arise." Through the practice of liveliness regarding ultimate sound, light, and light-rays, the *maṇḍala* of the three-fold embodiment of enlightenment shines forth in-and-by-itself. [The root text] continues, "Because the awakened mind-itself is empty and selfless, they arise as the empty appearances of the miraculous display." The awakened mind-itself is empty, without shape or color, yet this miraculous display of emptiness is unobstructed and the appearance of the five wisdom lights shines forth. [The root text] continues, "Primordial wisdom's self-awakened awareness is formless. Special insight [seeing beyond realizes] the liveliness of awakened awareness as the Enlightened Form-bodies." With respect to primordial wisdom's self-awakened awareness, the Enlightened Form-bodies are not something that is made to happen, but shine forth in various forms from practicing seeing beyond, on account of [realizing its] unobstructed liveliness. When it arises just as it is, [the root text adds] it is "like a rainbow painted in the sky." This refers to the five wisdom lights that arise much like a rainbow in the sky, or as the [root text] adds, "…like the unfolding of a rainbow-colored silk brocade." The light-rays shine forth in various ways, much like opening a rainbow-colored silk brocade." [The root text] continues, "…like the reflections arising in a mirror." The enlightened *Buddha*-bodies shine forth as various reflections in a mirror.

Commentary B:
B.2.5.2.2.2.2.1.2 **The Way the Experience of Clear-light Arises**

Second, [The way the experience of clear-light arises]. The root text says, "Through the purification of these light-rays, the *mandalas* of the three-fold embodiment of enlightenment self-arise." Through taking up the meditative experiences like this, the existence of the innate three-fold embodiment of enlightenment directly becomes evident, and their three respective *maṇḍalas* also arise—the *maṇḍala* of the enlightened body appearing as light, the *maṇḍala* of enlightened speech expressed as sound, and the *maṇḍala* of the enlightened heart-mind omnisciently knowing through the [purified] light-rays. The root text says, "Because the awakened mind-itself is empty and selfless, they arise as the empty appearances of the miraculous display. Special insight [seeing beyond realizes] the liveliness of awakened awareness as the Enlightened Form-bodies." Primordial wisdom's self-awakened awareness's (446) original purity is not made into a shape, form, or real attributes, but on the path of liveliness it expresses itself, or, from special insight into the magical display, the forms are empty forms like reflections in a mirror and not at all pervaded by all the conceptual thoughts. The enlightened completion body and the various enlightened emanation bodies arise. If they arise just as they are, they are "like a rainbow painted in the sky." The clarity is unadulterated, brilliant and splendorous, having the quality of light. Whatever arises as various is insubstantial. [As the root text says, it "is like the unfolding of a rainbow-colored silk brocade" whose clarity is beautiful and brilliantly colored. The brightness arises in a multiplicity of ways. [As the root text says], "Like reflections arising in the mirror," these visions arise in clarity without a real nature, and as insubstantial.

B.2.5.2.2.2.2.2 The Specific Explanation

Second, the specific explanation has four parts:

(1) how to take up whatever kind of meditative experiences,

(2) from these experiences how the clear-light of appearance arises,

(3) the close-to-the-heart instructions, and

(4) the positive qualities arising from the final direct appearance.

(349) Explaining the skillful means to practice liveliness is as follows: The golden fish of the moving mind is held captive in a net of light in the darkened chamber. The mirror of thoroughly lucid awakened awareness is shown to the opening space of clear appearances. Recollecting thought and ordinary mindfulness become like a spear that aims at the shield of clear-light appearances.

Commentary A:

A.2.2.2.6.2.2.2.2.2.2 Specific Explanation of the Close-to-the-Heart Instructions

The specific explanation of the close-to-the-heart instructions has three parts:

(1) explaining the practice of liveliness with respect to the three visions,

(2) explaining the specialness of familiarity, and (3) explaining the fruition of the close-to-the-heart instructions.

A.2.2.2.6.2.2.2.2.2.1 Explaining the Practice of Liveliness with Respect to the Three Appearances

[The root text] continues, "Explaining the skillful means to practice liveliness is as follows: The golden fish of the moving mind is held captive in a net of light in the darkened chamber." The movement of all the light-rays is because the eyes set [the visions] in motion, however unstable. These [visions] are set in motion inside of [the region of the gaze just below] the eyebrow [fence] and [the gaze] remains there without moving. [The root text] continues, "The mirror of thoroughly lucid awakened awareness is shown to the opening space of clear appearances." The eyes are illustrated with the metaphor of seeing into space, wherein seemingly external visions shine forth [in this space]. [The root text] continues, "Recollecting thought and ordinary mindfulness becomes like a spear that aims at the shield of clear-light appearance." This refers to the focus of the eyes on whatever [visions appear], and on the directionality of awakened awareness like a steady spear.

Commentary B:

B.2.5.2.2.2.2.2.1 How to Take up Whatever Kind of Meditative Experiences

First, [how to take up whatever kind of meditative experiences]. The root text says, "The golden fish of the moving mind is held captive in the net of light in the darkened chamber." For example, a fish moves in the water [freely] without direction. Relying on a fish net, the fish is held inside the water. Likewise, the movement of the mind's ordinary mindfulness has the support of the body and sense-organs, but when [the movement] is guided by the imprint of the light-rays of awakened awareness, the movement toward sense-objects is without direction [or reference point]. Externally, the essential point of means and path is the house of darkness. Internally, the essential point is that the gaze and [use of the eye] sense-organs purifies this darkness. Secretly, by relying on the self-radiance of the net of light-rays, and grasping [the realization of] that, special insight about clear-light is generated in the mind-stream. (447) Directly pointing out awakened awareness in-itself comes from relying on the six essential points. After practicing and taking up the meditative experiences, the clear-light comes, and you come to know it during [actual] meditation. The root text says, "The mirror of thoroughly lucid awakened awareness is shown to the opening space of clear appearances." For example, it is like holding space as a mirror. Internally, [the appearing visions] are clear and unadulterated, like the reflections of the sun, moon, planets, and stars. This awakened awareness and the eyes are interrelated. Take the lion's gaze and focus on the brightness of space. Externally, [focus on] how seeming appearance arises. Internally, the way [appearance] is generated in meditation is moment-by-moment. In this space, do the three [space-unifying] practices [the space of the sky, the space of the central channel, and the space of the real nature of mind]. This is called "the heart-blood guidance of the *samādhi* of clear visions in space." The root text says, "Recollecting thought and ordinary mindfulness becomes like a spear that aims at the shield of clear-light appearances." For example, an individual who has liveliness is like someone throwing a spear by initially aiming and then throwing the spear straight to the target. Likewise, the victory of awakened awareness comes from concentrating one-pointedly. Concentrate to plant the spear externally on the sphere of the light of the seeming external world, and internally on the spear of light of the [eye] sense-organs. By relying on this lamp and doing the three [space-unifying] practices, you generate the intense means of special insight. This is called "knowing the *samādhi* of the lamp of clarity-in-and-by-itself."

B.2.5.2.2.2.2.2.2 From these Experiences how the Clear-light of Appearance Arises

Second, from these experiences, how the clear-light of appearance arises has two parts:

(1) how the clear-light arises, and

(2) how to develop familiarity through meditative experience.

(349) At that time the seed of the Enlightened Form-bodies is seen. It arises like all the stars in the sky.

Commentary B:

B.2.5.2.2.2.2.2.2.1 How the Clear-light Arises

First, how the clear-light arises. The root text says, "At that time the seed of the Enlightened Form-bodies is seen. It arises like all the stars in the sky." (448) Thus, through taking up the meditative experiences, the seed of the Enlightened Form-bodies and the *Buddha*-fields arise in groundless-ground from the crystal-clear color energy drops of awakened awareness. With respect to daytime appearances, you see so many appearances of the energy drops of the offering tent of the five [rainbow] lights. For example, just as the panorama of stars arises in space, [so many] great and small, more or less, coarse and subtle, etc., [visions] arise in a way that is beyond all reflective thought.

Commentary A:
A.2.2.2.6.2.2.2.2.2.2.2 Explaining the Specialness of Familiarity

Explaining the specialness of familiarity is as follows: According to the root text, "At that time the seed of the Enlightened Form-bodies is seen." Because of taking up the meditation undistractedly, until the visions have become immeasurable and like a continuously flowing river, you will see the [great] energy drop of the basis, the arising of the Enlightened Form-bodies. [The root text] continues, "Like all of the stars in the sky." Like the appearance of innumerable crystals, seeing [the visions] is like all the stars appearing in the sky. The way appearance shines forth is that each of the five wisdoms is made up of piles of energy drops. (376) Because these are viewed as if casting rays of sunlight, you see the five wisdoms as innumerable energy drops. [The root text] continues, "When you are familiar with this and it becomes really familiar, you have the special distinction of the five [signs of familiarization]." This refers to the signs that come from having become acquainted and familiar with [the practice], and through this familiarity the five special signs of familiarity occur.

(349) First, appearances seem to proliferate. They are seen like concentrated and scattered mercury. Second, visions multiply like a wildfire, like the sun or moon shining forth in the space beyond. Awakened awareness is seen as a *mandala* of light. The energy drops are seen like tents of light. Third, the visions become quite extensive. The *mandala* of the sambhogakāya and the five enlightened families are seen. Fourth, the visions become complete. The *mandala* of the gesture [mudra] of spontaneous presence is seen. (350) The [pure] visions are seen as the *Buddha*-fields of light. See-

ing becomes an unshakable miraculous display.

Finally, the ultimate state of the visions shines forth. Light is the naturally arising light of awakened awareness, the way a rainbow arises by itself in empty space. Ultimate sound is the naturally occurring sound of awakened awareness, the way an echo occurs by itself in empty space. Light-rays are the naturally emitting rays of awakened awareness, the way the miraculous display of reflections appears in space. The Enlightened Form-bodies are the naturally-occurring form of awakened awareness, the way the form of the reflection of the moon arises over water.

Commentary A:

According to the text, "First, appearances seem to proliferate." This refers to [the vision of] all the energy drops. [The text] continues, "They are seen like concentrated and scattered mercury." Two connected together, three connected together, many connected together, and so forth. [The text] continues, "[Second], visions spread like a wildfire." The great seal of all the energy drops is, [as the text says], "like the sun or moon shining forth in the space beyond. Awakened awareness is seen as a *mandala* of light." This refers to seeing that is like seeing the eye of a peacock feather. [The text] continues, "The energy drops are seen like tents of light." This refers to seeing [the visions] as stacked up piles of light in the gateways of the eye [lamps]. [The text] says, "Then [third] the visions become quite extensive. The *mandala* of the *sambhogakāya* and the five enlightened *Buddha* families are seen." From the immeasurable energy drops, each of the five *Buddha* families becomes distinguishable. Each appears in a row like a child's smile, and [each has] its own skillful means. [The text] continues, "[Fourth], the visions become complete." Even though there are many energy drops, they become differentiated into each of the five *Buddha* families. Within each of the energy drops, each of the respective five *Buddha* families shines forth. The essence of awakened awareness is a single thread of compassion [extending throughout all existence]. The energy drops stay [stationary] like a string of pearls, and from inside of each of these, each of the five enlightened *Buddha*-bodies shines forth. [The text] continues, "The [pure] visions are seen as the *Buddha*-fields of light." The visions themselves are seen as the five wisdom lights, without [definable] characteristics. [The text] continues, "Seeing becomes an unshakable miraculous display." (377) The essence of awakened awareness is a single thread of compassion that remains unshakable and unwavering.

[The text] continues, "Finally, the ultimate state of the visions shines forth." When the ultimate state of the visions shines forth, they shine forth just as they are. [The text] says, "Light is the naturally arising light of awakened awareness, the way a rainbow arises by itself in empty space. Ultimate sound is the naturally occurring sound of awakened awareness, the way an echo occurs by itself in empty space. Light-rays are the naturally emitting rays of awakened awareness, the way the miraculous display of reflections appears in [empty] space. The Enlightened Form-bodies are the naturally occurring form of awakened awareness, the way the form of the reflection of the moon arises over water." You penetrate all falsehoods regarding appearance, and extinguish all falsehood about the mind. You decisively determine the close-to-the-heart certainty about the Enlightened Form-bodies. This refers to penetrating everything about appearance and extinguishing [all falsehoods] about the mind, as pertains to the three—ultimate sound, light and rays; the three enlightened *Buddha*-bodies; and the reflections [of the visions]. According to the close-to-the-heart instructions, all these are determined to be ultimate *bodhicitta*.

Commentary B:

B.2.5.2.2.2.2.2.2.2 How to Develop Familiarity Through Meditative Experience

Second, how to develop familiarity through meditative experience. The root text says, "When you are familiar with this and it becomes really familiar, you have the special distinction of the five [signs of familiarization]." Through taking up the meditative experiences on these appearances without distraction, becoming familiar with these in an unchanging way, and then becoming really familiar with these, you separate the dregs from the brightness of awakened awareness. Externally, through meditation, the appearance of clear-light visions comes, and internally, the original purity of awakened awareness and its lucidity increases. Then the five signs of the manner of arising directly become evident:

(1) the meditative experience of proliferating visions,

(2) the meditative experiences of multiplying visions,

(3) the meditative experience of quite extensive visions,

(4) the meditative experience of the completion of the visions, and

(5) the meditative experiences of the ultimate state of the visions.

(350) First, appearances seem to proliferate. They are seen like concentrated and scattered mercury.

Commentary B:

B.2.5.2.2.2.2.2.2.2.1 **The Meditative Experience of Proliferating Visions**

First, the root text says, "First, appearances seem to proliferate. They are seen like concentrated and scattered mercury." As described previously, practice the liveliness of awakened awareness of these visions undistractedly, and through taking up the meditative experiences, in the state of clear-light, these are merely grains of crystal-clear colored energy drops of awakened awareness. You encounter many of these—encountering two, encountering three, encountering many that appear, the heart-essence of awakened awareness, mere grains of energy drops, like filaments of energy drops, or silver-white threads, or filaments of white silk. (449) They stay like a string of very small grains. In the midst of these energy drops, the coarse types of enlightened *Buddha*-bodies are just projections and there they reside in a subtle way. At that time, these visions are like a waterfall gushing from a mountain, or like drops of water not staying but scattering or coming together. They arise and cease, scatter and come together, move and become agitated. Internally, too, there is occasionally the meditative experience of subtle one-pointedness, but since [the visions both] increase or decrease, there is likely to be doubt about the visions.

(350) Second, visions multiply like a wildfire, like the sun or moon

shining forth in the space beyond. Awakened awareness is seen as a *mandala* of light. The energy drops are seen like tents of light.

Commentary B:

B.2.5.2.2.2.2.2.2.2.2 The Meditative Experience of Multiplying Visions

Second, the meditative experience of multiplying visions. The root text says, "Second, visions multiply like a wildfire, like the sun or moon shining forth in the space beyond. Awakened awareness is seen as a *mandala* of light. The energy drops are seen like tents of light." These are viewed as mentioned previously. Take up the meditative experiences without distraction until integrating them into your mind-stream, and the clear-light of awakened awareness directly manifests itself. At that time, the lucid self-radiance of the *maṇḍala* of light, the essence of self-awakened awareness, is made clear, having a brilliance that is never obstructed. The external and internal body is made clear—the flesh, blood, muscles, wind channels, sense-organs, sense-supports—and become the unobstructed vessel of truth. These visions of clear-light arise externally everywhere in all directions and internally without obscuration. In these fields, the visions of white energy drops arise; the chain of energy drops surrounded by the offering tent of five [wisdom] lights arise; lucid, clear, and bright light-rays emanate; or a chain of three energy drops about the size of a bronze dish; an offering tent of energy drops like peacock eggs, and so forth. They arise more slowly and gently than before, and appear more stable for a moment. In the midst of this, a very subtle enlightened *Buddha*-body, (450) just the size of a very small grain, emerges for a little bit with just the slightest clarity. A white chain of energy drops and various colored energy drops also arise like light-rays. Internally, through the strength of the clarity of the practitioner's realization, these do not proliferate but become liberated in-and-by-themselves.

(350) Third, the visions become quite extensive. The *mandala* of the *sambhogakāya* and the five enlightened families are seen.

Commentary B:

B.2.5.2.2.2.2.2.2.2.3 The Meditative Experience of Quite Extensive Visions

Third, the meditative experience of quite extensive visions. The root text says, "Third, the visions become quite extensive. The *maṇḍala* of the *sambhogakāya* and the five enlightened families are seen." This refers to the direct manifestation of the most excellent clear-light arising just as it is. Through becoming familiar with awakened awareness and then becoming quite familiar, the impure and deluded visions cease through stopping the [elements] fire, water, earth, and wind, and the visions of the pure enlightened *Buddha*-bodies and *Buddha*-fields arise. The energy drops of the five [wisdom] lights are like building a tent of yak wool. These arise very slow and stably, and are not pervaded by even the smallest particle of reflective thought, however great or small. Then, the rows of each of the five multi-colored lights arise and the way each emerges becomes differentiated, like a lotus of light, or a *maṇḍala* of light made clear in each of the main directions, or the five lights of original purity rotating on the outer rim. Each gateway has its respective ornaments. Various filaments of light-rays spread from each gateway. These arise without the greatest or smallest pervasion of reflective thought linking them together, and in the center, each of the five *Buddha* families with their respective colors and ornaments arise, however complete or incomplete. Internally, by becoming familiar with one-pointed meditation on this, the objects known internally, all of *saṁsāra* and *nirvāṇa*, become the same taste of [ultimate] *bodhicitta*.

(350) Fourth, the visions become complete. The *mandala* of the gesture [mudra] of spontaneous presence is seen. The [pure] visions are seen as the *Buddha*-fields of light. Seeing becomes an unshakable miraculous display.

Commentary B:

B.2.5.2.2.2.2.2.2.2.4 The Meditative Experience of the Completion of the Visions

Fourth, the meditative experience of the completion of the visions. (451) The root text says, "The visions become complete. The *maṇḍala* of the gesture [*mudra*] of spontaneous presence is seen. The [pure] visions are seen as the *Buddha*-fields of light. Seeing becomes an unshakable miraculous display." Thus, the pure visions arise. Being purified by the liveliness of primordial wisdom's awakened awareness, the impure five aggregates become pure by leaving them in their own way and arise as the five deities. Having separated the pure elements from the dregs, seemingly real external appearances, when left in their own way, become pure and become directly manifest as the three-fold embodiment of enlightenment, and all the *Buddha*-fields exist in themselves as spontaneously present. Internally, these pure visions appearing by themselves arise impartially in three ways—externally, internally, and secretly—in the immeasurable *maṇḍala*, along with their thrones and their mansions. Externally, internally, and secretly, emanating from the five principal *Buddha* families, many visions arise. Whatever arises, the *sambhogakāya* and the *nirmāṇakāyas*, everything, [arises as] the ornaments, the throne, the major characteristics, the minor characteristics, all possessed with the three certainties, and emanate light-rays in the ten directions with immovable clarity. This is seeing immovably. Internally, these occurrences merely arise without meditation, without distraction, wherein the movement of the mind toward effortful thought of an object of meditation and an act of meditation is liberated.

(350) Finally, the ultimate state of the visions shines forth. Light is the naturally arising light of awakened awareness, the way a rainbow arises by itself in empty space. Ultimate sound is the naturally occurring sound of awakened awareness, the way an echo occurs by itself in empty space. Light-rays are the naturally emitting rays of awakened awareness, the way the miraculous display of reflections appears in space. The Enlightened Form-bodies are the naturally-occurring form of awakened awareness, the way the form of the reflection of the moon arises over water.

Commentary B:

B.2.5.2.2.2.2.2.2.2.5 The Meditative Experiences of the Ultimate State of the Visions

Five, the meditative experiences of the ultimate state of the visions. The root text says, "Finally, the ultimate state of the visions shines forth.

Light is the naturally arising light of awakened awareness, the way a rainbow arises by itself in empty space." Thus, the aggregates [of the physical body] having outflows and the enlightened *Buddha*-bodies and *Buddha*-fields without outflows arise. They arise as the liveliness of primordial wisdom's self-awakened awareness. Know this pure miraculous display of self-appearance. (452) The light is self-light like a rainbow. The sound is the self-sound like an echo. The light-rays are the self-rays like the rays of the sun. Form is self-form like reflections arising in a mirror. This brings the three visions to their ultimate end. This ends the close-to-the-heart instructions. What is to be purified has been purified. What is to be realized has been realized. There is liberation from the ordinary body and mind as the primordial wisdom of the enlightened body of the deity [of the *maṇḍala*]. Primordial wisdom's self-awakened awareness directly becomes manifest as the original purity and stainlessness of the *dharmadhātu*. By leaving awakened awareness in its own way, the *dharmakāya* becomes manifest. By attaining the arising of the *dharmakāya*, with [all] its unobstructed positive qualities and the *Buddha*-fields, and the two Enlightened Form-bodies, the three-fold embodiment of enlightenment becomes directly manifest. Awakened awareness is left in its own way. Deluded appearance is purified as mind. Delusion comes to its ultimate end. Ordinary mindful thought is liberated in its own way. Afflictive emotions arise as primordial wisdom. *Buddhahood* is attained and firmly implanted. Non-meditation becomes a state free of all distraction, and without grasping at conceptual thought. Non-meditation remains integrated into one's mind-stream. The ultimate end of the path is reached and the fruition directly manifests itself. This is why it is called "the ultimate state of the visions."

(350) [In this series of experiences/realizations] you penetrate all falsehoods regarding appearance and extinguish all falsehoods about the mind. You decisively determine the close-to-the-heart certainty about the Enlightened Form-bodies.

Commentary B:

B.2.5.2.2.2.2.3 **The Manner of the Close-to-the-Heart Instructions**

Third, the manner of the close-to-the-heart instructions. The root text says, "You penetrate all falsehoods regarding appearance and extinguish all falsehood about the mind." Because the magical display of the mind arises as the three—sound, light, and light-rays—you determine all these to be mind. The root text says, "You decisively determine the close-to-the-heart certainty about the Enlightened Form-bodies." The *sambhogakāya*, the *nirmāṇakāyas*, and the *Buddha*-fields, very much arise. Through the arising of primordial wisdom's self-awakened awareness, you make the determination that [all appearances] are mind.

(350) By penetrating and cutting through [all] delusion, delusion no longer exists. At this very moment the three-fold embodiment of enlightenment becomes evident [and stable], such that coming under the influence of the causes and effects of karma is [seen as] a great delusion.

Commentary A:

A.2.2.2.6.2.2.2.2.2.3 **Explaining the Fruition of the Close-to-the-Heart Instructions**

Explaining the fruition of the close-to-the-heart instructions according to the root text: "By penetrating and cutting through [all] delusion, delusion no longer exists. At this very moment the three-fold embodiment of enlightenment becomes evident [and stable]." There are conditions which make the three—ultimate sound, light, and light-rays—confused, so make a determination with the close-to-the-heart instructions that these three [visions] are mind. Now, even if you remain in *saṁsāra* delusion does not exist. For example, with respect to an illusion, if you know it [*saṁsāra*] as an illusion, this illusion does not deceive. With respect to a rainbow, if you know it to be without inherent nature, you don't chase after it. With respect to form-itself, if you know it as form-itself, you do not grasp it as some other [seemingly real] form. By making such a definitive determination, the aggregates [of the physical body nevertheless] are not discarded. (378)

(350) These [by-passing instructions] are the intense skillful means to enlightenment. These are the ultimate teachings for reaching

the end. They are the medicine for getting the [completely] purified [state of [enlightenment]. They are poison to those shrouded in ignorance.

(350) Therefore, these teachings are not taught to everyone and remain secret and hidden. For those with fortunate karma, these teachings are like pouring the white milk of a lioness into a bowl [for her lion cubs]. Those with less fortunate karma do not have the [proper] vessel. For them these teachings are like throwing a precious jewel into the mouth of a river crocodile. Yet, for thousands of eons these teachings can never be lost.

Commentary A:
A.2.2.2.6.2.2.2.2.3 **Explaining the Secret Pith Instructions**

To explain the secret pith instructions the root text says, "Coming under the influence of the causes and effects of karma is great delusion. These [by-passing instructions] are the intense skillful means to enlightenment." These instructions have been explained previously. When realized, all the causes and effects of karma are swept away and full *Buddhahood* is completed in a single instant. [The root text] continues, "These are the ultimate teachings for reaching the end. They are the medicine for getting the [completely] purified [state of enlightenment]. They are the poison for those shrouded in ignorance." These instructions are the plan for fortunate ones. For those less fortunate, they become poison. [The root text] continues, "For those with fortunate karma, these secret teachings are like pouring the white milk of a lioness into a bowl [for her lion cubs]." In general, these teachings are unequalled. There is nothing higher. They are uncommon and extraordinary. Much like the milk of a lioness, a common vessel cannot withstand them. [The root text] continues, "Those less fortunate do not have the [proper] vessel. For them these teachings are like throwing a precious jewel into the mouth of a river crocodile. Yet, for thousands of eons these teachings can never be lost." These teachings are very secret.

Commentary B:

B.2.5.2.2.2.2.4 The Positive Qualities that Directly Become Manifest

Fourth, the positive qualities that directly become manifest. The root text says, "By penetrating and cutting through [all] delusion, delusion no longer exists." You penetrate all conditions [supporting] delusion as self-appearance. (453) It is taught that it is impossible for delusion to exist. The root text says, "At this very moment, the three-fold embodiment of enlightenment becomes evident [and stable]." Through being recognized in-and-by-itself, the dharmakāya directly becomes evident. The Buddha-fields directly become evident. The enlightened emanations that subdue whatever various [delusions], and the two Enlightened Form-bodies, directly become evident. At this very time, the three-fold embodiment of enlightenment [becomes evident], [and deluded perception] comes to the end in its own way.

The root text says, "Coming under the influence of the causes and effects of karma is [seen as] a great delusion. These [by-passing instructions] are the intense skillful means to enlightenment." After that, all the [delusion] that has accumulated for incalculable eons becomes purified on this path, and one aspires [that all others attain] *Buddhahood*. This completes the conventional truth and indirect enlightened intention [of the *Buddha*], namely, from this, all obscurations [in all beings] become purified at once, and the causes and effects of delusion are released by these skillful means. By having recognized the innate existence of the three-fold embodiment of enlightenment in-and-by-itself, at this very time, *Buddhahood* becomes directly evident. This is why the intense means to reach the ultimate state, the definitive truth of *Buddhahood*, is taught.

B.2.5.2.2.2.3 The Instructions with the Authoritative Seal

Third, the instructions with the authoritative seal. The root text says, "These are the ultimate teachings for reaching the end." This refers to the fact that these instructions penetrate the profound essential points to reach the end of all vehicles. The root text says, "They are the medicine for getting the [completely] purified [state of enlightenment]." With respect to the proliferation of past karma, if the meaning [of these instructions] is explained, they become the medicine for attaining the [final] realization all at once. The root text says, "They are poison to those shrouded in ignorance." If they are taught to such individuals, they fail to develop the realization and turn away from them. They become the poison that binds them henceforth. The root text says, "Therefore, these teachings are not taught to everyone and remain secret and hidden. For those with fortunate karma, these teachings are like pouring the white milk of a lioness into a bowl [for her lion cubs]. Those with (454) less fortunate karma do not have the [proper] vessel. For them these teachings are like throwing a precious jewel into the mouth of a river crocodile. Yet, for thousands of eons these teachings can never be lost."

(350) This completes the Lamp of Pointing Out the *Buddha*-fields.

Samaya!

Commentary A:

A.2.2.2.6.3 **A Brief Summary**

As for the brief summary, the extensive explanation will do. [The text] concludes, "*Samaya!*" This completes the commentary on the fifth lamp.

Commentary B:

B.2.5.3 **The Conclusion**

Third, the conclusion. The root text says, "This completes the Lamp of Pointing Out the *Buddha*-fields. *Samaya!*" This means that for those who have not built the proper vessel, plant the secret authoritative seal [on these teachings]. This completes the commentary on the fifth lamp.

(6) The Lamp of the After-Death States

Sixth, The lamp of the after-death states has three parts:

(1) the teaching,

(2) the extended explanation, and (3) the conclusion.

(350) Homage to the *Buddha* Kun tu bZang po, who is the manifest *Buddha* of self-awakened awareness.

Commentary A:

A.2.2.2.7 The Lamp of the After-Death States

The ultimate truth of the lamp of the after-death states has three parts—homage, extended explanation, and brief summary.

A.2.2.2.7.1 Homage

Here is the explanation of the homage. [The root text] says, "Homage to Kun tu bZang po, who is the manifest *Buddha* of self-awakened awareness." This homage is about how the teachings from Kun tu bZang po, through the realization of self-awakened awareness, leads to *Buddhahood*. It is pointed out that awakened awareness knows itself and brings the victory [of *Buddhahood*] to itself [through its own intelligence]. Making a definitive determination [about awakened awareness] develops the belief [that it is always right here], and then to the assurance [that it can't be lost]. (379) [Then, based in that confidence,] the text explains that there is no after-death state but instead the manifestation of *Buddhahood*.

A.2.2.2.7.2 An Extensive Explanation

The extensive explanation has three parts—the brief, extended, and summary.

(350) Oh! Children of the Lineage! Here are the essential points on the lamp of the after-death states that show the way to encounter the crossroad between delusion and realization.

Commentary A:

A.2.2.2.7.2.1 A Brief Overview

[The root text begins], "Oh! Children of the Lineage! Here are the essential points on the lamp of the after-death states that show the way to encounter the crossroad between delusion and realization." These teachings are called "the essential points on how *saṁsāra* and *nirvāṇa* become divided:

(1) how the mind separates from the aggregates and the ordinary body,

(2) how liberation comes from the realization, and

(3) how delusion ensues when there is no realization." This passage is a brief summary of the teachings.

A.2.2.2.7.2.2 An Extended Explanation

Explaining the meaning in an extended way has three parts:

(1) how the mind separates from the aggregates and the ordinary body,

(2) how liberation comes from the realization, and

(3) how delusion ensues when there is no realization." This passage is a brief summary of the teachings.

Commentary B:
B.2.6.1 The Teaching

First, [the teaching]. The root text says, "Homage to the Buddha Kun tu bZangpo, who is the manifest *Buddha* of self-awakened awareness." This refers to those who have made the decisive and definitive determination that Kun tu bZang po is one's own mind, and who have become confident about this, so that they are said to become *Buddhas* without [cycling through] the after-death states. The root text says, "Oh! Children of the Lineage! Here are the essential points on the lamp of the after-death states." At the time of death when the mind separates from the body, all at once the body becomes an illusion. The mind becomes separated from the covering of obscuration by conceptual thought, and what appears to the senses are the groundless-ground and awakened awareness, [appearing] like the sun free of darkness, or like the sky free of clouds. This lamp arises without the covering of obscurations. The root text continues, "...that show the way to encounter the cross-road between delusion and realization." This refers to the fact that in the after-death states you encounter the crossroad to both the deluded realms of *saṁsāra* and the realization of Buddhahood. The root text continues, "These teachings are called 'the essential points on how *saṁsāra* and *nirvāṇa* become divided.'" This means that by acting with realization or without realization in the after-death state, *saṁsāra* and *nirvāṇa* respectively become separated or not.

(350) These teachings are called "the essential points on how *samsāra* and *nirvāna* become divided:"

(1) how the mind separates from the aggregates and the ordinary body,

(2) how liberation comes from the realization, and

(3) how delusion ensues when there is no realization.

Commentary B:

B.2.6.2 The Extended Explanation

Second, the extended explanation has three parts:

(1) how the mind separates from the aggregates and the ordinary body,

(2) an explanation (455) as to how the realization leads to liberation, and

(3) an explanation as to how delusion comes from being without realization.

1. There are two parts to the way the mind separates from the body:

(1) how the elements dissolve, and

(2) how the elements are absorbed.

(351) First, there are the teachings on how the elements dissolve, [and their relationship with the five vital organs at the time of death].

Commentary A:

A.2.2.2.7.2.2.1 How the Mind Separates from the Aggregates and the Ordinary Body

How the mind separates from the body has three parts:

(1) how the elements dissolve,

(2) how the elements are absorbed, and

(3) firmly establishing these teachings via the special essential points.

Commentary B:

B.2.6.2.1 **How the Mind Separates from the Aggregates and the Ordinary Body**

The first, [how the mind separates from the aggregates and the ordinary body], has two parts, as the root text says:

"(1) how the elements dissolve, and

(2) how the elements are absorbed.

(351) First, the earth element and its association with the constituents of the spleen dissolves and you lose body sensation. You can't hold up the left hand/arm without it falling, and an outflow [of fluid] begins from the nine orifices. Second, the water element and its association with the constituents of the kidneys dissolves and the ears no longer hear sound. You can't lift the left foot/leg. You no longer know how to control urination. Third, the fire element and its association with the constituents of the liver dissolves and the tongue loses taste sensation. You can't elevate the right hand/arm. Blood congeals in the nose. Fourth, the wind element and its association with the constituents of the lungs dissolves and the nose loses smell sensations. You can't lift the right foot/leg. Control over feces slips away. Fifth, the space element and its association with the constituents of the heart dissolves and the eyes no longer see forms. You can no longer lift the head. The secret wind drop slips away.

Commentary A:

A.2.2.2.7.2.2.1.1 **How the Elements Dissolve**

[The root text] says, "These are the teachings on how the elements dissolve." At the time [of conception] when the aggregates and sense-organs are just developing from above, the wind element comes from the space element, fire from wind, water from fire, and earth from water. At the time of dissolution [when dying in this realm] below, [the order is reversed] in that at first the earth element dissolves, then the water element dissolves, then the fire element dissolves, then the wind element dissolves, and finally the space element dissolves. With respect to the signs that the five elements are dissolving, the five vital organs degenerate. With respect to the five sense-organs, the five respective sense-objects become unclear. The five ancillary wind channels degenerate. The strength of the body is lost. The five vessels degenerate. There is a loss of control over the five outflows, which leak by themselves.

Commentary B:
B.2.6.2.1.1 The Teachings on How the Elements Dissolve

First, there are the teachings on "how the elements dissolve" [according to the root text]. When it happens that the four elements of the aggregates become absorbed, it begins with the space element. From space, the wind element; from wind, the fire element; from fire, the water element; from water, the earth element ends up becoming absorbed, and then it begins with the elements dissolving. First, earth, and from that water, and from that fire, and from that wind, and from that space dissolves. Then, with these five elements having dissolved, which internally served as a basis of support, the five vital organs degenerate. Externally, the five objects of sense-systems become unclear, and the interconnection between the five limbs degenerates, and [the limbs] lose their strength. As a result, the five vessels degenerate and the five outflows (e.g. desire, hatred, ignorance, view, and becoming) go their own way and are lost. If each of these were broken down into specifics, as the root text says, "First, the earth element and its association with the constituents of the spleen dissolves and you lose body sensation." Internally, the constituents of the earth element serve as the basis of support for the spleen. Externally, there are no longer any rough or subtle sensations coming from the body sense-organ. The root text says, "You can't hold up the left hand/arm without it falling and an outflow [of fluid] begins from the nine orifices." The once interconnected left branch wind channels from the spleen become separated. The outflows from the doors of the mouth and nose sense-organs leak out, as water from the mouth, and water from the nose. The root text says, "Second, the water element and its association with the constituents of the kidneys dissolves and the ears no longer hear sound. You can't lift the left foot/leg. You no longer know how to control urination." Internally, the constituents of the water element serve as the basis support for the kidneys. Externally, the ear sense-organ no longer hears sound. The once interconnected left branch wind channels from the kidneys become separated and you can't move your left leg. (456) As a result, control of urination is lost. The root text continues, "Third, the fire element and its association with the constituents of the liver dissolves, and the tongue loses taste sensation. You can't elevate the right hand/arm. Blood congeals in the nose." Internally, the constituents of the fire element serve as the basis of support for the liver. Externally, the tongue sense-organ no longer can taste. The once interconnected right branch wind channels from the liver become separated and you can't elevate the right arm. As a result you no longer control blood leaking from the nose. The root text says, "Fourth, the wind element and its association with the constituents of the lungs dissolves, and the nose loses smell sensations. You can't lift the right foot/leg. Control over feces slips away." Internally, the constituents of the wind element serve as the basis of support for the lungs. Externally, the nose sense-organ can no longer smell. The once interconnected right branch wind channels from the lungs become separated and you can't lift the right leg. As a result, you no longer control feces [and become incontinent]. The root text says, "Fifth, the space element and its association with the constituents of the heart dissolves, and the eyes no longer see forms. You can no longer lift the head. The secret wind drop [*gsang bar thig le*] slips away." Internally, the constituents of the space element serve as the basis of support for the heart. Externally, the eye sense-organ can no longer see visual forms. The once interconnected wind channels of the head and heart in this space become separated and you can no longer move your head. As a result, you no longer control the secret wind drops.

Commentary A:

A.2.2.2.7.2.2.1.2 **How the Elements are Absorbed**

The way the elements are absorbed is as follows:

[The root text says], "As the earth element is absorbed into the water element, (380) the strength of the body slips away." It is like sinking into the earth, weighted down by gold or a rock. The internal sign is that appearances that arise are like a mirage. Such appearances hold no support by the earth element and as such occur like self-deceptions.

[The root text says], "As the water element is absorbed into the fire element, the luster of the body [surface] slips away." The mouth becomes dry and there is intense dryness. The internal sign is that appearances arise like the early dawn. Such appearances are seen as more and more misty.

[The root text says], "As the fire element is absorbed into the wind element, the warmth of the body slips away." Ordinary consciousness becomes impermanent and well-being flashes on and off until becoming merely a faint glimmer, and this confused consciousness moves more and more into the vase.

[The root text says], "As the wind element is absorbed into the mind element, the [external cycle of the] breath is absorbed into the universal ground…" and there is no ordinary consciousness. The eyes roll up and turn back. The internal signs are that the breath stops moving, like a flame of a butter lamp [no longer flickering in the wind], and the states of non-conceptual stillness and bliss arise simultaneously.

[The root text says], "The mind [of ordinary consciousness] is absorbed into the universal ground as the breath [completely] ceases." The internal sign is that the external breath completely stops, but the internal breath has not completely stopped yet, and remains as a support to [subtle] momentary consciousness. Appearances arise like a cloudless sky. Because the stream of ordinary thought has been cut off, non-conceptual primordial wisdom arises, emptiness/clarity, not covered by any obscurations. This is why it is called "the after-death state of primordial wisdom." When the best masters are able to recognize [primordial wisdom] at this point [in the dying process], they become *Buddhas*. Ordinary people never come to recognize the vivid clarity of the *dharmadhātu* [at this point in the dying process].

Commentary B:

B.2.6.2.1.2 **The Way the Elements are Absorbed**

Second, is the explanation of absorption of the elements. The root text says, "As the earth element is absorbed into the water element, the strength of the body slips away." As a sign of its [the earth element] merging into the water element, the strength of the navel *chakra* wanes. The strength of the body is lost and the body becomes heavy. The [loss of] the earth element also makes the mind sink. Appearances in themselves become like a mirage. The pure essence of the earth element arises as a yellow light. The yellow light appears, and then dissolves on the path. The root text says, "Then, as the water element is absorbed into the fire element, the luster of the body [surface] goes." (457) The water element of the secrete *chakra* dissolves as a sign of its merging into the fire element. The mouth and nose become dry and the luster of the body is lost. A blue light appears on the path like the dawn. The root text says, "As the fire element is absorbed into the wind element, the warmth of the body slips away." The body's warmth comes to an end and speech becomes unintelligible. A red light appears over and over on the path like fireflies. The root text says, "As the wind element is absorbed into the mind element, the [external cycle of the] breath comes to an end and is given up." Unable to breathe, you grasp for something solid. The breath comes to an end, there is no [ordinary] consciousness left, and the eyes turn upward. A red-green appears over and over on the path like lightning flashes. The root text says, "The mind [of ordinary consciousness] is absorbed into the universal ground as the breath [completely] ceases, and body and mind separate." Darkness obliterates everything and the eyes blankly stare. The breath crackles [with the death rattle] and then ceases. A white light appears in bright space, dawning on the path like a whitish moon rising. After that the external breath stops. Externally, the six sense-consciousnesses stop. The sense-organs internally still move. The internal [subtle] breath does not stop. The previous consciousness becomes seven times more lucid and bright. Emptiness/lucidity arises without being covered by any obscurations. This is called "the after-death state of primordial wisdom." At that time, the best practitioners generate confidence about their realization. Middling practitioners generate radiance from meditating, holding their mindfulness. Lesser practitioners penetrate the essential point by generating the *samādhi* of the deities in their meditation, and by generating admiration, respect, compassion, etc. (458) One points this out in oneself and holds [the realization] in its own way.

(351) At the time of being in the jaws of death, there is [the opportunity] to eradicate the teeth of [distinctions like] pleasant/unpleasant. By such thinking there is great power to being propelled

by [either] good or bad [karmic ripening], [therefore] firmly plant the instructions in accordance with the vessel and capacity [of the practitioner] so there will be no delusion.

Commentary A:

The intermediate states between birth and death are where the mother and son meet. The root text says, "At the time of being in the jaws of death, there is [the opportunity] to eradicate the teeth of [distinctions like] pleasant/unpleasant." Happiness initially attained and remaining finally ends up in downfall in that it turns bad. The teeth of these distinctions are only eradicated at the time of death when the mind separates from the body. The root text says, "By such thinking there is great power to being propelled by [either] good or bad [karmic ripening]." At this time, acting by thinking good/bad makes you remain at that level, and there is also great power to being propelled by distinctions like superior/inferior. Therefore, it is very important to have thoughts that are firmly in compliance with the instructions. The root text says, "Firmly plant the instructions in accordance with the vessel and capacity [of the practitioner]." This refers to firmly planting the instructions to connect with the three [levels of mastery]—best, middling, and lesser [capacity]. Using the pith instructions, come to know this nakedly. [Using] both, know how to attain liberation from the realization. As the root text says, "Oh! Children of the Lineage! The way that liberation comes following the realization comes according to three capacities—best, middling, and lesser capacity."

Commentary A:

A.2.2.2.7.2.2.1.3 Firmly Establishing these Teachings via the Special Essential Points

[The root text] says, "At the time of being in the jaws of death (381) there is [the opportunity] to eradicate the teeth of [distinctions] like pleasant/unpleasant...but there is still a very strong tendency [to make distinctions] about good/bad recollections." This means that while in the jaws of death [during the dying process], you can attain liberation and subdue the teeth of wandering in the lower realms of *saṁsāra*, yet there remains a very great tendency to make distinctions between good and bad recollections. Those individuals who have practiced virtue, at the time of being in the jaws of death resist the tendency of the mind toward such recollections, and in so doing, because of their virtue, are not impelled into bad rebirths. However, those individuals who have practiced non-virtue, at the time of the jaws of death tend toward good recollections, but because of their non-virtue are not impelled into good rebirths. [The root text] says, "Firmly plant the instructions in accordance with the vessel and capacity [of the practitioner], so there will be no delusion." This means that at the time of death those individuals who have become firmly established, so as to have at least some measure of intellectual understanding of these instructions, are likely to make a connection [during the dying process] with the pith instructions of the Great Vehicle, which point out appearance as illusory; the instructions on immeasurable compassion that leads beyond all attachment and desire; the practice of taking refuge with trust, admiration, and respect; the skillful means of the non-ordinary *Buddhas* on consciousness-transference; and the devotional prayers that move beyond all hope of gain or fear of failure.

(351) Oh! Children of the Lineage!

1. The way that liberation comes following realization comes according to three capacities—best, middling, and lesser capacity.

Commentary A:

A.2.2.2.7.2.2.2 How Liberation Comes from the Realization [According to Capacity]

The explanation of how liberation comes from the realization pertains to the three capacities. [The root text] says, "Oh! Children of the Lineage! The way liberation comes from the realization comes according to three capacities—best, middling, and lesser capacity." This means that there are three ways liberation comes: the way for the masters, those of great capacity; the way liberation comes for those of middling capacity; and the way liberation comes for those of lesser capacity.

Commentary B:

B.2.6.2.2 How Realization Leads to Liberation

(351) First, those of highest capacity are like a garuda hatching or a lion cub. Having brought to completion the three livelinesses [rays, light, and ultimate sound], at the right moment as the mind separates from its close association with the body, it is possible to distinguish the brightness from the dregs with respect to the [five] elements so that the very depths of *saṁsāra* are shaken up, and delusion becomes self-purified. In the expanse of universal ground, like infinite space without any boundaries, primordial wisdom's awakened awareness arises, pervades and spreads everywhere like the sun. The magical display of the three-fold embodiment of enlightenment shines forth inexhaustibly like the rays of the sun, (352) and there is an unceasing gesture toward the benefit of sentient beings.

Commentary A:

A.2.2.2.7.2.2.2.1 Those of Great Capacity

[The root text] says, "First, those of highest capacity are like a hatching garuda or a lion cub. Having brought to completion the three livelinesses [rays, light, and ultimate sound], as soon as the mind separates from its close association with the body, it is possible to distinguish the brightness from the dregs with respect to the [five] elements." This refers to how all the impure elements become absorbed into the condition of the brightness of primordial wisdom and the *Buddha*-bodies. [The text] continues, "...so that the very depths of *saṁsāra* are shaken up, and delusion becomes self-purified." Out from under the aggregates, primordial wisdom comes forth upon completing [the practice] of liveliness, and as a result there isn't even the name of *saṁsāra* left, and the three-fold embodiment of enlightenment and *Buddhahood* becomes evident. When this increases, "universal ground, like infinite space without any boundaries, primordial wisdom's awakened awareness arises, pervades, and spreads everywhere like the sun. The magical display of the three-fold embodiment of enlightenment shines forth inexhaustibly like the rays of the sun, and there is an unceasing gesture toward the benefit of sentient beings."

Commentary B:
B.2.6.2.2.1 Those of Highest Capacity

First, the way liberation comes for those of highest capacity is as follows. The root text says, "Those of highest capacity are like a garuda hatching or a lion cub." Through realization of the three livelinesses you become like a hatching garuda that, while trapped when in the egg, is immediately able to fly once hatched. Through completing the three livelinesses you become like a lion cub that, while trapped in the womb, immediately jumps around once born. The root text says, "Having brought to completion the three livelinesses [rays, light, and ultimate sound]." This refers to the yoga of breaking the seal of the three—body, speech, and mind—at this very moment, so that these livelinesses become completed as an enlightened body, speech, and heart-mind. The human body transforms into previously concealed *Buddhahood*. The root text says, "At the right moment for the mind to separate from this close association with the body—which is the clear morning of the sixteenth day [of the Tibetan lunar calendar] wherein the sun and moon and stars all come together—that is when, in this way, *Buddhahood* comes. The way this flourishes is as follows: As the root text says, at the right moment, "it is possible to distinguish the brightness from the dregs...so that the very depths of *saṁsāra* are shaken up, and delusion becomes self-purified. In the expanse of universal ground, like infinite space without any boundaries, primordial wisdom's awakened awareness arises, pervades and spreads everywhere like the sun. The magical display of the threefold embodiment of enlightenment shines forth inexhaustibly like the rays of the sun, and there is an unceasing gesture toward the benefit of sentient beings."

(352) Second, for those of middling capacity, the [seeming] external appearance of [the elements] fire, water, earth, and wind ceases, and [internally] the appearance of the three—ultimate sound,

light, and light-rays—shines forth. Because they have become freed from the material body of flesh and blood, awakened awareness remains, unsupported and naked. The accumulation of delusion from [previous] karma, afflictive emotions, and discursive thoughts all cease. Universal ground remains without being covered by obscurations, and awakened awareness remains in-and-by-itself without obscuration.

Commentary A:

A.2.2.2.7.2.2.2.2 Those of Middling Capacity

There are two parts:

(1) the way of arising, and

(2) the way of liberation.

A.2.2.2.7.2.2.2.2.1 The Way of Arising

[The root text] says, "Those of middling capacity" are of two types:

(1) those who, at the time of death, stop "the [seeming] external appearance of the elements: fire, water, earth, and wind cease"; and

(2) those for whom "[internally] the appearance of the three—ultimate sound, light, and light-rays—shines forth." Having stopped the appearances of the seemingly ordinary world, the appearances of the three [visions]—ultimate sound, light, and light-rays—shine forth. [The text] continues, "Because they have become freed from the material body of flesh and blood, awakened awareness remains, unsupported and naked." In other words, because of becoming separated from the material body, awakened awareness remains in-and-by-itself, unclouded. For example, it is like the brightness of a crystal ball. [The text] continues, "The accumulation of delusion from [previous] karma, afflictive emotions, and discursive thoughts all cease. Universal ground remains without being covered by obscurations, and awakened awareness remains in-and-by-itself without obscuration." This refers to how at this point in time all ordinary awareness and thought becomes absorbed into the domain of groundless-ground, and awakened awareness remains absent of any conceptual thought.

(352) At that time, because the essence has been pointed out and there has been special insight [seeing beyond], and also having developed familiarity with it, the six paranormal abilities and six types of [extraordinary] mindfulness arise, and from that, enlightenment.

Commentary A:

[The text] continues, "At that time, because the essence has been pointed out…" With respect to seeing beyond, into the essence, (383) the practice has led to [all the] positive qualities [developing], and so at this time there is seeing beyond, so that the three [visions]—ultimate sound, light, and light-rays—shine forth. Recognizing all appearances as the self-appearances of the mind is like reconnecting with an old friend from the past. [The text] continues, "The six paranormal abilities and the six types of [extraordinary] mindfulness arise and from that, enlightenment." Having established the conditions for the three [visions]—ultimate sound, light, and light-rays—what shines forth goes beyond to the victory of knowing-awareness, and from that comes the clarity of the six paranormal abilities and the full measure of the six [extraordinary] mindfulnesses.

Commentary B:

B.2.6.2.2.2 **Those of Middling Capacity**

B.2.6.2.2.2.1 **At first, Liberation of the After-death State of the *Dharmadhātu***

Second, how liberation comes for those of middling capacity. Regarding those of middling capacity, at first, for those of middling capacity, there is no liberation in the after-death states, but there could be liberation from recognizing the clear-light in the after-death state of the *dharmadhātu*. How these two [respective paths] arise is the way to liberation or not. The root text says, "The [seeming] external appearance of fire, water, earth, and wind ceases." This refers to having stopped at that moment the [elements] of fire, water, earth, and wind, and the external and internal appearances of the container and its contents in one's own mind-stream. The root text continues, "…and [internally] the appearance of the three—sound, light, and light-rays—shines forth." This refers to the visions of the five lights and additionally that the light that shines forth is without direction, boundary, front or back, closeness or distance, middle or end. Regarding ultimate sound, from the sphere of awakened mind-itself comes the self-sound of emptiness within the *dharmadhātu*. This self-occurring sound expresses itself continuously. From the magical display of awakened awareness, the appearance of light-rays actively shines forth, and this activity of shining forth arises because there is no not-arising. The root text says, "Because they have become freed from the material body of flesh and blood, awakened awareness remains, unsupported and naked." (460) Through being freed from the obscuring activity of the appearing sense-objects and the obscuring activity of the material body, awakened awareness arises nakedly without support. The root text says, "The accumulation of delusion from [previous] karma, afflictive emotions, and discursive thoughts all cease. Universal ground remains without being covered by obscurations." The karma and afflictive emotions and all the deluded conceptual thoughts, without being rejected, become purified in their own way. Groundless-ground arises without obscuration like a cloudless sky.

(352) At that time, because the essence has been pointed out and there has been special insight [seeing beyond], and also having developed familiarity with it, the six paranormal abilities and six types of [extraordinary] mindfulness arise, and from that, enlightenment.

The six paranormal abilities are:

(1) Because awakened awareness remains without support, you develop clairvoyant knowledge of past, present, and future lives.

(2) Because the universal ground remains without obscuration, you develop knowledge of the causes and effects of karma.

(3) Because you have developed the eyes of divine sight, you develop knowledge of the [distinction between] pure and impure *Buddha*-fields.

(4) At the moment the visions of the three—ultimate sound, light, or light-rays—arise, there is the knowledge of the after-death

state of clear-light of the *dharmadhātu*.

(5) By having the essence [of mind] pointed out, you develop the knowledge that the mind-itself spontaneously shines forth as the three-fold embodiment of enlightenment.

(6) By having the insight pointed out, there is the knowledge of the three—ultimate sound, light, and light-rays—as self-appearing [in the mind] as manifestations of the corresponding three-fold embodiment of enlightenment.

Commentary A:
A.2.2.2.7.2.2.2.2.2 **The Way of Liberation**

[The text] continues, "Awakened awareness is seen naked and bare." Nobody sees this without all these teachings, yet you come to know the true face of awakened awareness in-and-by-itself, for example, like seeing your face in a mirror. [The text] says, "Realize the universal ground brilliantly without anything obscuring it." Realization of groundless-ground goes beyond, for example, like a child coming into a mother's lap [to be held]. [As the text] says, "Through such realization awakened awareness is held in its own way, and there is no chasing after [seemingly ordinary] appearances." This means that through the realization of the ultimate truth that groundless-ground is like [vast] space, you no longer chase after [seemingly ordinary] appearances, which have become the three—ultimate sound, light, and light-rays—just as a king does not pursue a common person. Because there is no chasing after the three visions—ultimate sound, light, and light-rays—[as the root text then] says, "These visions become self-liberated as illusions." If there is no grasping after the truth of these visions, they appear by themselves and become liberated by themselves, for example, like the sound of an echo. [The text] continues, "Due to the visions self-appearing and [immediately] becoming self-liberated, all delusion becomes self-purified." This refers to the three great visions appearing and becoming liberated in-and-by-themselves [automatically upon arising]. All kinds of confusing thoughts based on duality become purified in-and-by-themselves in the sphere of groundless-ground. These thoughts, for example, (384) are the rays of the sun coming from the sun itself, or like the reflection of the moon on the water coming from the moon. [The text] continues, "Due to the three-fold embodiment of enlightenment self-arising, ultimate truth comes in its own way by its own strength to benefit beings." The enlightened completion *Buddha*-body comes from the *dharmakāya*. The enlightened emanation *Buddha*-bodies come from the enlightened completion *Buddha*-body. Those going to ultimate truth activate [the realization] by its own force.

Commentary B:
B.2.6.2.2.2.2 Second, How Liberation Comes

Second, how liberation comes for those of middling capacity. The root text says, "At that time, because the essence has been pointed out and there has been special insight [seeing beyond], and also having developed familiarity with it, the six paranormal abilities and six types of [extraordinary] mindfulness arise, and from that, enlightenment." At this moment, as explained before, the ultimate truth of groundless-ground and awakened awareness has been pointed out. Through special insight into and having become familiar with the meaning of what has been pointed out as the self-appearance of the three [visions]—sound, light, and light-rays—the clear-light of the *dharmadhātu* arises in that after-death state, and the six paranormal abilities and six types of [extraordinary] mindfulness arise, and from that [full] *Buddhahood* arises. The root text says, "The first of the six paranormal abilities is: because awakened awareness remains without support, you develop clairvoyant knowledge of past, present, and future lives." Being free of the obscuring activity of the material body, awakened awareness remains without support, as does consciousness of past, present, and future lives. The root text says, "Because the universal ground remains without obscuration, you develop knowledge of the causes and effects of karma." Because in groundless-ground reflections arise in the mirror free of the effects of karma, there is the knowledge of all kinds of effects of karma. The root text says, "Because you have developed the eyes of divine sight, you develop knowledge of the [distinction between] pure and impure *Buddha*-fields." By attaining the eyes of the deities that transcend the eyes of the flesh, there is the extraordinary knowledge of the *Buddha*-fields and of the five families of pure beings and the realms of the six types of impure beings. (461) The root text says, "At that moment, the visions of the three—ultimate sound, light, and light-rays—arise, and there is the knowledge of the after-death state of clear-light of the *dharmadhātu*." Through the conditions by which the three great visions arise, there is the knowledge of the after-death state of the clear-light within the *dharmadhātu*. The root text says, "By having the essence [of mind] pointed out, you develop the knowledge that the mind-itself spontaneously shines forth as the three-fold embodiment of enlightenment." At the time awakened mind-itself is pointed out, *Buddhahood* arises in this after-death state, such that there is recognition that the three enlightened *Buddha*-bodies exist innately in one's own mind. The root text says, "By having the insight pointed out, there is the knowledge of the three—sound, light, and light-rays—self-appearing [in the mind] as manifestations of the corresponding three-fold embodiment of enlightenment." At that time, through having pointed out the special insight of appearance of the clear-light as self-appearance, there is recognition of the three enlightened *Buddha*-bodies in this after-death state as [manifestations of] the three livelinesses. It is like meeting an old friend you knew before.

(352) **The Six Types of Mindfulness are:**

(1) **mindfulness of consciousness-transference at the very first moment [of dying];**

(2) **mindfulness of being in an after-death state;**

(3) **mindfulness of awakened awareness staying without support;**

(4) **mindfulness of the lama's oral teachings [after one has died and when they are needed];**

(5) **mindfulness of everything that self-appears to be ultimate sound, light, and light-rays; and**

(6) **mindfulness of one's own mind as being [the mind of a full] Buddha.**

Awakened awareness is seen naked and bare. Realize the universal ground brilliantly without anything obscuring. Through such realization, awakened awareness is held in its own way, and there is no chasing after [seemingly ordinary] appearances. The essence

is not intentionally engaging these visions. By not intentionally engaging these, these visions become self-liberated (353) as illusions. Due to the visions self-appearing and [immediately] becoming self-liberated, all delusion becomes self-purified, and the three-fold embodiment of enlightenment self-arises. Due to the three-fold embodiment of enlightenment self-arising, ultimate truth comes in its own way by its own strength to benefit beings.

Commentary B:

The six extraordinary mindfulnesses are as follows. The root text says, "Mindfulness of consciousness-transference at the very first moment [of dying]." At that very moment, through the conditions of pointing out and the arising of the three visions, that is when mindfulness of consciousness-transference comes. The root text says, "Mindfulness of being in an after-death state." In the after-death state there is knowledge of [actually] being in an after-death state. The root text says, "Mindfulness of awakened awareness staying without support." At that moment, through what had been pointed out, there is the mindfulness of awakened awareness staying without support. The root text says, "Mindfulness of the lama's oral teachings [after one has died and when they are needed]." Through what was previously pointed out, there is the mindfulness of the teachings cutting off the after-death state. The root text says, "Mindfulness of everything that self-appears to be ultimate sound, light, and light-rays." As before, there is the mindfulness of the meaning of what had been pointed out about the three visions as self-appearing. The root text says, "Mindfulness of one's own mind as being [the mind of a full] *Buddha*." (462) As previously taught, regarding the subject of the mother and son, there is the mindfulness of the ultimate truth of what had been pointed out, namely the meaning of the three livelinesses as *Buddhahood*. Thus, the six supernormal abilities and the six extraordinary mindfulnesses occur because of the causes and conditions by which the clear-light becomes liberated in the after-death state of the *dharmadhātu*. The way to get liberation from these conditions is as follows. The root text says, "Awakened awareness is seen naked and bare." Through the conditions by which self-appearance is known, primordial wisdom's awakened awareness, free of any covering by conceptual thought, is realized bare and naked. The root text continues, "Realize the universal ground brilliantly, without anything obscuring." Groundless-ground, which never experiences obscuration by delusion, by its brilliant transparency, is realized. It is like the sun rising in a cloudless sky. The root text says, "Through such realization, awakened awareness is held in its own way, and there is no chasing after [seemingly ordinary] appearances." Thus, the victory of the realization of awakened awareness ends up in its own way. There is no chasing after the radiance of the visions. The root text continues, "The essence is not intentionally engaging these visions. By not intentionally engaging these, these visions are liberated in-and-by themselves as illusions." By not engaging in these three as [externally] appearing objects, they appear in-and-by-themselves and are liberated as illusions. The root text says, "Due to the visions self-appearing and [immediately] becoming self-liberated, all delusion becomes self-purified." Due to appearances becoming liberated, all delusion is purified in-and-by-itself. For example, you know a rope to be a rope, and it is not apprehended as an emanation [of a snake]. Through delusion having become purified, the three Enlightened *Buddha*-bodies arise in and by-themselves. The root text says, "…due to three-fold embodiment of enlightenment self-arising." Through the purification of all delusion, the three enlightened *Buddha*-bodies arise in-and-by-themselves. For example, it is like the sun that has been obscured by clouds that suddenly are being cleared away. Then the sun becomes evident. The root text says, (463) "Ultimate truth comes in its own way by its own strength to benefit beings." Through the three enlightened *Buddha*-bodies arising like the heart of the sun, enlightened activity spreads everywhere impartially like the rays of the sun, and you become able to distinguish the characteristics [of specific skillful means] for the purpose of helping sentient beings.

(353) Third, those of lesser capacity, although they have entered the gateway of these instructions, because they have less realization, they do not recognize the clear-light of the *dharmadhātu* in the after-death state. Due to the karma of previous existence, they remain deluded in the after-death state. Through the influence of

these pith instructions, however, they may attain a body associated with a favorable rebirth. By purifying the proliferation of karma, they may be able to wipe away the habitual karmic propensities of previous existences, and they may therefore be able to attain freedom in one lifetime.

Commentary A:

A.2.2.2.7.2.2.2.2.3 The Way Liberation Comes for Those of Lesser Capacity

[The root text] says, "Those of lesser capacity, although they have entered the gateway of these instructions, because of having less realization...." This means they often come under the influence of laziness and apathy. Their familiarity is weak and their realizations are small. [The text] continues, "So they do not recognize the clear-light of the *dharmadhātu* in the after-death state. Due to the karma of previous existences, they remain deluded in the after-death state." At the time during the dying process when the three visions arise in the clear-light of the after-death state of the *dharmadhātu*, they do not know that these [visions] appear in-and-by-themselves and have no substantiality. They see these as independently existing and as real. Therefore, the brightness of the three visions—ultimate sound, light, and light-rays—fades and disappears. Instead, these visions presently become the dregs [of appearance]. [The text] continues, "Through the influence of these pith instructions, however, they may attain a body associated with a favorable rebirth. By purifying the proliferation of karma, they may be able to wipe away the habitual karmic propensities of previous existences, and may therefore be able to attain freedom in one lifetime." This means that through the power of having purified karma to the point of cleansing all past habitual karmic propensities, they become emancipated from all karmic traces in their mind-streams, and only good remains.

Commentary B:

B.2.6.2.2.3 Those of Lesser Capacity

Third, the way liberation arises for those of lesser capacity. For those of lesser capacity, the root text says, "Third, those of lesser capacity, although they have entered the gateway of these instructions, because of having less realization, they do not recognize the clear-light of the *dharmadhātu* in that after-death state." They are taught the instructions but have a small intellect, and their level of familiarity is weak. Even though the clear-light arises in the after-death state of the *dharmadhātu*, they do not recognize it, and there is no liberation at that moment. The root text says, "Due to the karma of previous existence they remain deluded in the after-death state." Karma first arises in life and death and appears again in the after-death state. From even the slightest delusion, these appearances end up appearing in their own ordinary way, yet these actually arise as the purity of the three visions. They arise as clear-light for those who remain in bliss, with the clarity of their *yi dam* and the prophecies of their lama. The root text says, "Through the influence of these pith instructions, however, they may attain a body associated with a favorable rebirth." Through the positive benefits that come from merely hearing the instructions, they remember them at that moment and take up the meditative experiences, and through having these pith [instructions] and their own influence, will enter the gateway of a most favorable rebirth. They are fortunate to obtain a god or human body. The root text says, "They may therefore be able to attain freedom in one lifetime." (464) Having this special sublime wisdom, they will have an extraordinary birth, and at the age of twenty-five, thirty-five, or forty-five, will have developed the meditative experiences and realizations, and at the age of fifty-five or sixty-five or thereafter will develop and disappear as rainbow body light, and will have attained *Buddhahood* in this same life or in the first after-death state.

(353) Oh! Children of the Lineage!

The teachings on the way delusion ensues for those who do not have the realization: Ordinary people do not enter the gateway of these instructions, [and so] under the influence of bad karma, they never recognize the natural state or essence [of the mind]. Mov-

ing wind [of conceptual thought] rises up and stirs up the ocean of awakened awareness. Habitual karmic propensities, like rippling water, stir up the swelling waves of conceptual thought. The universal ground remains obscured by delusion, like clouds covering the sky. Awakened awareness remains covered by afflictive emotions, like the sun shrouded by darkness.

The three—ultimate sound, light, and light-rays—are seen in delusion as something other than the visions. Because of previous good or bad karma, what is seen appears as duality [with pure realms "out there" resulting from virtuous karma, and impure realms "out there" resulting from non-virtuous karma]. These individuals [after death] see their former form-body, which is [actually] a mental body [after death], as if it were corporeal, with all of their sense-organs [still] operative, fully unhindered. Without any remaining support, there is no protector who protects, as if an infant were abandoned by a mother. [For them] the after-death state is like being shrouded in the darkness of delusion, an ocean of suffering spreading everywhere. Abandoning the bliss [of the ocean of awakened mother consciousness] is like a fish [drying out] in hot sand.

The habitual karmic propensities activate the winds that propel [such beings] along the journey to [rebirth in] whatever of the six realms [of existence] and whatever location [in that realm], and thus [you are propelled] continuously [throughout cyclic existence] like a [perpetual] water wheel or a horse circling [round and round in its corral]. Without any means of protection, where is the hope in these three realms? Without any opportunity for liberation, they remain unconscious, mired in the lower realms. Those who bear in mind the negative consequences of such delusion, thereafter forsake worldly concerns. Such fortunate children of the lineage develop enthusiastic perseverance on the path.

Commentary A:

A.2.2.2.7.2.2.3 **How Delusion Ensues When There is No Realization**

[The root text] says, "Oh! Children of the Lineage! The teachings of the way delusion ensues for those who do not have the realization. Ordinary people do not enter the gateway of these instructions, [and so] under the influence of bad karma, they never recognize the natural state." (385) This means that under the influence of bad karma, they fail to recognize primordial wisdom in the after-death state. [Even after-death] they remain in their ways of an unconscious or intoxicated state-of-mind. Thus, in the after-death clear-light, at the time the visions of the three—ultimate sound, light, and light-rays—shine forth, they fail to recognize these visions as the self-appearance of mind. Having passed to the other side [after-death], they still see these appearances in their own mind-stream as really existing, and they see the three visions—ultimate sound, light, and light-rays—as too real and as having specific characteristics. Through the conditions that make [such confusion], the three visions—ultimate sound, light, and light-rays—arise as the appearances of *saṃsāra*, namely from not knowing awakened awareness. [The text] says, "Moving wind [of conceptual thought] rises up and stirs up the ocean of awakened awareness." After the mind separates from the body, at that time you remain in a state of clear-light. Here, groundless-ground stays like a cloudless sky or like a still, immovable ocean. When a fresh wind rises up, without a previous wind, the ocean becomes agitated. Under the influence of not recognizing awakened awareness and the confusion that ensues, you come to know the movement of the ordinary sense-mind in the sphere of groundless-ground. These movements are fresh, without previous movements. Knowing these movements of the ordinary sense-mind is like the winds on the ocean. Groundless-ground is similar to the ocean that becomes agitated. [The text] continues, "Habitual karmic propensities, like rippling water, stir up the swelling waves of conceptual thought." From the liveliness of groundless-ground, habitual karmic propensities arise one after another like ripples on the water, and after that, conceptual thought gets stirred up like waves swelling on the ocean. [The text] says, "The universal ground remains obscured by delusion, like clouds covering the sky." Groundless-ground is like the sky and confusion is like clouds covering the sky. [The text] adds, "Awakened awareness remains covered by afflictive emotions, like the sun shrouded by darkness." (386) Awakened awareness is like the heart of the sun. Afflictive emotions are like darkness that obscures the sun. Deluded appearances like this arise in the after-death state.

[The text] continues, "The three—ultimate sound, light, and light-rays—are seen as something other than the visions." This means that the three—ultimate sound, light, and light-rays—are held to be real. Then from these three all sorts of deluded appearances come forth. [The root text] says, "Because of previous good or bad karma, what is seen appears as duality." For those individuals with good karma, what arises appears like the sun arising at daybreak, very lucid light; sound heard by the ears; a sense of being elevated upwards; or like coming into a flower garden. Such individuals will take a higher birth. For those individuals with bad karma, what arises appears as if obscurations keeps piling up, like being enveloped by darkness, like dark blue light without hearing any sound, like being struck by icy rain, a blizzard, lightning and hail, or a rain of arrows, accompanied by various sounds of being struck and killed, and falling down and crying out in pain. When such impure appearances arise, it leads to descending and staying in bad rebirths. [The root text] continues, "These individuals [after death] see their former form-body, which is [actually] a mental body, as if it were corporeal." Sentient beings who have this experience [after dying] become freed from this fettered body, but have a mental body that seems corporeal. Such an individual [retains] the thought that he has not previously died, and sees the body as if it were [actually still] existing. [The root text] continues, "...with all of their sense-organs [still] operative, fully unhindered." At that present moment, there is no letting go of the five sense-organs that bind the individual. With respect to the ordinary storehouse mind [i.e., the confused experience of groundless-ground],[33] the five sense-objects arise at once. Such individuals in the after-death state experience the body as still existing, but the objects of the sense-mind are unimpeded. These three [livelinesses] are empty, but, impelled

---

33. *kun gzhi'i rnam shes pa*: "ordinary storehouse mind." This term is used when confusion remains as to the groundless-ground [*kun gzhi*], so that ordinary storehouse mind becomes the depository for the ripening of habitual karmic propensities. At some other point in time, all these karmic impressions will arise sooner or later as virtue/non-virtue, higher/lower, etc. (387)

by the force of *saṁsāra* in that instant, these appear as the various scenes of the magical display of the recollections of the ordinary sense-mind. All that seems to exist externally and internally is taken as real instead of as the unimpeded transparency [of liveliness], and so this becomes the force of further wandering into rebirths. [The root text] says, "Without any remaining support, there is no protector who protects." The degree of suffering for those sentient beings in the after-death states is due to their not having any remaining support. It is like trying to carry on with lungs but no flesh. Being without a protector who protects, [according to the root text] is said to be like "an infant abandoned by a mother." [The text] says, "It is like being shrouded in the darkness of delusion, an ocean of suffering spreading everywhere." This ocean of confusion and suffering spreading everywhere is like a fish or bird unable to withstand being caught in a net or cage yet trying to get free. [The text] says, "The habitual karmic propensities activate the winds that propel [such beings] along the journey to [rebirth in] whatever of the six realms [of existence], and whatever location [in that realm]." [Migration] becomes, [as the root text says], "like a perpetual water wheel or horse circling [round and round in its corral]. Without any means of protection, where is the hope of compassion in the three realms?" Those without even an instant of [positive] habitual karmic propensities from good karma arising out of groundless-ground never find the birthplace of those lamas gone to bliss. [The text] says, "Without any opportunity for liberation, they remain unconscious, mired in the lower [realms]." Because they wander limitlessly in the realms of *saṁsāra* and there is no occasion for liberation, [the root text says], "they become mired" in suffering that they are unable to endure. [The root text says, "Those who bear in mind the negative consequences of such confusion, thereafter forsake worldly concerns. Such fortunate children of the lineage develop enthusiastic perseverance on the path." (388) They set a firm resolve to develop whatever skillful means they do not have to turn back confusion, and to learn the close-to-the-heart [instructions] undistractedly on the path.

Commentary B:
B.2.6.2.3 An Explanation as to How Delusion Comes from Being Without Realization

Third, the root text says, "The teachings on the way delusion ensues for those who do not have the realization. Ordinary people do not enter the gateway of these instructions." When the mind separates from the body, at that time they remain in a state of the clear-light of awakened awareness. Yet, [as the root text says], being "under the influence of bad karma," they do not recognize the natural state that is never covered by obscuration. The root text says, "Moving wind [of conceptual thought] rises up and stirs up the ocean of awakened awareness. Habitual karmic propensities, like rippling water, stir up the swelling waves of conceptual thought." At that time, through the winds of conceptual thought rising up and moving, the ocean of awakened awareness begins to move, the water of habitual karmic propensities becomes fiercely agitated, and then the waves of conceptual thought become agitated. The root text says, "Groundless-ground remains obscured by delusion, like clouds covering the sky." Groundless-ground is like the sky that is clouded by delusion and obscured by the darkness of death. There is no clarity. The root text continues, "Awakened awareness remains covered by afflictive emotions, like the sun shrouded by darkness." Primordial wisdom's awakened awareness is like the sun that is obscured by afflictive emotions and from being covered over it does not appear. The root text says, "The three—ultimate sound, light, and light-rays—are seen in delusion as something other than the visions." The self-appearing objects, being illusions, arise from the liveliness of awakened awareness as the three great visions, and although they arise as self-occurring, they are seen as something other and as real. (465) The root text says, "Because of previous good or bad karma, what is seen appears as duality." With respect to the three—sound, light, and light-rays—arising from groundless-ground, from good karma these arise as purely seen visions, like the immeasurable light of the *Buddha*-fields and the Enlightened Form-bodies. From bad karma they arise as impurely seen appearances, like the depths of sinking into darkness and fear. The root text says, "These individuals [after death] see their former form-body, which is [actually] a mental body [after death], as if it were corporeal." For those bound by their karma, even though they do not have a body, it seems real. From the ripening of habitual karmic propensities in dreams they have the support of a mental body, and it appears in one of three aspects—as the body from their previous existence, or it seems to stay just the way it was in the after-death state, or it seems to appear as an external body. The root text continues, "…with all of their sense-organs [still] operative, fully unhindered." Without the support of the senses, it seems as if all the senses are complete. Their subsequent view and conduct [is determined by ripening] habitual karmic propensities, and in accordance with that karma there is no womb. They seem to reside in a world of rocky mountains, yet there is no support to this. They can travel anywhere just by thinking. The strength of this miraculous display of karma is the cause of the six classes of beings and where they reside. Each of these wanders inside the after-death state and, not having the pure vision of a god, they do not see and view [this karmically created world] as something other. In this after-death state they will have their measure of pure and impure [experiences]. The root text says, "Without any remaining support, there is no protector who protects, as if the infant were abandoned by the mother." They suffer because they are without the level of support of awakened awareness, like an insect that gets destroyed as soon as it enters life. Without the moisture of support, they suffer because they are searching for a body to support them. (466) They suffer because they are without any guardian to protect them, like a mass of fish swimming in the all-pervading ocean of suffering. The root text says, "[For them] the after-death state is like being shrouded in the darkness of delusion, an ocean of suffering spreading everywhere. Abandoning the bliss [of the ocean of awakened mother consciousness] is like a fish [drying out] in hot sand. The habitual karmic propensities activate the winds that propel [such beings] along the journey to [rebirth in] whatever of the six realms [of existence] and whatever location [in that realm], and thus [they are propelled] continuously [throughout cyclic existence] like a [perpetual] water wheel or a horse circling [round and round in its corral]." Thus, their suffering increases without measure. Through the ripening of their own karma by itself, if their minds become disheartened by the means by which they protect themselves, they should remain in a state of compassion. The root text says, "Without any opportunity for liberation, they remain unconscious, mired in the lower realms."

They wander without beginning and without end in *saṁsāra*. They experience immeasurable suffering. Oh! Victorious Ones! The root text continues, "Those who bear in mind the negative consequences of such delusion, thereafter forsake worldly concerns." The appropriate practice is to imagine the negative consequences of delusion and *saṁsāra* with its suffering, and then reflect on escaping from the hardships of this, and so forth. Cast off the seeming appearances of the ordinary world. The root text says, "Such fortunate children of the lineage develop enthusiastic perseverance on the path." Be encouraged to use these instructions and skillful means on this profound path to turn away from *saṁsāra*. To take up the meditative experiences, generate enthusiastic perseverance.

(354) Thus, either from such realization *Buddhahood* comes, or lacking such realizations wandering in *samsāra* comes. Both [types of] individuals encounter the jaws [of death] and the after-death states, but the essential difference is how *samsāra* and *nirvāna* become divided [through lacking the realization].

Commentary A:

A.2.2.2.7.2.3 **A Brief Summary**

[The root text] says, "Thus, either from such realization *Buddhahood* comes, or lacking such realization wandering in *saṁsāra* comes. Both [types of] individuals encounter the jaws [of death] and the after-death states, but the essential difference is how *saṁsāra* and *nirvāṇa* become divided [through lacking the realization]." This passage clearly finishes the summary. This completes the commentary of the sixth lamp.

Commentary B:

B.2.6.3 **Conclusion**

Third, a conclusion. The root text says, "Thus, either from such realization (467) *Buddhahood* comes, or lacking such realization wandering in *saṁsāra* comes. Both [types of] individuals encounter the jaws [of death] and the after-death states, but the essential difference is how *saṁsāra* and *nirvāṇa* become divided [through lacking the realization]." This refers to making a determination about the lamp at the time of the after-death states [in such a way that the realization] flourishes.

Commentary A:
A.3.0 Concluding Practices
A brief summary of the concluding practices has three parts:

(1) explaining the greatness of these instructions,

(2) explaining how to find and keep up these instructions, and

(3) explaining the lineage of these instructions.

Commentary B:
B.3.0 Overall Conclusion
Third, the [overall] conclusion has five parts:

(1) the positive qualities that ensue from these great instructions,

(2) how whatever of this is explained,

(3) how the enlightened emanation body came to teach,

(4) the way followers attain the positive qualities, and

(5) a summary of the basic import of the teachings.

(354) Oh! Children of the Lineage! These are the pith instructions on the six essential points of [ultimate] *bodhicitta*.
   It is the lamp for those whose minds are without [realization].
   It is the mirror for those who cannot see the mind.
   It is the iron hook that grabs the mind for those who have a runaway mind.
   It is the nail for those with scattered minds.
   The mind is firmly established in lucidity for those whose minds are dull.
   It extracts the benefit for those whose minds are adrift.
   It is a yoke for those whose minds are too unruly.
   It is a key for those whose minds are locked shut.

Commentary A:
A.3.1 Explaining the Greatness of These Instructions
[The root text] begins, "Oh! Children of the Lineage! [These are the

pith instructions on the six essential points of [ultimate *bodhicitta*]. It is the lamp for those whose minds are without [realization]." For example, if you hold up the flame of a butter lamp, you can see directly what has not been seen. Likewise, these pith instructions are like holding a lamp to self-occurring primordial wisdom. The plain, naked [truth] of each of these [lamps] has been explained for those whose minds are without [realization], and they have been explained to self-purify all the qualities of the view to look into the belly of emptiness. [The text] says, "It is the mirror for those who cannot see the mind." For example, if you can't see your own face, take a more careful look in the mirror. These instructions directly explain the natural state of groundless-ground and awakened awareness with its refined awakeness through which the mind is not seen in its old ways but anew. (389) [The root text] says, "It is the iron hook that grabs the mind for those who have a run-away mind." This refers to the mind not staying, and chasing after sense-objects instead. These instructions are explained to see self-occurring primordial wisdom nakedly, so that the mind stops doing this in-and-by-itself. [The text] says, "It is the nail for those with scattered minds." This refers to those whose clarity of mind had faded but who now become free of that. These instructions pertain to how co-emergent primordial wisdom shines forth in-and-by-itself. They show how ultimate truth neither unites with nor becomes separated from the three times. [These instructions] are like getting hit by a nail for those whose minds are not free. [The root text] says, "The mind is firmly established in lucidity for those whose minds are dull." These instructions on self-occurring primordial wisdom are like the sun shining forth. Because they show a refined awakeness, all the features of laxity and dullness become purified in-and-by-themselves. [The root text] says, "It extracts the benefit for those whose minds are adrift." There is no advantage to failing to recognize [the true nature of] the mind, so [once recognized, it leads to] so-called "confidence." These instructions show how compassion exists in its own right. They show the plain, naked [truth], as if discovering a crystal jewel that was [already] held in hand. Through the meditative experiences and realizations that ensue, it is like the infant [of individual consciousness] meeting the [ocean-like] mother [consciousness]. [The root text] says, "It is like a yoke for those whose minds are too unruly." This so-called "unruliness" is like a wild horse that is suitable to ride. These instructions explain how self-occurring primordial wisdom becomes evident. [The root text] says, "It is a key for those whose minds are locked shut." (390) Those whose minds are caught up in suffering are said to have "locked" their minds. These instructions explain how self-occurring primordial wisdom becomes evident by showing the full extent of everything that has arisen in the mind as liveliness. Through this realization, all the characteristic ways of suffering in the mind are left in their own way and the mind is liberated in-and-by-itself.

Commentary B:

B.3.1 The Positive Qualities that Ensue from These Great Instructions

First, the positive qualities that ensue from these [great instructions]. The root text begins, "Oh! Children of the Lineage! These are the pith instructions on the six essential points of [ultimate] *bodhicitta*." The root text says, "It is the lamp for those whose minds are without [realization]." If you hold up these lamps, it is like seeing [everything] just as it is, as insubstantial. These instructions affect seeing one's own mind and, lacking independent reality, seeing the ultimate truth of the [mind's] essence-itself just as it is, directly and nakedly. The text continues, "It is the mirror for those who cannot see the mind." If you have looked into a mirror and do not see an image, it is because the seeing is the image. By means of these instructions those who cannot see the mind are enabled to directly see the three [visions]. The root text says, "It is the iron hook that grabs the mind for those who have a run-away mind." Just as an iron hook holds onto some material substance, when the mind does not stay, but instead moves toward mental content and runs away, these instructions enable you to take hold of the mind. The root text says, "It is the nail for those with scattered minds." Nakedness means there is no mistake, which enables you to become firmly established in and inseparable from the truth. These instructions put an end to thought elaboration, to become inseparable from truth. They enable you to become firmly established nakedly, inseparable from the truth. The root text says,

"The mind is firmly established in lucidity for those whose minds are dull." Through being shown how awakened awareness directly becomes evident (468) [all] sinking and dullness is purified in its own way and this enables you to see lucidity in-and-by-itself. The root text says, "It extracts the benefit for those whose minds are adrift." For those who did not recognize [awakened awareness], but who have come to recognize it, it allows them to conduct themselves on the basis of groundless-ground and awakened awareness, and enables mother and son to meet at this very moment. The root text says, "It is a yoke for those whose minds are too unruly." [These instructions] tame those with agitated minds, and from the ensuing tranquility, it enables them to become calm. The root text says, "It is a key for those whose minds are locked shut." Through untying the unyielding chains, it enables you to make a firm determination about the great [teaching] of self-appearing/self-liberated.

(354) Oh! Children of the Lineage! In future times, assess whether to hold back or pass on [these instructions]. Build the vessel according to [the appropriate level] of capacity. This practical guidebook has been given to those individuals of fortunate karma to be their unmistaken [guide].

Commentary A:

A.3.2 Explaining How to Find and Keep up These Instructions

[The root text] says, "Oh! Children of the Lineage! In future times, assess whether to hold back or pass on [these instructions]. Build the vessel according to [the appropriate level] of capacity." This practical guidebook has been given to those individuals of fortunate karma to be their unmistaken [guide]"

Commentary B:

B.3.2 How Whatever of This is Explained

Second, how whatever of this is explained. The root text says, "In future times, assess whether to hold back or pass on [these instructions]." This refers to being careful with the authoritative seal, which has been conferred upon you. The root text says, "Build the vessel of [the appropriate level] of capacity." This refers to the three capacities [best, middling and lesser]. Those who are shown these instructions, think in accordance with them, and bring them into whatever [they experience], will integrate these into their mind-stream. The root text says, "This practical guidebook has been given to those individuals of fortunate karma to be their unmistaken [guide]." This practical guidebook about the path is for individuals who have built [a proper] vessel, and is said to be the one guidebook for becoming liberated quickly. It is explained to those having the blessing and authorization [to practice].

(354) Then, the *nirmāṇakāya* [enlightened emanation body of Tapihritsa] transformed like a rainbow fading in the sky, and disappeared.

Commentary A:

A.3.2

The root text says, "Then, the *nirmāṇakāya* [enlightened emanation body of Tapihritsa] transformed like a rainbow fading in the sky, and disappeared."

Commentary B:

B.3.3 **How the Enlightened Emanation Body came to Teach**

Third, how the Enlightened Emanation Body came to teach. The root text says, "Then, the *nirmāṇakāya* [enlightened emanation body [of Tapihritsa] transformed like a rainbow fading in the sky, and disappeared." Having spoken these instructions to fortunate individuals, to subdue [their delusion] for whom he had come at that time, this enlightened emanation body came into the expanse to fully accomplish the benefit of others, and then became like a rainbow fading in the sky. (469)

(354) Then, Guru sNang bzher Lod po, through the close-to-the-heart [instructions], made the determination of awakened awareness, and transformed his [former] spiritual pride into many standard and supreme spiritual accomplishments.

Commentary A:

A.3.3 **Explaining the Lineage of These Instructions**

The way the lineage is explained is as follows: [The root text] says, "Then, Guru sNang bzher Lod po, through the close-to-the-heart [instructions], made the determination of awakened awareness, and transformed his [former] spiritual pride into many standard and supreme spiritual accomplishments."[34] This is the explanation up to this point on the six essential points of *bodhicitta*, as [given] from the sacred speech of Kun tu bZang po just as it is, and taught [the lineage] directly from the mouths of accomplished lamas. I, Au Ri, designed this [commentary] to make [the teachings] a little bit clearer. *Sarvamangalam!*

Commentary B:
B.3.4 The Way Followers Attain the Positive Qualities

Fourth, the way followers attain the positive qualities. The root text says, "Then, Guru sNang bzher Lod po, through the close-to-the-heart [instructions]." These [instructions] are for followers who have the right karmic connection, so as to become liberated from the full measure of their bondage [to *saṁsāra*]. If you make a decisive determination to know [the meaning] definitively, you will be free of the arrogance of self-inflation, have a strong belief, and come to attain the full realization in a single life time. Spiritual pride is transformed into very "many standard and superior" magical displays of positive qualities. The superior positive qualities include the final accomplishment of everything about the view, intent, meditative experience, and realizations, and having primordial wisdom's awakened awareness become directly evident. The standard positive qualities include having many very special qualities, such as the power and blessing of the magical display, the signs of accomplishment, the paranormal abilities, and so forth.

(354) Be guided by this oral transmission free of the stains of [ordinary] words. This completes the teachings on the Six Lamps of the Great Completion. *Sarvamangalam!*

Commentary B:

---

34. Commentary reads *rdzu 'phrul*: "magical displays." The root text reads *dngos grub*: "yogic accomplishments." The commentary is more consistent with compassion toward other beings.

B.3.5 A Summary of the Basic Import of the Teachings

Fifth, a summary of the basic import of the teachings. The root text says, "Be guided by this oral transmission free from the stains of [ordinary] words. This completes the teachings on the *Six Lamps of the Great Perfection*." The "oral transmission lineage" refers to those having heard the profound truth of these instructions for reaching the final state, and in hearing them, pass them on. "Be guided by this oral transmission" refers to the unbroken oral transmission by those having the realization. Their gift-waves of influence never fade into the mist.

Do not follow only after the meaning of the words or the teaching lineage. Do not interrupt this lineage transmission. Do not be influenced by demonic forces. Because these authoritative teachings are not hidden in the earth [as discovered treasure texts], they are extraordinarily special. "Great completion" refers to making a connection with the highest, unexcelled view, and through these instructions sentient beings are elevated to *Buddhahood* with all its positive qualities. According to these teachings, there is completion [of all these positive qualities of a *Buddha*] as spontaneously present. (470) "Lamp" refers to making clear what has been unclear regarding ultimate truth, of which these instructions are very special. "Completion" means that its words are without remainder, and that the intent of the ultimate meaning is finally completed. These instructions from the *Zhang Zhung* Oral Transmission of Great Completion offer an explanation of the heart-blood pith instructions to guide followers. This serves the purpose of setting forth the intent and meaning of the Six Lamps in a way that never contradicts what has been described by all the previous *Mahāsiddhas* and the practices of the holy realization-holders. [These were given] to Bru meditator rGyal ba g.Yung Drung through the meditative experiences of the great meditator known as 'Og blon bKra' shes Rab. Having made a request through greatly endeavoring with trust, admiration, and respect, [this request is fulfilled] by completing this composition written in words.

From the Oral Transmission
of Zhang Zhung

"The Six Essential Points of *Bodhicitta* for Practice"

Transmitted from the Lineage of
Ya ngal Gong bkra ba

translated under the guidance of
His Holiness the thirty-third
Menri Trizin

by Geshe Sonam Gurung
and Daniel P. Brown, Ph.D.

for Pointing Out the Great Way Foundation

The Six Essential Points of *Bodhicitta* for Practice

(479)

Homage to Kun tu bZang po, who bestows the clarity of self-awakened awareness.

From the oral transmission, this is the mirror of the mind. This is the lamp for reaching the endpoint of ultimate truth. These notes on these essential points of the pith instructions have six parts. The first pertains to the lamp of the universal ground that stays. The essential point is recognizing the universal ground that stays just as it is. The second pertains to the lamp of the fleshy heart. The essential point is self-awakened awareness that stays in the universal ground arising from within [the heart-space]. The third refers to the lamp of the soft white channel. The essential point is [seeing] transparent primordial wisdom in whatever occurs along the path. The fourth refers to the lamp of the fluid eyes of the extensive lasso. The essential point is seeing whatever arises from the sense-gateways nakedly as [the liveliness of] awakened awareness. The fifth refers to the lamp of pointing out the *Buddha*-fields. The essential point is making a close-to-the-heart determination about the three-fold embodiment of enlightenment in whatever meditation is done along the path. The sixth refers to the lamp of the after-death *bardos* for reaching the boundary between delusion and realization. The essential point is the way to differentiate between *saṁsāra* and *nirvāṇa*. These are the six.

[Basis, Path, and Fruition Pith Instructions]

These can be condensed into three [essential] pith instructions pertaining to the manner of arising in the four lamps. The three pith instructions are: (1) the mother, the purified empty unborn essence, like space; (2) the son, the self-clarity the primordial wisdom's awakened awareness, free of obscuration, like the heart of the sun; (480) and (3) the inseparable pair of mother and son that stays, non-dual emptiness/clarity, like the sun arising in the sky.

With respect to the natural state that is the essence of the universal ground, the three visions—ultimate sound, light, and light-rays—from the liveliness of this [awakened awareness] they arise like self-appearing illusions. Through realizing the natural state of this just as it is, all the positive qualities of *nirvāṇa* arise. [However,] by not realizing this just as it is, all of the faults of *saṁsāra* arise in-and-by-themselves. However, when the manner of this arises unobstructedly [without mental engagement], this becomes the basis of all the faults and positive qualities in this universal ground. What is called "universal ground" refers to the pith instruction on the basis.

The pith instruction on the path is such that the basis is the non-duality of emptiness/clarity. This stays innately and primordially. By pointing this out through these profound pith instructions, this is the unmistaken view you recognize. Being mindful of this [view] and remembering it without distraction, this is meditation. Through this view and meditation, you bring into the meditation and skillfully meditate such that the three clear-light visions appear—ultimate sound, light, and light-rays. Through the gazes and skillful means of this profound path, instantly the visions of clear-light and sound should arise. Through familiarity [with this meditation] and the skill of practice, the signs [of progress] along the path won't be mistaken. There are many ways that this clear-light arises, and this becomes many visions of the celestial palaces of the *Buddha*-fields and the enlightened bodies. Furthermore, sound becomes the self-sound of [lively] awakened awareness, like an echo. Light becomes the self-light of [the liveliness of] awakened awareness, like a rainbow. Light-rays become the self-rays of [the liveliness of] awakened awareness, like reflections [in a mirror]. The enlightened bodies become the self-form of [the liveliness of] awakened awareness, like a water-moon. By understanding that, you make a determination about deluded [perception]. (481) The origin of false appearance is emptied. You find the root of the foundation of *saṁsāra* and *nirvāṇa*. The universal ground is free of being covered by obscurations. This is the pith instruction for awakened awareness to arise nakedly. This is the path pith instruction.

The fruition pith instruction follows: The universal ground and awakened awareness stay innately as the *dharmakāya*, with the great original purity of the inseparability of emptiness/clarity. Within that [expanse], the innate spontaneous presence of the three visions—ultimate sound, light, and light-rays—and the five primordial wisdoms, are the enlightened body of the *sambhogakāya*. For those who have this realization as compared to those who do not, the [ordinary] six sense-objects do not arise as well-known [ordinary] objects. This becomes the *nirmāṇakāyas*. Thus, you accomplish the three-fold embodiment of enlightenment that is innate within you [as part of your *Buddha*-nature]. By practicing the meditation of this path and becoming familiar with the meditation, you completely cut through *saṁsāra*. Deluded [perception] becomes purified in its own way. In the expanse of space, free of all divisions and boundaries, the universal ground is like the sky. Primordial wisdom's awakened awareness arises and saturates everything like the sun [rising]. The magical display of the three-fold embodiment of enlightenment arises inexhaustibly like sun-rays. Then, serving the welfare of sentient beings goes on forever.

Furthermore, according to your capacity there are three times for liberation.

Those of best capacity [when dying] take their last external breath but still have an internal [subtle] breath, and become liberated at that time. Those of middling capacity become liberated in the *bardo* of the *dharmadhātu* when they recognize the three visions—ultimate sound, light, and light-rays. Those of lesser capacity remain in cyclic existence for one more favorable rebirth and become liberated after that. This completes the pith instruction of basis, path, and fruition. (482)

[The Manner of Arising of the Visions]

The manner of arising of the four lamps follow: In the non-dual lively emptiness/clarity of the universal ground, the visions of the three—ultimate sound, light, and light-rays—arise unobstructedly. The experience of the realizations has four ways of arising. The first is that the three visions—ultimate sound, light, and light-rays—are spontaneously present in the universal ground. The second is that the three visions—ultimate sound, light, and light-rays—arise from incidental conditions. The third is that signs of progress in the three visions—ultimate sound, light, and light-rays—occur along the path. The fourth is that these visions—ultimate sound, light, and light-rays—arise during the after-death states.

(1) Spontaneously present in the universal ground means that they arise in the universal basis from [the liveliness of] primordial wisdom's self-awakened awareness. The three visions—ultimate sound, light, and light-rays—arise as spontaneously present. Furthermore, they arise like clear-light in clear space. Ultimate sound arises from the domain of empty space. From inside this non-dual state, light-rays emanate. It stays in the place of the heart, like a dark ruby offering tent with a crystal lid. Arising from that is the lamp of the soft white channel that extends to the eye sense-gateways. The universal ground has not been created or made by anyone. Because here, the three visions—ultimate sound, light, and light-rays—arise as liveliness, it is therefore referred to as "natural clear-light." You should realize this as the manner of arising in the universal ground."

(2) The manner of arising from incidental conditions: By depending on these essential points of the pith instructions and skillful means, the three visions—ultimate sound, light, and light-rays—which naturally exist in the universal ground, directly manifest themselves. By depending on what is pointed out, light is self-light, rays are self-rays, and ultimate sound is self-sound.

(3) Here's how the signs of progress manifest along the path. When separating the brightness of awakened awareness from the residual dregs [of the ordinary mind], if you know this brightness of mind, the sign of progress that arises is that there are many such visions of ultimate sound, light, and light-rays. (483) It is held because of the serviceability of the wind element.

As a sign of the earth element, it arises like smoke. As a sign of the fire element, it flashes like lightning, a glow-worm, or a firefly. As a sign of the wind element, it arises like a mirage. As a sign of the water element, it is like the moon rising. As a sign of the space element, it is like a cloudless sky. Furthermore, it is like a rainbow, a leaf, or a flower, indeterminate forms of sentient beings, energy drops, and spheres of light. And the enlightened bodies of the *Sugatas*, the *nirmāṇakāyas*, come in the form of the *vinaya* [monks], *sambhogakāya* in the form of the five *Buddha* families, etc. Unfathomable visions arise. You see the many *mandalas* and *Buddha*-fields. The darkness of night no longer obscures. The light of this clear-light outshines everything. When seeing [the visions], there is no difference between daytime and nighttime, and no difference [with the visions] seen near or far. Many things happen, such as reading other's minds and so forth. In brief, everything in saṁsāra and nirvāṇa becomes clear-light. Thus, you cut off any deviation from the supreme view regarding whatever seems to arise as substantial. You should know [everything] as the liveliness of mind. Until you reach the endpoint [of the path], become more familiar and acquainted with [this view].

(4) What happens during the after-death *bardos* is that the mind and the physical substance of the body separate. Externally, the appearance of [the elements] fire, water, earth, and wind cease. Internally, the three visions—ultimate sound, light, and light-rays—arise. Up to five days after the deluded appearances [of the outside world] cease, the visions of the five lights arise. These are called "the main five lights." There is the white light of emptiness primordial wisdom, (484) the yellow light of mirror-like, the green light of sameness, the red light of discriminating, and the blue light of all-accomplishing primordial wisdom. Their meaning is primordial wisdom. Their sign is the five lights. These are referred to as "the essence of the five lights." From these five lights the five *Buddha* families become clear. From the white light, the deities of the gShen lha family, from the yellow, gSas rje, from the green, Gar gsas, from the red, gNam gsas, and from the blue, rGod gsas. These are called the "five lights of the families that proliferate." Each of these respective lights is associated with one of the five families. Each of these respective five lights emit another five lights. They are called "the flaming five lights," [yet] color and form arise as indeterminate. They are called the "five lights of emanation." Various forms made from these five colors occur like reflections [in a mirror]. Furthermore, these five lights arise without a center or edges. They arise like a rainbow appearing in the sky. The light-rays arise as an indeterminate magical display, like opening a cloth of silk brocade. The light that flares up and emanates appears as light-rays. The sounds heard are loud and harsh, and some are like melodious vibrations, the way self-occurring continuous thunder sounds. With respect to these three visions—ultimate sound, light, and light-rays—they are not taken as out there or as real. [However], if you become afraid of

or attached to them, you will not cut off the *bardo*. Therefore you should know [the visions of the *bardo*] as self-occurring illusions.

This completes [the teachings] on the manner of arising of the lamps.

Homage to Kun tu bZang po, whose self-awakened awareness is free of [all] obscurations!

This practical guide to the unmistaken path is for those of fortunate karma. Six essential points for practice will be explained. (485) Identifying the universal ground has two parts:

(1) pointing out the natural state where the brightness of awakened awareness is separated from the residual dregs [of the ordinary mind], and

(2) recognizing the conditions [that support] delusion, and making a determination about delusion.

The first has two parts:

(1) separating the brightness of awakened awareness from the residual dregs [of the ordinary mind], and

(2) pointing out the natural state.

Separating the Brightness of Awakened Awareness From the Residual Dregs

First, from one's depths fearing birth and death, you should abandon the activities of everyday life. Carry your lama on your crown. For those who have fortunate karma, take up the practice of meditation in an isolated spot in a mountain hermitage. Start with the preliminary practice of taking refuge and generating *bodhicitta*. Meditate on impermanence. Offer the *mandala* prayers. These preliminaries come first.

Then, sit on a comfortable seat. The essential points of the body are to set up the essential five body posture points in a natural way. The essential point of speech is to hold the reins on the horse of the winds. Hold the soft wind. Press down the upper wind and restrain the lower wind. The essential point of the gaze is to set it up [so everything arises] in its own way as the gateway of the [eye] lamps. Set up the gaze on the surrounding space with the eyes not closed, not fluttering, with alertness. The essential point of the mind is that the mind is free of any analysis about external sense-objects, free of examination internally on awareness, not chasing after the past or future. Don't follow the past. Don't anticipate the future. Stay in the present, free of grasping. Set up [the mind] in a state like space. By setting up the mind accordingly, in the right way for however many days, first, the signs of stability of mind arise before the [eye] sense-organs. "Then, separating the brightness of awakened awareness form the dregs [of the ordinary mind] reaches full measure. Having dissolved the dregs into the domain of space, (486) the brightness of the light [of awakened awareness] becomes clear. Having taken away the outer covering of conceptual thought, awakened awareness arises nakedly. Having purified the mass of conceptual thought, primordial wisdom [arises] free of obscuration." As the root text explains, many visions of the three—ultimate sound, light, and light-rays—appear.

Pointing Out

Second, pointing out thus refers to separating the brightness of awakened awareness from the dregs [of the ordinary mind]. The brightness of the mind is pointed out as the non-dual pair, clarity/emptiness, like the sun rising in the sky. The pure emptiness of the universal ground is pointed out like pure space. The mother, the universal ground, is pointed out as the unborn expanse. The self-clarity of awakened awareness, free of obscuration, is pointed out to be like the heart of the sun. The son, awakened awareness, is pointed out to be unobstructed primordial wisdom's self-awakened awareness. The clarity itself is the very essence of emptiness. The emptiness itself is the unobscured clarity. Mother and son are pointed out to be inseparable, like the sun rising in the sky. The non-duality of clarity/emptiness is pointed out as the *dharmakāya*. From that state, the seemingly deluded afflictive emotions and conceptual thought, the recollections, and ordinary mindfulness, everything of the various [events] that arise, is pointed out to be like clouds in the sky, without a foundation, and rootless, as self-occurring and becoming self-calm.

Furthermore, as mentioned in the root text and the *gZer bu* [*Twenty-One Nails*], the three-fold embodiment of enlightenment, and the three—space, domain of space, and expanse—are pointed out by the three [methods] explaining the meaning, metaphors, and signs [occurring during meditation]. Having it pointed out like this develops confidence that the clarity/emptiness of awakened awareness is like space. Being mindful like this again and again develops the clarity in meditation practice. By the three restraints, all distraction is abandoned. By the three ways of keeping it loose, the conceptual mind settles down. By the three means to set it up, you hold the base of awakened awareness. (487) Through the three ways of disconnecting [from mental engagement], the [ripening] of habitual karmic tendencies is interrupted. By the three ropes, you extend familiarity with this state. Through the three skillful means of abandoning, the meaning [of the essential point] won't degenerate. By the three visions, you develop skill in the liveliness of awakened awareness. By the three liberations, you let go of duality. Through the three ways free of obscuration, you reach the full measure of the fruition. This explains the meditation practice.

Delusion

Second, identifying the conditions of delusion and making a determination about delusion has two parts.

Identifying the Conditions of Delusion

First, recognizing the conditions of delusion is knowing that the base of delusion is the universal ground and awakened awareness. Knowing the conditions [that support] delusion are the three visions—ultimate sound, light, and light-rays—and knowing that the cause of delusion is ordinary mindfulness and recollections. Furthermore, the objects [of appearance], the three—ultimate sound, light, and light-rays—at the time they arise are not understood as the many manifestations of the liveliness of awakened awareness. External appearances are seen as having self-inherent existence, and through that you become deluded. For example, it is like seeing your own form in the water [and not seeing it as a reflection]. By not knowing it as your own form, it arises as something other than you. By seeing it as something other in this example, the nakedness of awakened awareness is covered in the clothes of conceptual thought. For example, it is like clouds covering the sun. Therefore, failing to recognize self-awakened awareness to be like the sun, this failure is like the [sun] seeming to be covered in darkness. The meaning of the universal ground being like space becomes obscured. Just as the sun sets, the sky is obscured by darkness. This is co-emergent failure to recognize awakened awareness [moment-by-moment].

Furthermore, the designation "failure to recognize" has two parts.

(1) Everything that appears occurs as delusion. (488)

(2) The three visions—ultimate sound, light, and light-rays—are self-appearing illusions, but by taking them as real and becoming deluded, you establish the conditions of delusion. These are the conditions [that support] delusion.

Making a Determination About Delusion

Second, determining the origin of delusion is such that by looking at the basis of delusion in the universal ground, it stays as pure empty space. By looking at awakened awareness, it appears as clarity/emptiness, and because it stays it cannot exist as the basis for delusion.

Because you have depended on the pith instructions, the conditions that support delusion regarding looking at the three visions—ultimate sound, light, and light-rays—that arise, you see these as self-appearing illusions, and therefore, they do not become the fault of delusion. The cause of delusion is ordinary recollections and ordinary mindfulness, but being groundless and rootless, these move like a breeze, self-empty [in the atmosphere]. [In this way] the cause of delusion does not exist. What is pointed out is such that the causes and conditions that support delusion never existed and are free of having their own essence. Because these do not inherently exist, delusion does not exist. Because delusion becomes like a dead son in a dream, you make a decisive determination about delusion.

Meditation on the Heart-Lamp

The meditation practice for self-awakened awareness to arise from within its depths [the heart lamp] is to experience the universal ground free of obscuration, to not experience any delusion with respect to awakened awareness, and have it stay in the heart primordially; and what stays in the universal ground right now is the clear space, seen in that space. Inside the clear space of the dark ruby offering tent with its crystal lid, it stays in the tent of the clear appearance of light. This is called "taking hold of the channel of the heart." Externally it stays as an eight-sided jewel. Internally it stays as an eight-petalled lotus. In the center of this, in the domain of space, it stays like five spheres of rainbow light. The universal ground and awakened awareness stay unmixed into anything whatsoever, stainless, the great original purity. (489) This is called "the thumb-sized clarity of primordial wisdom." With respect to it staying like a butter lamp inside a pot, the three visions—ultimate sound, light, and light-rays—stay like the light-rays of the butter lamp. Thus, even though the king of awakened awareness arises from the depths, for example, if there is no door to the treasury you don't see the treasure inside the treasury. Likewise, if you do not know how to view the mind, self-awakened awareness does not become clear. At the doorway to this [eye] lamp, keep the mind loose and let whatever arises go its own way. Through looking nakedly at the essence of awakened awareness, awakened awareness will be directly realized as self-clear and free of any grasping for it.

Practicing to get the transparency of primordial wisdom [focuses] on the essence wherein the universal ground and awakened awareness stay primordially. Staying means staying in the center of the heart. The path is where [primordial wisdom] self-occurs, arising in the channel path. By that, from many different channels, many different visions arise from the liveliness of awakened awareness. Furthermore, there are three main channels, six *chakras*, like the trunk [of a tree], which divides into five main branches, three hundred and sixty branch channels, twenty-one thousand tributary channels, and eighty-four thousand [minor channels] like leaves. [Here in the channels] is what arises as the multitude [of visions] from the mind's liveliness. When these [visions] arise in this way, the ordinary [person takes] deluded conceptual thought as the liveliness. To those on the path, the meditative experiences and realizations are [taken as] liveliness. To *Buddhas,* primordial wisdom also arises impartially as liveliness. As such, there are many channels, but the lamp of the [soft white] channel is the [upper] central [channel]. The non-dual clarity/emptiness of awakened awareness arises like the sun rising in a cloudless sky, and as such it arises as the immense transparency of primordial wisdom. Furthermore, inside the central channel, if you hold the mind and energy drops with the wind, you will have many meditative experiences (490) and realizations from the liveliness [of awakened awareness], and many visions of clear-light.

The way to practice the meditation is to take a crossed-legged posture, let the mountain meet the ocean [pull in the stomach to the spine], join the tongue to the upper palate, the eyes turned upward, make the breath soft, and control it so it settles into itself, and through that, from both the right and left side channels, the wind moves downward like blowing it into the intestines. Through that, the winds, mind, and energy drops become mixed, enter into the central channel, and move upward in the form of light. Imagine this comes out from the Brahma aperture, and dissolves into space. Then focus the mind on this space. Through meditating like this over and over again, you separate the brightness of awakened awareness from the dregs [of the ordinary mind]. The king of awakened awareness arises nakedly, the outer skin of conceptual thought falls away, and you see your own true face of self-occurring primordial wisdom. You purify the darkness of failing to recognize awakened awareness and delusion. You completely reverse the three realms and nine levels, and so forth. Many positive qualities will develop.

Practicing Seeing Awakened Awareness Nakedly

The practice of seeing awakened awareness nakedly has two parts:

(1) pointing out seeing the essence nakedly, and

(2) pointing out seeing the clear-light nakedly.

Pointing Out Seeing the Essence Nakedly

First, pointing out seeing the essence nakedly is through both awakened awareness staying in its stainless original purity, and through the liveliness through which the light-rays and five primordial wisdoms stay. The basis stays in the center of the heart. The path comes from the path of the channels. Because these arise in the fluid eye lamps, this is when the brightness of awakened awareness separates from the dregs. From the mind held loosely at the gateway of the [eye] lamps and letting [whatever arises] go its own way, you are looking at awakened awareness, and therefore the emptiness/clarity of the universal ground is like [vast] space without inside or outside. You then see the vessel of primordial wisdom nakedly. (491) You come to see the self-clarity of awakened awareness nakedly and unborn, free of obscuration, like the heart of the sun.

Pointing Out Seeing the Clear-Light Nakedly

Second, pointing out the clear-light: By both holding the wind a little bit, and both eyes unwavering, press on the gateways of the eye lamps. When first holding the breath at the time of filling, various lights and rays arise. These are pointed out to be self-rays. Once you completely expel the breath and keep the mind loose and [the eyes] unwavering, the five rainbow lights arise. This is pointed out to be self-light. At the end, when exhaling the breath, without blocking the gateways, you take the view the same as previously [and allow whatever arises to arise] unobstructedly at the gateways, and through that, the characteristics of the light-rays go their own way and become liberated. This is pointed out as the self-liveliness of awakened awareness.

Making a Close-to-the-Heart Determination

Practicing making a close-to-the-heart determination for meditating on the path just as it is, and for the three-fold embodiment of enlightenment, has two parts: (1) pointing out the three-fold embodiment of enlightenment, and (2) making a close-to-the-heart determination.

Pointing Out the Three-fold Embodiment of Enlightenment

First, pointing out. It is pointed out that the three enlightened *Buddha*-bodies reside in you, as innate and primordial within you.

Making a Close-to-the-Heart Determination about the Three-fold Embodiment of Enlightenment

Second, making a close-to-the-heart determination has two parts.

Determining the Dharmakāya

With respect to pointing out awakened awareness's essence-itself, you make a close-to-the-heart determination about the *dharmakāya*, and with respect to what has been pointed out about awakened awareness's seeing beyond, you make a close-to-the-heart determination about the Enlightened Form-bodies. First, the essence-itself of awakened awareness is pointed out by the three lamps. By the lamp of the universal ground that stays, you recognize the basis. By illustrating the lamps with metaphors, you convey the symbolic meaning of the examples used. (492) Through the lamp of the signs of primordial wisdom, the various signs [of meditation progress] are pointed out.

Determining the Enlightened Form-bodies

Second, pointing out awakened awareness that sees beyond. Making a close-to-the-heart determination about the Enlightened Form-bodies has two parts: pointing out and making a close-to-the-heart determination.

The first is pointing out the three visions—ultimate sound, light, and light-rays—to be clear-light. By meditating on that, the brightness comes forth, [and the dregs] become exhausted. Then, pointing out the first two—light and light-rays—and then pointing out ultimate sound. Pointing out ultimate sound is also known from the mouth of the teacher.

The first has three parts:

(1) external pointing out the brightness of the elements with the sup-

port of the lamp of existence,

(2) internal pointing out of the brightness with the support of the fluid eye-lamp, and

(3) secret pointing out of the brightness of the illusory body with the support of the three—channels, winds, and energy drops. This comes from the mouth of the teacher.

Second, the meditation practice has three parts:

(1) the conceptual mind that moves [with thought] is mastered by focusing the mind on the continuous self-occurring sound.

(2) The mind that remembers the past and prepares for the future is the mind in concentration one-pointedly, free of distraction, on all these various visions as light.

(3) The liveliness of self-clear awakened awareness, free of obscuration, is such that you should practice on the various events that arise as light-rays and become familiar with it.

Furthermore, specific practices and skillful means for liveliness have been shown. Focus the mind on the spheres of light that appear or on the sky.

The essential point of the body is to have it remain stable, free of distraction. The essential point of the gaze is the eye sense-organs. The essential point of the winds is holding them. The essential point of the mind's visualization is meditation with all four [essential points].

First, within this clear-light (493) the seed-[syllables] of the Enlightened Form-bodies arise from within the energy drops, like all the stars and planets in the sky. After becoming familiar with this, there are five specific ways of becoming familiar. [These five levels of visions] are:

(1) increasing,

(2) multiplying,

(3) flourishing,

(4) completion, and

(5) reaching the endpoint of the visions.

From such familiarity, the [after-death] visions reach full measure and reach their endpoint. The full measure of reaching the endpoint is in seven days for those of best capacity, twenty-one days for those of middling capacity, and one cycle of the moon and ten days for those of lesser capacity. Whatever meditative experiences of visions arise, they occur gradually [for most practitioners]. Relying on these meditative experiences means depending on the pith instructions. Thus, the three visions—ultimate sound, light, and light-rays—are such that the energy drops are strung together like a rosary, the Enlightened Form-bodies and celestial palaces, the *mandala* of the *Buddha*-fields and so forth [arise from within these energy drops]. If you know all of this as the liveliness of awakened awareness, and its manner of arising, you have made a close-to-the-heart determination of the mind being without inherent nature. Seeing the five [wisdom] lights manifest directly is mentioned in another note. Practicing meditation on the *bardo* is for those who have recognized [awakened awareness] in this life, and have strong practice, and are of best capacity.

[The Lamp of the Dying Process and After-Death Bardos According to Capacity]

Those of best capacity are given the instructions that the many self-arising events of primordial wisdom all have the same taste. The internal breath has not [yet] been cut off. At the time the external breath is cut off [when dying] *Buddhahood* will occur. Especially at that time, it is very important to review the instructions.

Those of middling capacity, who have moderately strong practice, are shown the instructions to not be attached to or desirous of the three visions—ultimate sound, light, and light-rays—and [that these visions during the after-death *bardo* of the *dharmadhātu*] are like self-appearing illusions. (494) They will become liberated in the *bardo* of clear-light. Those of lesser capacity and weak practice have admiration and respect for their own tutelary deity (*yi dam*) and lama. They are given the instructions of consciousness-transference. Because of these [instructions], for them the appearances of the *bardo* of rebirth will still arise, but they will have pure visions, so they are reborn in a place where the teachings have spread or will be reborn into a pure realm. After one more rebirth they will attain emancipation [from cyclic existence]. These are the pith instructions that cut off [cyclic existence] within one *bardo*.

Conclusion

This completes what is known as "the six essential points for practice." These teachings should be shown to those whose mind-streams are suitable vessels for their lama, and who have completed the manner of arising of the meditative experiences and realizations. It is not given to more than one [person in this way]. This is a single transmission [from heart-to-heart]. If these are given to two or more people [in a way that weakens their potency, you will incur] the wrath of the *ḍākinī*s.

These have been introduced and transmitted from the lineage of the great lama Ya ngal Gong bkra ba.

Sarvamangalam!

From the Oral Transmission of Zhang Zhung
"Pointing Out the Six Energy Drops"

Transcribed by gTsang pa Bye Bral

translated under the guidance of
His Holiness the thirty-third
Menri Trizin

by Geshe Sonam Gurung
and Daniel P. Brown, Ph.D.

for Pointing Out the Great Way Foundation

Pointing Out the Six Energy Drops

(693)

Homage to all those glorious [masters] who, from their meditative experiences and realizations, have become liberated, and, out of kindness guide sentient beings out of their suffering without exception, and show the bliss of the *dharmakāya* that is within you.

These are the pointing out instructions from the *Zhang Zhung* oral transmission [lineage]. These are the root of all teachings. These are also the epitome of all vehicles. These extract the vital essence of all pith instructions. These are the practical heart instructions of all the *ḍākinīs*. These extract the refinement from all the vehicles. These bring clarity to the mind-streams of both self and others. Even if it is written down, it is kept secret. These are the instructions for pointing out the six energy drops. Indeed, these really are the six energy drops that are the very root of the pith instructions.

With respect to the energy drop of the universal ground that stays, it is pointed out how [the realization of] awakened awareness occurs. If the universal ground is not pointed out, the full extent of delusion [arising from] the storehouse mind never ends. With respect to the energy drop of the heart, the natural state of awakened awareness is pointed out. If accordingly you do not meditate on this, then you won't make a determination about the natural state of awakened mind-itself. With respect to the energy drop of the soft white channel, the [liveliness of] awakened awareness along the [channel] path is pointed out. If it is not recognized along the path, you will not separate the brightness of awakened awareness from the residual dregs [of the ordinary mind]. (694) With respect to the energy drop of the fluid eye lamps of the extensive lasso that brings clarity [of the visions], the signs of [progress in the visions from the liveliness] of awakened awareness are pointed out. If [the visions] to be made clear do not become manifest through the eyes, you will not make a determination about the clear-light. With respect to the energy drop that points out the [purified] *Buddha*-fields, these are pointed out as an example of the [liveliness] of awakened awareness. If accordingly, this example does not manifest, the [deluded] elaboration of energy drops will never come to an end. With respect to the energy drop of the after-death *bardo*, the dissolution of the elements in the mind and consciousness-transference of the mind are taught. These are the six energy drops according to the root text.

The Energy Drop of the Universal Ground

First, meditation practice. These are the instructions for those of sharpest capacity. Staying (*gnas pa*) refers to the fact that the *dharmakāya* never not pervades everywhere. Therefore, the universal ground, empty and identityless, remains unwavering. Whether it seems to move or not move, it is just the mind moving. Whether it seems to change or not change, it is just the mind changing. From this empty [expanse], light comes forth. From the light-rays that emanate free of clouds, the purity of the elements, the pure brightness of this light comes forth as the five [wisdom] lights. The physical body having hatred and desire no longer ripens. [However, the mind] becomes trapped inside of the elements. The body becomes trapped in the mind. The mind becomes trapped in the body. [The mind] is like a fish trapped in a net. The way in which the physical body and mind become connected is the way that delusion comes forth. The universal ground itself is the *dharmakāya*. To realize this, it needs to be pointed out. So first make a determination about the natural state of this universal ground.

The pointing out of awakened awareness has three parts—its meaning [as found in the scriptures], metaphors, and signs [of progress in meditation]. The metaphor is to set up [the mind] on a clear mirror wherein [reflections in the mirror are viewed] as mirror-like primordial wisdom. This [inseparable] clarity/emptiness is the *dharmakāya*. Next, it is pointed out that the five primordial wisdoms are spontaneously present.

Pointing out the signs [of meditative progress] is such that the visions manifest before the eye [lamps]. (695) Staying also refers to [awakened awareness] staying inside the precious heart. Then, the path of the soft white channel is made clear. This radiance then arises in the eye sense-organs. With respect to the objects seen, various signs [of progress in the visions] arise. The time to point these out is when you are separating the brightness from the dregs with respect to the elements. The essential points of the body are important. Hold the breath a little. Both [eyes focus] on the object without moving. At the gateways [to the visions, namely the eyes], you press [the surface of the eye balls]. First, holding the breath and then when [the breath] is active, that is when various light-rays arise. These are pointed out to be the *nirmāṇakāyas*. When the breath is of short duration, through the mind being kept loose [yet focused] and without moving, then the various five rainbow lights arise. This is pointed out as the *sambhogakāya*. At the end, when you exhale the breath, without pressing the gateway of clear-light [the eyes], by looking into the empty space in a carefree state, the three visions—ultimate sound, light, and light-rays—are pointed out as coming from the liveliness of the *dharmakāya* in the universal ground.

With respect to pointing out the meaning, this universal ground is non-conceptual and does not inherently exist. Through the power of what is pointed out like this, [these visions] arise as the unobstructed liveliness of awakened awareness. The [ordinary] mind of mindfulness is liberated into the non-dual. This is stark naked *dharmakāya*. This is like [the expanse of] the sky. Awakened awareness is like the sun. Its vivid radiance is amazing. This completes what is called "the instructions of the first energy drop."

The Energy Drop of the Fleshy Heart

With respect to the energy drop of the fleshy heart, the path of meditation has three parts. As the external elements are forming, [the mind] stays in the internal physical body. The physical body, likewise, is like the celestial palace of the deities. The diaphragm is like a silk scarf [that frames] the lower courtyard. Above that (696) is the upper courtyard [of the *mandala*]. The lungs, like an eight-petalled lotus, are the walls [of this bodily palace]. Inside the lungs, like an eight-petalled lotus, is the precious jewel of the heart. The outside is a triangle. The inside is an octagon complete with eight sides. On the cushion of the white and red, the fat and the red fleshy precious heart tissue is like a tent of rubies. Inside that is the window of primordial wisdom. There is where the energy drops of the expanse abide. This is referred to as "the preciousness of the heart-space where awakened awareness stays." By referring to it as "staying," the signs of shape and color are not taken as being inherently existing. They are neither eternal nor taken to be real. It is also not nihilistic in that it is aware and clear. It is beyond all boundaries and so no center exists. Self-occurring primordial wisdom has no origin [or source]. The root text says, "Homage to the three-fold embodiment of enlightenment, the *dharmakāya*, the *sambhogakāya*, and the *nirmāṇakāyas*," and to the deities of great depth. [This means that the threefold embodiment of enlightenment] is free from all extremes of eternalism and nihilism. In being without any inherent nature, it is nevertheless clear. Because this mindfulness is unobstructed, it is called "the energy drop that sends forth various emanations." It is clear, but it is empty. It is empty but it is clear. It is called "energy drop (*thig le*)" because it is natural clear-light.

There are two ways this is pointed out. What is called "pointing out" (*ngo sprod*) refers to pointing out guided by the characteristics of the words [in the scriptures], and guided by the enlightened deity bodies. It is pointed out as clarity/emptiness, and meditating with intense mindfulness clearly on the present mind that is without characteristics.

First, [pointing out the characteristics of] the words has two parts. Because the body gestures are like the lining [of the *mandala*], you make the body gestures.

Focusing the mind (697) on the words is like nailing them down. Therefore, the heart that holds the channels is [where you discover] the *maṇḍala* of the great energy drop of the expanse. There you focus on the natural clear-light that is about the size of a mustard seed, as if light-rays of a white *A* were drawn by a [fine] brush, and a *HUNG* [is drawn] that contains the five primordial wisdoms. Furthermore, the very essence of these words is the enlightened deity body. This very deity, too, is called "emptiness." It is pointed out that the awakened mind-itself and the *dharmadhātu* are inseparable as clarity/emptiness. This is called "the essence of clear-light."

Pointing out, free of characteristics, is such that you should know it manifesting in the present moment or in a short time thereafter. [It is known] as unobstructed livelinesss.

Its lucidity is co-emergent *Buddhahood*. Mindfulness is brought into meditation practice by the power of the pith instructions. Enlightened intention, free of any taste of arising clarity, is such that whatever appears brings forth the brightness of the *dharmakāya*. Having had this pointed out as such, you meditate on the emptiness/clarity. These are the definitive instructions that can bring a person to the direct [result].

This completes the instructions on the second energy drop.

The Energy Drop of the Soft White Channel

With respect to the energy drop of the soft white channel, pointing out the path of awakened awareness has four parts. In general, these four aggregates of the physical body are like a net of channels. These are the four channels that make you able to function. In these is where *bodhicitta* resides like the trunk of a sandlewood tree, which is like nothing else. This one root has three branches, (698) which extend from the secret place and then extend to the Brahma aperture. The heart channel is like a pillar [about the thickness of] ten white silk threads or ten horse-tail hairs. "Energy drop" refers to the radiance of the five primordial wisdom [lights], and to the two secret winds of the clarity of awakened mind-itself that resides there. Once you have delineated the channels, hold the wind, and through that the entire existing world is made clear, without outside or inside. As if holding a [precious, crystal-clear] *amalaki* berry in the palm of your hand, this is the energy drop that helps us to read others' minds. What is referred to as "mind" is such that, in each moment, the wind and awakened awareness reside in this channel. Once you have this experience you will complete the entire liveliness of the three-fold embodiment of enlightenment.

Having activated [this liveliness] through the winds, which are the agent of activation, you ride the horse of the unborn [seed-syllable] *A*, like blowing breath on a mirror, until it comes out from the path of the channel. The breath with [the sound of] "*HA*" comes out from the mouth. Awakened awareness rides from the unborn horse and comes out from the [fluid] eyes-lamps. Furthermore, awakened awareness of the male comes out the right eye and awakened awareness of the female comes out the left eye.

Pointing out refers to pointing out this clarity/emptiness as the essence of clear-light. The five lights are the natural clear-light. It is pointed out as radiance or liveliness.

The appearance of the ultimate sound and light-rays are pointed out as the magical display. Even now these subtle light-rays exist as clarity/emptiness and are pointed out as mother and son. At the time of the after-death *bardos*, this is the fertile ground for practice using these pith instructions. Through having these subtle light-rays pointed out as clarity/emptiness, the full strength of the unwavering immortal *dharmakāya* is born. (699) This completes the instructions on the third energy drop.

The Energy Drop of the Fluid [Eye-Lamp] of the Extensive Lasso

With respect to the energy drop of the extensive lasso, there are four parts to pointing out the signs [of progress of the liveliness of] awakened awareness. What is referred to as "the fluid [eye lamp] of the extensive lasso" pertains to the light-rays [seen at the surface] of the left and right fluid [eye lamps]. It is called "manifesting in the eye [lamps]" because it is the gateway for the manner of arising of primordial wisdom, which is the pure elemental radiance of the five elements. It is called the "energy drops of the extensive lasso [of the eye lamps]" because it is like pure water, [symbolizing] the balance of the elements. It is called "energy drop" because it arises from the eye lamps no longer obscured by outside or inside. It is called "energy drop" because it is a clean crystal egg that is transparent and unobscured.

What is referred to as "signs" refers to the universal ground, wherein the unwavering *dharmakāya* is made clear, and the signs of both Enlightened Form-bodies arising are made clear in the pure light in the channel. The signs arising at the gateways of the eyes refers to making clear the natural five [wisdom] lights in the eyes. This completes the instructions on the fourth energy drop.

The Energy Drop of Pointing Out the Buddha-fields

What is referred to as "the energy drop wherein the *Buddha*-fields are pointed out" is such that in the very first moment [the visions appear] the many light-rays and subtle lights that arise are pointed out as the *nirmāṇakāyas*. In the second moment, what is pointed out is the naturally clear clear-light and the subtle *sambhogakāya*. In the third moment, you make a determination of the meaning of the natural state. The liberation of the characteristics of ultimate sound and light [occurs from not mentally engaging] and letting them go their own way. These are pointed out as the *dharmakāya*. (700) Thus, the progression of the essential points of the pith instructions is conveyed right within the universal ground. These indeed bring about the end of the causes for going to the lower realms and eradicate the conditions [that support] suffering.

The energy drop of the karmic activity of the elements is pointed out as an example of [the liveliness] of awakened awareness. This has four parts. The elements are both outside and inside. The sun and moon are the essence of the external elements. The two eyes are the essence of the internal elements. Both these energy drops are natural clear-light. The brightness of the [light of] the five primordial wisdoms is clear without obscuration. The sun and moon are metaphors for the clarity of the lamp. The sign is the eye-organs. The meaning refers to the appearance of the clear-light.

There are four categories for recognizing the clear-light that manifests: season, right time, essential body points, and the winds. The season refers to the autumn winds. The right time refers to the morning and afternoon. Investigate on the auspicious day with the clear sky [for sun- or sky-gazing]. At that time, pray to your lama [do Guru Yoga].

When you generate impermanence in your mind-stream, make the essential body points. There are four.

(1) The first is like a lion, so make the crouching dog posture. [Expel] the lower wind and hold the winds. Let the ocean meet the rock [pull the stomach back to the spine]. Because there is no activation [of the wind] in the left [side channel], the gateway of sublime knowledge closes. Then, focus [the eyes] on the external energy drops at the gateway where great skillful means is made clear. At that time, in about thirty-five seconds transparent clear-light arises externally and internally—blue, white, yellow, red, and green—like painting a rainbow in the sky. At that time, a deep conviction arises in your meditative experience as if the mother and son have become one. Because [everything] is made clear outside and made clear inside (701) it is called "transparent."

(2) When you recognize it and remain with the mind and body in a state of being at ease, the body assumes the posture like a stretched out elephant. In addition to the previous, the upper wind is then pressed down. Hold the mind on the [eye] lamp wherein you see the clarity of

sublime knowledge. Both thigh channels face each other. After twenty-five times alternating each side, then the light of the celestial palaces arise. This is the time referred to as "the immense clear-light without outside or inside."

(3) Furthermore, in a state wherein both the body and mind are soft and at ease, [the posture] is held the same way as a sage. The wind is likewise held soft and smooth. By focusing both [the right and left eyes] of skillful means and sublime knowledge on the external energy drops, after twenty-three times, the extraordinary external and internal clear-light of the deities and the *nirmāṇakāyas* (enlightened emanation bodies) are generated. Through that, this is the time referred to as "uninterrupted awakened awareness of the external and internal." Through making a determination that this never changes or shifts, the meditation experience arises like finding a precious jewel.

(4) Furthermore, this is the time the ease of body and mind is let go. The body is like a duck moving sideways. In addition, regarding the previous wind, press the upper wind, and churn the middle wind. This becomes like the eyes of primordial wisdom. At that time the visions of the deities arise within the clear-light. Make the determination that the meditative experience is like reaching a precious island of gold. With respect to the deities and enlightened bodies that have been pointed out, make a determination about them.

(5) Now is crossing over. The essential point is to assume the posture of the antelope climbing on the rocks for elevating [the winds] in the channels. (702) By the two [eyes] of primordial wisdom, the external and internal spaces become mixed.

Pointing out through intense means is the essential body points of shooting like an arrow, shaking, and bouncing, and the doors of the channel opening wherein the three—the enlightened deity bodies, the clear-light, and awakened mind-itself—become the primordial *Buddha* in the expanse of space. The three—clarity, emptiness, and bliss—become the meditation practice, and indeed bring out its purification. Being free of conceptual thought that causes delusion, it follows that liberation comes in a non-conceptual state. Even the very elaboration as to what has been pointed out is cut off. Even those who have great realization are free of grasping concepts, such as thinking "This is the realization." Such clarity doesn't have even the smallest particle of conceptual thought. This completes the instruction on the fifth energy drop.

The Energy Drop of the After-Death Bardo

The energy drop that makes clear the after-death *bardo* has three parts:

(1) the etymology,

(2) the energy drop that makes clear the *bardo*, and

(3) focusing the mind.

[First], with respect to the definitive meaning of *bardo*, [*bar* means between and *do* means two]. At that time you can't stay in your own place.

[Second] what is called the "energy drop that makes clear." The time refers to when the mind and body separate at the jaws [of death]. The finality [of life] is when the elements in the body dissolve. The [coarse] breath leaves from the nose and mouth [and ceases]. This is the time the mind leaves from the eyes. The clarity is when the brightness [of awakened awareness] separates from the residual dregs [of the ordinary mind], and the object known is the clear-light [of dying]. At that time, the three [possibilities] are: staying, ceasing, or becoming clear. It stays as the essence of clear-light. It arises as liveliness and emanations. What ceases are the manifestations of the seemingly existing world [of this life]. This is the place where [the elements supporting] the mind dissolve. There are three [distinctions]. Those of best capacity (703) subsume under clarity/emptiness the essence of the subtle light-rays of clear-light. On that occasion, by remembering that you have died, and through the strength of your current meditation practice, no panic is generated. [Third], Then, you set up the mind in an unconstructed way, unwavering.

For those of middling capacity, there are six [points]—three escorts, and three people who accompany you. The three escorts are the objects of mind, which arise as the three [visions]—ultimate sound, light, and light-rays. Earlier [the sound] comes. Then, later [the light-rays], and then the two join together. The three attendants are the lama, the tutelary deities (*yi dam*), and the *ḍākinīs*. The benefits [of having these attendants] are such that the lama shows the path and fruition of *Buddhahood*. The tutelary deities rescue you from falling into the six realms. The *ḍākinīs* show [the path] by signs and prophesies. These individuals point out the path.

For those of lesser capacity, there are three [kinds of] people who drop you off: dropping you off according to your own meditation experience; dropping you off by the instructions of someone else; and dropping you off by the compassion of your lama. For the person of lower capacity, give these kinds of instructions. A person who is in the jaws of death should set up his body comfortably. Let them meditate on their own tutelary deity (*yi dam*), and then remember their lama as an object brought to mind, and bring admiration and respect to him. First, come to realize without delusion [the preciousness of] the person [the lama] whom you admire and respect; and at the moment you give up your last breath, come to ride on the horse of [the indestructible essence of your consciousness], the [seed-syllable] *A*, such that the clear-light [of this *A*] is transferred into the heart of the deity [on the top of your crown]. In fact, there is no [substantial] cause of transferring and no cause of dissolving this consciousness], but set up [the mind] such that all the light-rays are in a state of emptiness/clarity. (704) Mix the ultimate sound and light into the enlightened deity bodies as inseparable. Set up [the mind] in a state of the *dharmadhātu*, free of mental construction, [in a way that is] free of all extremes of contemplation, expression, or visualization focus.

The pith instructions of the six energy drops of a single lineage are now completed.

May auspiciousness and virtue spread far. I, the yogi from gTsang [Central Tibet], transcribed it.

Samaya! Samaya!

Bibliography

A. Tibetan Works Used:

rDzogs pa chen po zhang zhung snyan rgyud las sgron ma drug gi gdams pa zhugs [*Instructions on the Six Lamps from the oral transmission of Zhang Zhung Great Completion*]. (No date.) Root text by Tapihritsa & sNang bzher Lod po. Dolanji, India: Menri Monastery, 331-354, block print version.

rDzogs pa chen po zhang zhung snyan rgyud las sgron ma'i grel ba nyi 'od rgyan bzhugs so [*The Ornamentation of Sunlight Commentary from the oral transmission of Zhang Zhung Great Completion*]. (2010) Au Ri, Dolanji, India: Menri Monastery, Bon Dialectical School, 27: 319-390..

rDzogs pa chen po zhang zhung snayn rgyud las sgron ma drug gi dgongs don 'grel bzhugs so [*The Intention and Ultimate Meaning Commentary*] (2010). Bru sgom rGyal ba g.yung drung. Dolanji, India: Menri Monastery, Bon Dialectical School, 27: 391-470.

rDzogs pa chen po zhang zhung snyan rgyud las bynag chub sems kyi gnad drug ces bya ba'i lag len bzhugs so [*The Six Essential Points of Bodhicitta*]Transmitted from the Lineage of Yan gal Gong bkra ba, in *rdzogs pa chen po zhang zhung snyan rgyud bka' rgyud skor bzhi* [*Four Cycles of the Authoritative Lineage of the Oral Transmission of Zhang Zhung Great Completion*]. (2010) Dolanji, India: Menri Monastery, Bon Dialectical School, vol. 27, 479-494.

rDzogs pa chen po zhang zhung snyan rgyud kyi ngo sprod thig le drug pa bzhugs so. [*The Six Energy Drops*]. Transcribed by gTsang pa Bye bral in *rDzogs pa chen po zhang zhung snyan rgyud bka' rgyud skor bzhi* [*Four Cycles of the Authoritative Lineage of the Oral Transmission of Zhang Zhung Great Completion*]. Dolanji, India: Menri Monastery, Bon Dialectical School, vol. 27, 693-704 (2010).

B. Western Works:

Achard, Jean-Luc (2017). *The Six Lamps; Secret Dzogchen Instructions of the Bon tradition*. Somerville MA: Wisdom Publications.

Chongtul Rinpoche (trans.) (2012). *The instructions on the Six Lamps extracted from the oral transmission of Zhang-Zhung Great Perfection*. Unpublished manuscript. New York: Bon Shen Ling.

Tenzin Wangyal Rinpoche (No date). *The instruction of the Six Lamps from the oral transmission of Zhang Zhung*. Unpublished manuscript. Virginia: Ligmincha.

www.ingramcontent.com/pod-product-compliance
Lightning Source LLC
Chambersburg PA
CBHW062057280426
43673CB00085B/459/J